The Moving Target

The Moving Target

What Every Marketer
Should Know About Women

Rena Bartos

THE FREE PRESS
A Division of Macmillan Publishing Co., Inc.
NEW YORK

Collier Macmillan Publishers
LONDON

Copyright © 1982 by Rena Bartos

All rights reserved. No part of this book may be reproduced or
transmitted in any form or by any means, electronic or mechanical,
including photocopying, recording, or by any information storage
and retrieval system, without permission in writing from the
Publisher.

The Free Press
A Division of Macmillan Publishing Co., Inc.
866 Third Avenue, New York, N.Y. 10022

Collier Macmillan Canada, Inc.

Library of Congress Catalog Card Number: 81-70148

Printed in the United States of America

printing number

1 2 3 4 5 6 7 8 9 10

Library of Congress Cataloging in Publication Data

Bartos, Rena.
  The moving target.

    1. Women as consumers—United States.
2. Women—Employment—United States.   3. Women in
advertising.   I. Title.
HC110.C6B33   658.8′348   81-70148
ISBN 0-02-901700-9   AACR2

For Harold—who never believed in labels

Contents

Preface

Now that this book is in print it seems almost inevitable that it should have been written. It is the culmination of a series of professional activities conducted on behalf of my company, J. Walter Thompson, to further our understanding of the changing women's market.

In the early 1970s I was engaged in a series of studies of consumer segments which we labeled "Special Markets." The purpose of the Special Markets Program at Thompson was "to identify the marketing opportunities suggested by life styles or cultural patterns, to study the characteristics that set those groups apart, and to apply this knowledge in specific marketing actions."

Although none of us realized it at the time, the first seeds of this book were sown at a luncheon I gave early in 1973. I had invited a number of professional women at J. Walter Thompson to join me in deciding whether or not working women represented a viable consumer market and whether we should do something about it. This task-force group included media specialists, senior creative women, and account executives.

As a result of our early informal meetings, there was an overwhelming consensus among the group that the working women's market did, in fact, warrant our attention. The first tangible result of our examination was a presentation called "Working Women: The Invisible Consumer Market." As time went on we conducted an in-depth media analysis of the women's market, which compared working women to nonworking women. At that point our study of working women was expanded to include housewives. The concept was re-titled "The Moving Target," because that seemed better to encompass the scope and dynamics of the women's market.

About a year after these activities were begun, a number of working documents had been developed. These included a media analysis, an examination of the buying behavior of working and nonworking women, and a creative review of the imagery of current advertising in a number of product categories.

Another moment which pushed the Moving Target concept closer to book form occurred early in 1974 in a conversation with Ted Wilson

(Edward B. Wilson, former chairman of J. Walter Thompson Company). He suggested that I "put everything you've learned about women in one master document." I was surprised, flattered, and challenged by his suggestion and said that I would try it.

Several months later I brought forth a fairly boring compendium of all the information I had gathered relating to various aspects of the women's market. It was far more like a college term paper than a professional communication from an advertising agency.

I turned to the Creative Department for help and was fortunate that a superb writer named Ellen Currie (who is currently a vice president and associate creative supervisor at J. Walter Thompson) waded through my endless material and synthesized it into what turned out to be the first formal publication on the subject, which we called *The Moving Target.* This brochure was issued by J. Walter Thompson as part of a series of professional communications. I am grateful indeed to Ellen for her sense of clarity, style, and economy of expression. I am also grateful to Carolyne Diehl (currently a vice president and creative director at J. Walter Thompson) for the taste and flair with which she designed and executed the visual aspects of the brochure.

Another moment that might mark the genesis of this book occurred some years later. In the fall of 1976 David Ewing, executive editor for planning of the *Harvard Business Review,* invited me to do an article on the women's market. He said he had heard through the grapevine that I had some interesting ways of segmenting women, and he thought is was high time that the *Harvard Business Review* published something on the subject.

I was very honored at this invitation and accepted it with enthusiasm. One of the conditions, of course, was that anything I submit to them not have appeared elsewhere. It so happened that literally twenty-four hours earlier I had made a commitment to do an article for the *Journal of Marketing.* That article was to deal with the impact of employment on women's consumer behavior. Therefore, the challenge was to develop an article dealing with much the same material but from a totally different perspective.

I completed the *Journal of Marketing* article first and then proceeded to attack the *Harvard Business Review* assignment. I decided to set it in the broader concept of the underlying assumptions that marketers bring to their definitions of target groups. My working title for this article was "The Challenge of Our Assumptions." After an intensive editorial process that occurs when working with the *Harvard*

Business Review, the final title was "What Every Marketer Should Know About Women."

After that article appeared, several publishers expressed interest in having me expand it into a book. Some months later I did decide to undertake this awesome task, and the present volume is the result. Since so much of the content of this book is intertwined with my professional activities on behalf of J. Walter Thompson, there is no way to separate the two. Actually, I would never have made the commitment to write it if I had not been encouraged to do so by the present management of the J. Walter Thompson Company. I am grateful to Don Johnston, chairman and chief executive officer, and Wayne Fickinger, president and chief operating officer, of the J. Walter Thompson Company for their support and encouragement not just in undertaking the development of this manuscript but throughout the implementation of the program of which this book is just one expression.

I would also like to express my sincere gratitude to a number of people who contributed to this ongoing project over the years. First, the earliest task force consisted of many people who are no longer at J. Walter Thompson and, for that matter, no longer in the industry. I would like to say thank you to my former associates at J. Walter Thompson: Ann Wright, former vice president, media, currently retired; Berta Best, former vice president and associate creative director, currently retired; Susan Procter, currently vice president and creative supervisor, BBDO, Inc.; Joyce LaTerre, vice president, associate media director, Lord, Geller, Federico, Einstein, Inc.; Bette J. McCabe, senior vice president, Hill & Knowlton; Sys Morch, international director of marketing, American Home Products; and Amelia Grinstead, media manager, The Pillsbury Company.

My thanks to my current Thompson colleagues: Ruth Downing Karp, senior vice president and creative director; Jeanne Maraz, vice president and management supervisor; and Catherine Ames, vice president, executive television producer.

In 1978 the original *Moving Target* brochure had gone out of print. We had continuing requests for it and decided that it should be brought up to date rather than reissued. The first brochure was written before the New Demographics concept had been implemented. Therefore, it made good sense to include the new insights provided by the New Demographics concept in the current version of the brochure. My thanks to Lorelle Burke Grazis, currently vice president and creative supervisor, Ted Bates & Company, Inc., for developing the second version of the brochure. I am grateful for her creative and editorial skills in bringing that brochure to a successful conclusion. My thanks also to Peter From for the design and implementation of the graphics and visual aspects of *The Moving Target II.*

My thanks to John Bonnell, Nancy Denious, and William Moore for their superb counsel and implementation of all of the graphic materials I use in my public presentations of the Moving Target concept. Many of the illustrations in this book are samples of the superb work done by this team. My particular thanks to Bill Moore for bringing some abstract concepts to life through his perceptive and creative cartoon sketches, such as those included in Chapter 18.

A special note of appreciation to two warm friends and professional colleagues for their creative and aesthetic counsel and guidance throughout the development of all aspects of this program. My thanks to Wilson Seibert, international creative director, for his perceptive and graceful description of the Moving Target on the jacket of this book. Thank you to Bernard Owett, senior vice president and creative director, for his unfailing taste in all aesthetic matters and his generosity in sharing of his time and his talent in counseling on the visual aspects of this book. I am grateful to my former JWT colleague Bob Hungerford, executive vice president and co-creative director of Bradley, Dimmock and Hungerford, for developing the cover graphics which capture the spirit of the Moving Target.

I am grateful to the two professionals who assisted in all of the analysis and technical processing of the data presented in these chapters and the great wealth of data on this subject not included in the present volume. They are Robert Cohen, currently a doctoral candidate in the Sociology Department at Columbia University, who functioned as my assistant during the period from June 1976 to September 1978, and to Dr. Cathy Pullis, who succeeded Bob Cohen in this capacity and has worked with me from August 1978 to the present time. My special thanks to Cathy for her painstaking and patient processing of all the myriad details that go into bringing a text like this to completion. I am most grateful to her for her invaluable assistance. And, finally, many thanks to my superb secretary, Peg Lang, without whose infinite patience, concern, and warm cooperation this project would never have been brought to fruition.

RENA BARTOS
October 1981

I

Changing Women

Chapter 1

The Quiet Revolution

There is a simple demographic fact at the heart of a quiet revolution that has affected almost every man, woman, and child in the United States. The ripple effect of that one demographic fact could eventually touch almost every institution in our society and every aspect of our daily lives.

The ultimate shape of the quiet revolution resulting from the surge of women entering the work force is not yet clear to any of us. We are living through a period of accelerating social change. None of us has the perspective of those future social historians who will be able to define the ultimate effects of that change.

Professor Eli Ginzberg, Chairman of the National Commission for Manpower Policy, calls it "the single most outstanding phenomenon of the twentieth century." He agrees that we cannot predict the ultimate consequences of this phenomenon. He goes on to say that the secondary and tertiary consequences of "that outstanding phenomenon" are really unchartable.

The eminent sociologist David Reisman says it is not a single phenomenon at all but a multiple series of parallel phenomena. He calls the changes that have occurred in women's lives "the women's movements" rather than "the women's movement." Professor Reisman says: "I regard the women's movements—and I insist on the plural— as the most important of my time. And it's not true, as some say, that they're over. They have become so much the fabric of the country that one no longer thinks of them as a movement."[1]

The dramatic rise in the number of women in the work force is one of the more obvious changes that has occurred. It is this phenomenon that I term "the quiet revolution." But it would be too narrow and simplistic a view to assume that the unprecedented flood of women into the work force in recent years is the only real change that has taken place. The dramatic increase in the number of working women is one symptom of a more fundamental change in women's self-perceptions.

Traditionally women have been identified in terms of derived status. Their lives were defined in terms of whose daughter they were and whom they married. It is only in recent years that even the happiest of wives and mothers has also yearned for a sense of self-identity that goes beyond her family role. This is one of the strong motivators that has drawn some women into the work force, other women into the pursuit of mid-life education, and still others into encouraging their daughters to seek goals different from the ones they themselves held in their formative years.

A dramatic example of this change is found in the contrast between Margaret Trudeau and the wife of Joe Clark, the recent Prime Minister of Canada. Mrs. Clark, a lawyer and the mother of a small daughter, prefers to retain her maiden name. She and her husband appear to have a close marriage based on partnership and mutual respect.

Contrast this with Margaret Trudeau, whose courtship and marriage to Pierre Trudeau was in true fairy tale tradition—the beautiful, obscure young girl courted by the famous, attractive, dashing statesman. After a whirlwind courtship she married her Prince Charming, moved into the residence of the Prime Minister, and raised a family. The headlines have reminded us that she did not live happily ever after. Ironically, even in her current separation from Trudeau, her identity is defined only in terms of her former relationship to him. Without it, no one would be interested in whether or not this unknown young woman danced at Studio 54 or not. This is a classic example of derived status.

So many changes have occurred in women's lives in the last decade that it is difficult to remember the way we were only a few years ago. The forces that were unleashed in the last few years will continue into the 1980s and beyond. Someone has said, rather inelegantly, that once you squeeze the toothpaste out of the tube it can't be put back. That describes what has happened with women's self-perceptions and aspirations. There is no turning back.

The flood of change has touched the lives of almost every woman in this country to some extent. The changes have not affected all of us in the same way. We are not all at the same stage of the life cycle, and we are not all cut out by the same cookie cutter. The women in our country are wonderfully diverse.

Two major attitudinal changes in public opinion that have occurred are revolutionary in relation to the values with which many of us grew up. Nine out of ten people in this country think it is perfectly all right for a couple to decide not to bring children into this world if they don't care to. And more than half of the people in this country think it is all right for a man and woman to live together without marriage if they care for each other.[2] This means that young women today have many more options than women thought they had in the past. It is not always easy to tread an uncharted path.

Some fundamentals do not change. Marriage and family life will continue, but the context may be different. Whether the young women of today marry at all or marry later, I think many of them will marry. Their reasons may be different from those of yesterday's brides. They will marry not because it is expected of them, nor to snag a meal ticket, and not because it is the only option available to them. If they do marry, it will probably be because they really want to join their lives with those of the men that they marry. I think there will be more of a spirit of sharing and partnership and more openness in marriage.

There could be new areas of conflict, particularly in homes where both husbands and wives are pursuing serious careers. In some cases this could lead to weekend marriages. While that is not an appealing thought to the traditional-minded, we should remember that many very traditional marriages are also weekend marriages to all intents and purposes. Think of all the wives alone in the suburbs coping with the responsibilities of housekeeping and bringing up children while their husbands are off on business trips. Perhaps a marriage where each partner has a sense of accomplishment during the time of separation can lead to a greater appreciation of the other in the times when they are together.

While there is no doubt that many of the wives flooding into the work force are propelled by economic motivations, it cannot be economics alone that is keeping many of them there. We might contrast the present situation with the Depression years of the 1930s. In those days if wives worked, it was because their husbands were unemployed and they went to work temporarily to help cope with an emergency situation. It was the norm in those days for the husband to support his wife and for the wife to keep the home fires burning.

Of course, we have always had some women seeking professional careers even though their husbands could support them. But a generation ago those women were swimming against the tide. Eyebrows were raised. It was assumed that perhaps their husbands were not able to support them or that something was wrong with their marriages. Such women paid their dues in order to pursue careers by becoming "supermoms." They tried to prove to their friends and neighbors that they could do it all and do it superbly. They had the best-kept homes and the best-raised children, and they served superb gourmet dinners. They and their husbands assumed that the home was solely the responsibility of the wife. If she chose to work outside the home, she took on a second job.

Currently the situation has flip-flopped. These days wives of some of the most affluent, achieving men are distinctly uncomfortable in social situations when someone asks them: "And what do you do?"

One of the other key factors in the change is the close link between education and women's presence in the work force. The more education a woman has the more likely she is to be at work. Conversely, women at the lowest educational level, whom one might assume are in the greatest financial need, are least likely to be working.

In the past few years most of the Ivy League colleges have opened their doors to women. Every year the ratio of men to women in those colleges comes closer to equality. A generation ago only about three out of every ten college students were women, while today as many women as men are enrolled in colleges and universities. In the past few years there has been an enormous acceleration in the number of women seeking advanced training in professions that were normally considered male bastions: medicine, law, architecture, engineering. The ratios of women to men are far from equal in these graduate schools, but the proportion is growing every year.

Another element in this complex mix is the fact that our population is living a greater number of years, and people are far more vigorous at those advanced ages than in previous generations. In the days when women defined their roles as wives and mothers, they tended to raise larger families and did not have very many years left after that biological function had been fulfilled. Today, with small families, the child-raising years are a relatively short interlude in a woman's life span. Therefore, the energy of many middle-aged women needs outlets beyond the traditional nurturing role.

In the past such women turned to volunteer work, which is still, of course, an important outlet for many women in our society. But, increasingly, middle-aged women are seeking to renew old skills or develop new ones and find second careers for themselves in the world of work.

In addition, women in our society tend to outlive men. Since most women marry men somewhat older than themselves, we are left with more widows than widowers. Even if these widows have lived in the most traditional life style, when widowhood comes their children are grown and out of the nest, and they are, in effect, suddenly unemployed.

The changes that are manifested in so many aspects of life interact with each other, so it is difficult to separate cause and effect. Many of the attitudinal and behavioral changes that have occurred in the homes of working women spill over into the households of traditional-minded housewives. Even the most traditional housewives want to share in the family decision-making process. They want to have a greater voice in how the family spends its money.

The pendulum has swung so that all of us, full-time housewives and working women alike, are more casual in the way we keep house, the way we entertain, and the way we interact with our families. As these changes have happened, many of the old stereotypes are giving way. American women are no longer depicted as the dominating, silver-cord mothers castigated by Philip Wylie or the obsessive housewife like the heroine of *Craig's Wife,* whose emphasis on perfection left no room for humanity in her beautifully kept house.

The symptoms of change that I have described are not manifest to exactly the same degree in every household in America. However, they reflect a fundamental change in women's lives. My prediction is that these changes will not go away.

In the following pages I shall document the most obvious manifestation of change, the increased presence of women in the work force.

When Did It Start?

There have always been women at work in our country. However, historically they were a rather minor factor in the labor force. At the turn of the century 18 percent of all workers in our country were females. By 1940 they had inched up to a level of 25 percent participation. The pace began picking up in the gray flannel 1950s. It accelerated in the 1960s and reached a crescendo in the 1970s. By 1980 the number of women in the labor force had not equaled that of men. However, they were fast approaching equality in numbers, if not in rewards. In 1980 42 percent of all workers in our country were women.

So far we have been considering the proportion of workers in our country who are women. Another way to look at this revolutionary demographic fact is to consider the proportion of women in our country who are workers.

Even at the turn of the century some women were working women. Back in 1900 one out of every five women in the United States was in the work force. If this number is modest, it is also somewhat startling.

Exhibit I

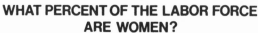

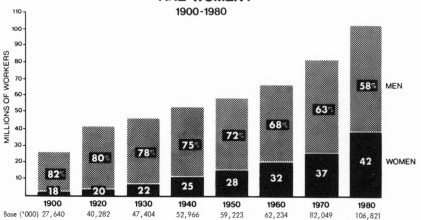

Source: U.S. Census Bureau, Bureau of Labor Statistics

It challenges the assumption that many of us had that prior to World War I women were totally home-oriented and never ventured out into the world of work.

The reality is that by 1920 just under one in four American women were at work, and by the 1940s just over one in four were in the work force.

This historical review, which charts the change at ten-year intervals, does not reflect the explosion that occurred during World War II. In the period from 1942 to 1945, more than 6 million women joined the labor force to serve the needs of a highly mechanized wartime economy, crossing almost every traditional male job boundary.[3]

As the historian William Chafe describes it, "women ran lathes, cut dies, read blueprints, and serviced airplanes. They maintained roadbeds, greased locomotives, and took the place of lumberjacks in toppling giant redwoods. As stevedores, blacksmiths, foundry helpers, and drill press operators, they demonstrated that they could fill any job, no matter how difficult or arduous."[4]

Things were never quite the same again. True, when the war was over, women welcomed their heroes back with an enthusiastic return to domesticity. Returning veterans bought their share of the American dream in an uprecedented flight to the suburbs.

The women's magazines extolled the glories of "togetherness."

They were full of tips on cooking, sewing, home decorating, and all the domestic arts. Large families became the ideal. The baby boom was under way.

In spite of the intense emphasis on hearth and home, there was a sharper rise in the percentage of women in the work force from 1940 to 1950 than had occurred in any previous decade since the beginning of the century. But this was only a preliminary to the main event.

From 1950 to the present, at every ten-year interval, the percentage of women in the labor force surged ahead at a steady increase of 20 to 21 percent. By 1980 more than half of all women in the United States sixteen and older were going to work.

But not all nonworking women are housewives. Even as we consider the fact that 52 percent of all women were in the work force at the end of 1980, we must realize that this simple statement of fact is an understatement. By basing our analyses on all women in our country sixteen and over, the universe includes women who are too young or too old to be actively involved in the world of work. This is illustrated dramatically by the occupational profile of all women aged sixteen and over in the United States in 1980.

This explodes the common assumption that if a women isn't in the

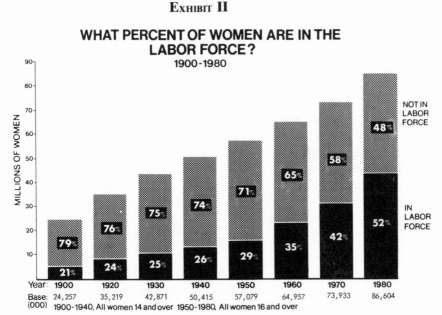

Exhibit **II**

WHAT PERCENT OF WOMEN ARE IN THE LABOR FORCE?
1900-1980

Source: U.S. Census Bureau, Bureau of Labor Statistics

Exhibit III

OCCUPATIONAL PROFILE
OF AMERICAN WOMEN: 1980

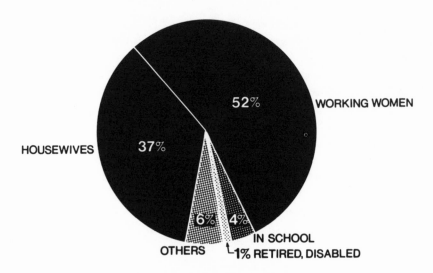

Source: Bureau of Labor Statistics. Jan., 1981
Base: All women 16 and over = 86,604,000

work force she must, of course, be at home keeping house. The realities are that while just over half of all women were going to work in 1980, only 37 percent were full-time homemakers. The remainder were too young or too old to be actively involved either in work or in keeping house. Four percent were still in school; 1 percent were retired or disabled, and, therefore out of the mainstream. The base also includes 6 percent who represent that mysterious group that the Bureau of the Census labels as "others."

Working Women Have
Become the Majority

Once we remove the schoolgirls and grandmothers from our consideration, we see that the ratio of housewives to working women is a dramatic 41 to 59 percent! *Working women are no longer the exception. They are the rule.* The overwhelming majority of all women in our country are in the work force. A woman who is old enough to be out of school and young enough to be unretired is one and a half times more likely to be at work than staying home and keeping house.

Historical trends of this more realistic perspective of the ratio of working women to full-time homemakers cannot be projected back prior to 1948. That was when the Bureau of Labor Statistics first began identifying which nonworking women were full-time housewives and which ones were in school, retired, disabled, or "others."

Back in 1948 the ratio of housewives to working women was slightly less than two to one in favor of housewives. During the 1950s and the 1960s, the majority of women were engaged in keeping house. The pace picked up rapidly at the very end of the 1960s, and at the beginning of the 1970s there were almost as many women going to work as staying home and keeping house. The momentum accelerated even more dramatically in the 1970s. Exhibit V depicts the ratio of housewives to working women at two-year intervals since 1948, when the data first became available.

Eхнiвiт IV

RATIO OF HOUSEWIVES TO WORKING WOMEN: 1980

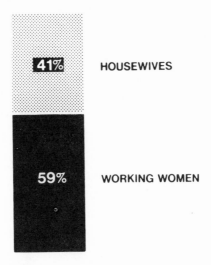

Base: All women 16 and over in the labor force or keeping house = 76,422,000
Source: Bureau of Labor Statistics, Employment and Earnings, Jan.,1981

Exhibit V

EXHIBIT V

RATIO OF HOUSEWIVES TO WORKING WOMEN
1948-1980

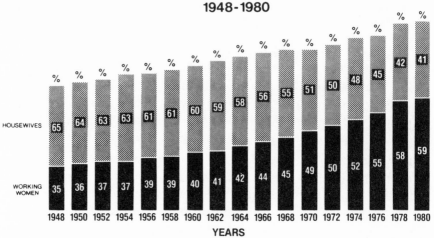

BASE (000) 50.054 51.324 52.511 53.470 54.786 56.284 57.73o 59.288 60.789 62.563 64.446 64.427 66.589 68.643 70.233 72.474 76.442

SOURCE BUREAU OF LABOR STATISTICS OF THE U.S., EMPLOYMENT & EARNINGS REPORTS, JAN., 1971-81
BASE TOTAL ACTIVE WOMEN 16 + YRS (EITHER WORKING OR KEEPING HOUSE)

There was never more than a 1 or 2 percent increase in the proportion of American women in the work force at these two-year intervals until the fateful year 1968. As a matter of fact, in two instances there was no change at all. While the absolute number of women in the population rose consistently from year to year, between 1952 and 1954 the proportion of all women who were working outside the home remained at a constant 37 percent level. Again, from 1956 to 1958 the level remained constant at 39 percent.

The most dramatic rise occurred between 1968 and 1970, when the proportion of working women rose four full percentage points in two years. In 1968 the ratio of housewives to working women stood at 55 to 45 percent. Two years later the ratio was 51 to 49 percent. After an absolute fifty–fifty tie in 1972, working women became the majority. Increases were particularly sharp in the latter half of the decade. Between 1974 and 1976 and again between 1976 and 1978, the percentage of working women rose by three percentage points. In the six years between 1974 and 1980 the proportion of working women increased by seven percentage points.

Where did they all come from? Who are the women who have flooded into the work force in recent years? What kinds of women caused this remarkable revolutionary phenomenon?

Looking backward again, we observe that while there have always been women in the work force, for the most part they were unmarried women. There was almost a tradition that a young single woman might work for a few years between school and marriage while waiting for "Mr. Right" to come along. If he never appeared, or if her marriage was terminated by the husband's death or the misfortune of a divorce, the poor thing might return to the work force in order to support herself.

For the first thirty years of this century, the Bureau of Labor Statistics simply reported which women in the work force were married and which were not.

Starting in 1930 the Bureau told us which of those unmarried women had never married and which were formerly married. Therefore, we could identify precisely how many unmarried women were single and how many were either widowed or divorced.

As can be seen in Exhibit VI, the proportion of unmarried women at work in our country remained fairly constant throughout the years. But beginning in 1940 there was a rise in the number of women going to work. The pace accelerated in the 1960s and 1970s. This new influx of women into the work force was due to married women, who entered or reentered the world of work in ever increasing numbers.

Exhibit VI

MARITAL STATUS OF WORKING WOMEN
1900-1979

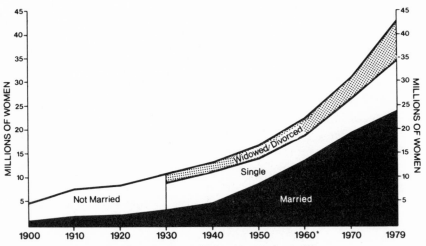

Source: Employment and Training Report to the President, 1978. Current Population Reports, 1980
*First Year Alaska and Hawaii Included

Starting in the mid-1970s, the marital pattern of working women began to shift somewhat. There was a slight leveling out of married women and a fairly sharp increase of unmarried women, both single and formerly married. I speculate that this is due to the shift in the marital composition of our population rather than to a return of married women to the home. There are simply more people, both men and women, either delaying marriage or leaving it. Therefore there is a wider pool of unmarried women available for work. However, married women have been the main source of the ''quiet revolution'' described in these pages.

Which wives have entered the work force? What kinds of women are they? So far we have been talking about the marital status of working women. We have identified which working women are married and which ones are not. Let us now consider working wives. In the early 1900s working wives were a very tiny minority of all married women. At the turn of the century only 6 percent of all wives went to work. From the anecdotal material available, our impression is that most of them were at work for reasons of sheer economic necessity. They probably longed to take their places as full-time homemakers.

The percentage of working wives increased slightly from decade to decade, but the rate of increase was extremely low. By 1940, at the beginning of World War II, only 16 percent of all married women went to work.

Ten years later fewer than one in four married women were in the work force. Then the movement began. By 1960 almost one in three married women were working wives. By 1970 two in five married women went to work. At the end of 1980 half of all married women were in the work force. Remember, those married women who were not working included women of all ages. As we have seen earlier, some of these wives were not available to go to work because of either age or the state of their health.

The ''quiet revolution'' has indeed penetrated the households of married couples throughout America.

Perhaps *the greatest* revolution *of all has been a social* revolution. This is reflected by the kinds of married women who have in fact entered the work force in recent years. I report this particular phenomenon with very little joy. However, the facts are that the greatest rate of growth of married women entering the work force came from those with very young children. This, of course, represents rate of growth, not the absolute level of such women in the work force.

The rate of growth is so steep because a generation ago most

Exhibit **VII**

WHAT PERCENT OF WIVES GO TO WORK?
1900-1980

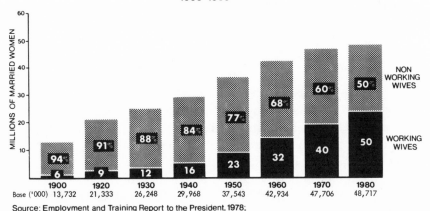

Base ('000) 13,732   21,333   26,248   29,968   37,543   42,934   47,706   48,717

Source: Employment and Training Report to the President, 1978;
Current Population Reports, 1980

women with young children simply did not go to work. They automatically assumed that they would stay home and care for those
children. Their husbands, friends, neighbors, and the rest of society
shared that assumption.

Exhibit **VIII**

GROWTH OF WORKING WIVES
BY PRESENCE AND AGE OF CHILDREN
Percentage Increase: **1948–1980**

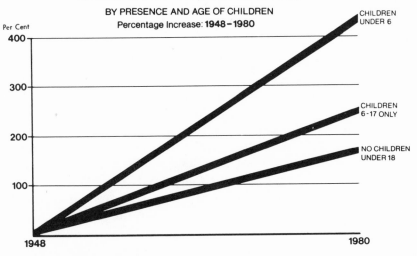

Source: Employment and Training Report to the President, 1978;
Current Population Reports, 1980

This change may be the most revolutionary one of all of the demographic facts reported in this chapter. It was so unexpected that it caught some of the pundits in the Bureau of Labor Statistics and other governmental groups by surprise. When these experts forecast which women would enter and remain in the work force and which women would not, they assumed that women would behave as they had previously. Therefore, in projecting past behavior they naturally assumed that women with young children would stay at home.

This is one example of how none of us can assume that past behavior is a prediction of anything. As the social context changes, so must our forecasts. Several erudite articles were written by forecasters explaining why they had so underestimated the number of women who would be in the work force by the late 1970s. According to their predictions, by 1980 some 48.4 percent of all women sixteen years and over would be in the work force. In fact, we reached that level at least two years earlier.

As the 1970s ended and we entered the 1980s, more than half of all women sixteen and over were going to work. So our forecasters had missed the mark by a very large margin indeed.

Who Is a Housewife?

One of the problems with the neat categorizations of people in demographic groupings is our tendency to believe that the labels are mutually exclusive. We have seen that many full-time homemakers have left their kitchens and flooded into the ranks of working women. Therefore, even as the percentage of full-time homemakers has declined, the percentage of working women who are also housewives has increased. To define which women in our country are housewives, we can start with the base of 41 percent of all active women who keep house full time.

However, to complete the picture we must also consider the additional 34 percent of working women who are married. Even if we define a housewife very narrowly as a married woman, we still ought to reckon with the working housewife, because today when a girl gets married, living happily ever after does not necessarily mean staying barefoot and pregnant! Approximately three out of five working women are married.

For the pragmatic observer who is willing to look at the facts, mar-

EXHIBIT IX

THE "HOUSEWIFE" MARKET

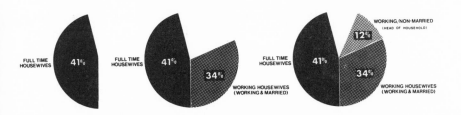

SOURCE: BUREAU OF LABOR STATISTICS EMPLOYMENT & EARNINGS, JANUARY 1981 UNPUBLISHED DATA

BASE: ALL WOMEN 16 AND OVER WHO ARE IN LABOR FORCE OR KEEPING HOUSE = 76,442,000

ried women who work represent a potential increment of 83 percent over the entire universe of full-time housewives in America. Further, if we are willing to challenge the assumption that a woman must be living in wedded bliss in order to keep house, we might note that some 12 percent of all active women are unmarried working women who are also heads of their own households. The unmarried working female head of household represents an additional increment of 29 percent to the basic "housewife" segment.

Thus, a little simple arithmetic shows that working housewives, both married and not, add a potential 112 percent increment to our definition of the American housewife.

To sum up, we see that the simple demographic fact of the number of women in the work force today is, in fact, the basis of a quiet revolution. Simple Demographic Fact Number One tells us that:

- 52 percent of all American women go to work. More than half of all women in our country are at work. Working women are the dominant female group in our society today; they outnumber full-time housewives by a ratio of three to two.
- Not all women who are out of the work force are necessarily housewives. We must remember that some females are too young to go to work; they are still in school. And some are too old or too infirm to be working; they are retired or disabled.
- And four out of five women who do go to work also keep house! We can no longer assume that it is only full-time homemakers who are housewives in our society.

Notes

1. Nan Robertson, "A Sociologist 'Emeritus' Who Is Far from Retired," *New York Times,* December 14, 1980.
2. *The Yankelovich Monitor* (annual) (New York: Yankelovich, Skelly, and White, 1980). *The Yankelovich Monitor* is an annual study of social trends that was begun a decade ago and now provides us with ten years of trend data relating to all sorts of social issues, values, and attitudes.
3. Robert Atwan, Donald McQuade, and John W. Wright, eds., *Edsels, Luckies, and Frigidaires: Advertising the American Way* (New York: Dell, 1979), p. 8.
4. William Chafe, *The American Woman* (1972), as cited in Atwan, McQuade, and Wright, *Edsels, Luckies, and Frigidaires,* p. 8.

Chapter 2

Why Women Work

What has spurred the sharp and continuing influx of women into the work force? The explanations are usually economic. Some observers speculate that women have gone to work because of dire economic necessity. Others refer to the need to keep pace with inflation. Some attribute the surge of women into the work force to the desire of some wives to have a little mad money of their own.

The assumptions underlying these explanations as to why women work appear to be that no woman would go to work if her husband could support her and that only those unfortunate women who have not yet snared a husband or who have had the bad luck to lose one must enter the job market.

Implicit in the latter assumption, of course, are still others. The working woman who finally succeeds in landing a mate will, of course, prefer to stop working and become a full-time homemaker. Or, even if the young wife works for a year or two after marriage, she will surely leave her job when she has started a family.

The very fact that we ask why women work implies that there is something remarkable or unexpected or unnatural in their doing so. I can't remember hearing any discussions or reading any articles on why men work. We all assume that men are not responsible members of society unless they work at something. We expect even men who have inherited great wealth to lead productive working or professional lives. Gloria Steinem writes: "It's a question rarely directed at male workers; their basic motivations of survival through personal satisfaction are largely taken for granted. (Indeed, men are regarded as "odd" and, therefore, subjects for sociological study only when they don't have work of their own, even if they are rich or can't find jobs, even if they are poor and untrained."[1]

We expect men to work. We expect women to be wives and mothers, supported by their husbands. Until very recently any deviation from this pattern was considered exceptional and outside the norm.

There is no single clear-cut answer to the question of why women work. The answers may be found in a combination of objective demographic facts, economic realities, and sharply changing values and aspirations.

As we examine the apparently contradictory explanations as to why women do or do not go to work, we find an apparent conflict between those who believe the motivations are economic and those who believe they are attitudinal. Some of these apparently conflicting reasons for working are inextricably intertwined.

Economic Necessity

Sheer economic necessity as the basic motivation for women working has always been with us. There are women in the work force who have always done the unpleasant, difficult menial jobs in our society. For these women, true liberation would be a chance to get up off their knees, stay home, and take care of their own families.

One example of this "drudge" motivation for working was quoted in a poignant excerpt in *The New York Times* from *Women of Crisis, Struggle, and Hope,* a book by Robert Coles and Jane Hallowell Coles. The woman quoted is a cook and housekeeper for a prominent and affluent Cambridge family. She discusses her employer, a woman who works in public relations and is involved in a number of cultural activities in her community. She quotes her as saying that she used to do volunteer work but now feels that she should go to work as men do. The housekeeper says: "My husband thinks she's crazy and so do I. If I had money, I'd quit this job and go home and stay home for a thousand years. I would be with my kids and not someone else's. It doesn't make sense. The missus says she has to get out and work or else she'll stagnate . . . her favorite word. She's always worrying about stagnating."[2]

This moving comment dramatizes the socioeconomic divergence between those women who work only because they really have to and those women who yearn to get away from a life of volunteerism and into the real world of work.

Even the most traditional-minded among us admit that most unmarried women (whether single, widowed, or divorced) must work to support themselves. What we may not realize is that more than four out of every ten women in our country are not married.

Howard Rosen, Director of the Division of Research and Development, Employment and Training Administration, U.S. Department of Labor, says: "The myth in our society is that most women do not have to work. Many people believe that women are in the labor force to help their families acquire luxuries. Some people believe that when we have recessions women should leave the labor force so that men who head families would have an easier time in finding jobs."[3]

Obviously, unmarried women must work to support themselves. They do not have the luxury of choice. An increasing number are responsible not only for themselves but for their families as well. Rosen points out that our country has the highest divorce rate in the world. The rate of divorce has doubled since 1950. This means an increasing number of households are headed by divorced or separated women. There has also been a phenomenal rise in the number of babies born out of wedlock. The increase in the number of unmarried mothers accounts for one-fifth of the post-1970s households headed by women.

In 1978 the National Commission on Working Women conducted a study entitled "National Survey: A Focus on Working Women." The sample was a cross-section of all women in and out of the work force. The purpose was "to identify the problems, needs, and concerns of all American women and to discover how they feel about working." An article in the October 11, 1979, issue of *Woman's Day* reported on that study: "For many single women and many single mothers, divorcees and widows, the motive for working is simple: *a paycheck* is *the only thing* that keeps them off the relief rolls."

To quote Mr. Rosen again: "Marital disruption is oftentimes an economic catastrophe for women. About one in four white families becomes poor when a marriage is broken. The situation for black women is far worse."[4]

The experiences of two of the divorcees who participated in the study give eloquent testimony to the impact of divorce on the economic status of a family:

"I am a member of the 'working-class divorced poor,' demoted from a ten-room house and housewife/mother status, and an income of $23,000 a year to a four-room apartment with one bedroom (the other child in the dining room, and me in the living room with no privacy), working-mother status and an income of $8,000 a year plus $2,700 child support. Two male lawyers and one ex-husband figured I could go to work full time when the children were in school full time. There is just a little two-hour discrepancy, though. They are in school six hours, I must work eight. So a small fortune is spent on babysitters.... It has taken me four years to establish credit in my name. ... I am angry, but at least I know what I am angry about.''

"I am a 45-year-old woman who stayed home with her children and raised them. I thought I was secure because my husband had been in the military for twenty years, and we retired here in Florida. He walked out on us when my boy was fourteen and my girl thirteen. We had no warning of this and of course I had to go out and get a job. . . . Hope your survey will help working women because a lot of us out here are pretty desperate and would appreciate any help we could get. I, like many others, do not want charity, food stamps, etc., as I am able to work. Speaking for myself, I would like to be able to feel I have job security and respectability in what I do. I pray to God every night just to keep me well, at least until my children are launched.''[5]

Doesn't this confirm the assumption that women who work are working for reasons of sheer economic necessity?

Indeed it does. But it does not account for the dramatic rise in the number of married women who have entered the work force in the past decade. Many of these are economically motivated as well. According to the Bureau of Labor Statistics, a majority of working wives are also working for reasons of economic necessity.

The Second Paycheck

Two-paycheck marriages have become a fact of life. In 1980, half of all husband–wife families had two or more paychecks. The dramatic rise in the porportion of working wives is illustrated by the increase in multiworker families since 1955.

Howard Rosen calls the traditional view of the breadwinner husband a myth: "Let us turn to another mythical being, the macho man who supports his wife out of his own earnings. If his wife works, it is to acquire luxuries." The *Woman's Day* article concurs: "The widespread belief that women take paying jobs outside their homes to fulfill

TABLE 2-1. Percentage of Two-Paycheck Households

	1955	1960	1965	1970	1975	1980
Husband/wife households with two or more paychecks	25%	29%	33%	39%	44%	50%

SOURCE: U.S. Census Bureau.

themselves, because they don't cherish their husbands, and care deeply about their children is absolute nonsense. The overwhelming majority work for exactly the same reason men do: they need the money."

Testimony to the essential character of that second paycheck was voiced by two wives quoted in *Woman's Day.*

"One Oregon writer expressed it clearly: 'Perhaps, in the higher wage brackets, women can work because they want to, or enjoy job fulfillment, but all the women I've ever worked with worked because they 'have to.'"

"Lots of women are angered by the assumption of others that they work for trivial reasons. Said one Oklahoman: "Several of my employers (always male) think that we only work for luxuries, new curtains, knickknacks, etc. I work to put food on the table! I don't know any young women who can afford not to work." And some wives report that it is pressure from their husbands that sends them out to work or keeps them in the job market.

"An Idaho wife described the sort of game she felt was too often played: It didn't matter how a wife 'really felt,' she said, 'or how busy she was at home. She was made to feel lazy if she didn't bring home a second paycheck. . . . "If you went to work, we could do this, afford that, buy this." And worse yet—'So-and-So's wife has a good job! Boy, is she great—why can't you do that?'"

"'I'm tired of working . . . have worked twenty-eight of my forty-six years," said one, "but my husband is scared we would starve without my salary. . . . I feel as if I am in a trap.'"[6]

So far the picture looks grim. It seems to confirm the economic necessity theory. Gloria Steinem terms this "womenworkbecause-wehaveto" as one word, one key on the typewriter, an economic form of the acceptably "feminine" stance of passivity and self-sacrifice.

However, the purely economic explanation of why women work doesn't jibe with some of the facts. *The more education a woman has, the more likely she is to be in the work force.* Surely all of those college-educated women aren't living at subsistence levels. True, unmarried women work to support themselves whether they have had advanced education or not. However, the greatest proportion of working wives are found among families with total household incomes of $25,000 to $50,000 a year. There is a good deal of evidence that it is the wife's earnings that have moved the family up the economic ladder. But this is hardly economic necessity.

There has been a dramatic change in perceptions and attitudes that is still not acknowledged by the perpetrators of the myth. After all, if economic necessity were the sole motivation for women to work, married women would never seek employment unless their husbands were incapacitated or unemployed. The assumptions about the husband as breadwinner and the wife who works only to meet an emergency had some validity during the late Depression. Wives who went to work in those years returned to the home as soon as their husbands returned to the work force. Gloria Steinem describes the change in our social values since that time:

"Then, of course, the one-job-per-household seemed justified, yet the concept was generally used to displace women workers and create intolerable dependencies. (As it still would be. If only one salary is allowable per family, guess who is likely to get it?) That Depression experience, plus the energy and example of women who were finally allowed to work during the World War II man-shortage, led Congress to reinterpret the meaning of the country's full-employment goal in the Economic Act of 1946. It became 'employment of those who want to work, without regard to whether their employment is, by some definition, necessary. This goal applies equally to men and women.'"[7]

Since their husbands are employed, that second paycheck is in most cases an extra paycheck. These wives claim to be working for economic reasons, for the good things of life, so that they can improve the family standard of living or maintain it in the face of rising inflation. It is only when we look deeper and examine which of these women who are working for that second paycheck would truly prefer not to go to work and which ones would truly prefer to remain in the work force that we can really understand the dynamics of why they work.

Beyond the Paycheck

Clearly there is something beyond the paycheck that motivates many women to work. Some evidence of this may be found in responses to a question asked by the Newspaper Advertising Bureau in its studies of working women conducted in 1971 and again in 1979.[8] Working women, many of whom had previously explained that they were working because they needed the money, were asked whether they would choose to stay home or continue working if they could receive the same amount of money that they earned at work.

A consistent three out of five working women said they would prefer to work even if money were no longer the issue. Not surprisingly, women in professional and managerial occupations were more likely

TABLE 2-2. Percentage of Working Women Who Would Continue to Work Even If They Could Receive the Same Amount of Money to Stay Home

Total working women	61%
Professional/managerial	66%
Clerical/sales	62%
Blue collar	57%

SOURCE: *Women, Work, and the Markets of the '80s,* Newspaper Advertising Bureau Project, 1979.

than any other group to want to continue to work. However, there was less difference than one might expect in preference for work between women in less glamorous and jobs and those in prestigious occupations.

As this study comments, "money, of course, is an important reason for working, but it is difficult to isolate the strictly monetary reasons for working since money has symbolic meanings (such as a measure of achievement) as well as practical consequences."

In spite of the fact that "in a culture that still values the homemaker role, many women are likely to publicly emphasize monetary reasons for work," between 1971 and 1979 both working women and nonworking women who said they might go to work were less likely to say that the reason they work or want to work is because they "have to work."

In 1971 slightly fewer of the women who said they were working for reasons of sheer economic necessity would have continued to go on working if they could receive the money, than of those who said they did not have to work. In 1979 the level of commitment to continued work of women who needed to work was almost identical to that of women who did not have to work.

The Roper Public Opinion Poll[9] asked a similar question of women

TABLE 2-3. Work Because Need Money

	WORKING WOMEN		NONWORKING WOMEN WHO MIGHT WORK	
	1971	*1979*	*1971*	*1979*
Have to work	45%	39%	37%	24%
(Base)	(661)	(736)	(121)	(242)

SOURCE: *Women, Work, and the Markets of the '80s,* Newspaper, Advertising Bureau Project, 1979.

TABLE 2-4.   Interest in Continuing Work
(Working Women by Need for Money)

	HAVE TO WORK		DO NOT HAVE TO WORK	
	1971	1979	1971	1979
If same money were provided without working:				
Would go on working	55%	62%	63%	64%
Would stop working	42	33	31	28
Don't know	3	5	6	8
(Base)	(286)	(272)	(296)	(358)

SOURCE: *Women, Work, and the Markets of the '80s,* Newspaper Advertising Bureau Project, 1979.

in February 1978: "Regardless of whether both are possible, would you *prefer* to have a job outside the home or would you *prefer* to stay home and take care of the house and family?" *Two out of three working women* said they *would prefer to continue working,* even if it were economically possible for them to stay at home.

Further confirmation of the relative strength of economic and non-economic motivations for work is reflected in an analysis of trends in the *Yankelovich Monitor.*[10] Ever since 1972, Yankelovich has been asking employed women whether they work *primarily* to derive income, primarily as a source of enjoyment, or primarily to be independent.

The noneconomic reasons have predominated through the years. In 1980, 28 percent of working women said they were working primarily for the income. About two in five said they worked primarily as a source of enjoyment, and one out of three said they went to work in order to be independent.

When we examine the work motivations of working women who consider their work just a job with those who are career-oriented,* a fascinating picture emerges. Job-oriented women are far more likely than career women to say they go to work because they need the money. This is more true of the unmarried women in the job category than working wives.

Career women are far more likely than women who say their work is just a job to say that their primary reason for working is that they en-

*We term these categories "the New Demographics." This will be discussed in detail in Chapters 7 and 8.

joy the work. This is particularly true of unmarried career women: 80 percent say that enjoyment is the primary reason that they work. Conversely, independence is almost twice as important to job-oriented women as to career women. In both cases *married women are more likely than their unmarried sisters to stress independence.*

What are the attractions of work that would keep these women out of the home even if money was no longer the issue?

There Must Be Something More to Life than the Kitchen Sink

Some working wives are motivated less by what they are going toward than what they are getting away from. Their reasons for working are to escape from the confining, narrow lives available to them as full-time homemakers.

These are the women who perceive work as a passport that will take them out of the kitchen and into the world. They say they are restless and don't have enough to do at home, they are bored with housework, they are too lonely at home, or they feel taken for granted when they are full-time homemakers. These are negative reasons for seeking broader horizons and activities outside the home.

In recent years there has been a subtle shift away from the negative desire to get out of the house toward a more positive response to the attractions and satisfactions of the working experience. The pair of studies conducted by the Newspaper Advertising Bureau in 1971 and 1979 provide insights into this change in emphasis.

In 1971 some of the strong noneconomic reasons for work reflected the frustrations that working women perceived in the narrow horizons of a homebound life. They said they were restless and did not have enough to do at home. They found housework boring and found life at home too lonely.

The Attractions of Work

In 1979 working women were more likely to cite the positive attractions of the working experience as reasons for going to work, whether or not they needed the money. They appreciated the social stimulation provided by work. They were more likely than in 1971 to say that going to work enabled them to get out and meet new people. They also responded to the sense of accomplishment and self-development that occurred when they went to work. They gave more emphasis in 1979 than in 1971 to the fact that work enabled them to do something worthwhile. They said they appreciated working because they learned new things.

However, the most significant change that occurred between 1971 and 1979 was a heightened perception that work connotes independence. The two out of three working women who told Roper that they would prefer to have a job outside the home even if they didn't need the money were clearly seeking horizons broader than those they found in the role of a full-time homemaker. They craved the social stimulation of being with other people. Beyond that they said that working helped them find personal fulfillment. Or they said that working gave fuller expression to their sense of self-worth than would be possible if they stayed home.

Identity

No matter which aspect of "broader horizons" reasons for work was expressed by these working women, it becomes clear that for many of them going to work represents opportunities for self-expression and achievement of a sense of self beyond their traditional roles as wives and mothers.

"I feel I have talents or abilities in addition to taking care of a house or children."

"I think I am a more interesting person because I get outside the house."

"Working outside the house is more interesting than staying home and taking care of the house."

"I want to be more independent, to have a part of my life that is mine, and not involved with my family."

"I have more of a sense of accomplishment working at a job than I would being a housewife."

The yearning for an identity beyond that of their traditional family roles is so deeply intertwined with the economic motivations for going to work that they cannot be separated. *This surge toward a sense of self is a fundamental part of the surge of women into the work force.*

The question of work as identity is an assumed part of men's lives. Just as we never analyze why men work, we never question what work means to their sense of self-worth. Some clues to the relationship between work and identity can be found in studies of how people adjust to retirement. There is much anecdotal evidence that many retirees experience a feeling of trauma and loss when they leave their working identities behind and move into the nonstructured world of nonwork. Conversely, as many women move into the working world, they begin to bloom with a new sense of self-worth.

One of my favorite examples of this attitude came from a receptionist employed at my company a few years ago. She was a well-groomed middle-aged woman from the Bronx. She stopped me one morning as I got off the elevator to comment on some publicity that had appeared about one of my speeches on working women. She said that many of her friends and neighbors could not understand why she went to work because, "after all, my husband can afford to support me."

"They don't understand that my children are grown and out of the house," she continued, "and I really don't like to sit home all day and watch television or play bridge. Although this isn't a very important job, it gives me a reason to get up in the morning, a place to come, a reason to get myself dressed and out of the house." It was clear that for this woman work did not fulfill any career ambitions, but it did give her a clear sense of focus and personal identity.

At the other end of the socioeconomic scale, in 1979 I had an interesting conversation with Alice Weber, who was then president of the Association of Junior Leagues. That organization traditionally recruited its members from the more privileged segments of our society.

She told me that almost half of the Association's members were currently working. Therefore, the organization has to adjust the hours of its meetings and the nature of its programs to accommodate the schedules of its working members. Mrs. Weber was, of course, a full-time volunteer herself. She told me something about her responsibilities as AJL president. Her work and travel schedule was as intensive as that of the most active corporate executive. I asked her what she planned to do when her year in office was over. She said to me, "Frankly, I plan to go to work for pay. I don't think I could ever be happy functioning solely as a volunteer any more."

Today Alice Weber works as the executive director of a three-hospital cancer program in Toledo. Her résumé was based solely on her experiences as a volunteer. Her husband, Edward F. Weber, is a freshman congressman representing the Ninth District in Toledo. She was an active participant in his campaign, as she puts it, "doing everything from stuffing envelopes to sharing in strategy decisions."

An example of the transition from professionalism to volunteerism and back again is cited in Lindsy Van Gelder's article "Five Good Motives."[11] This gives fascinating testimony to the symbolic meaning of working for a paycheck as compared to doing the same work as a volunteer. She quotes a geriatric social worker who has pursued her profession both as a volunteer and as a paid professional worker: "'When my children were very small and I needed flexibility, I worked as a volunteer at various hospitals, doing the exact same work I had always done professionally. It was tremendously interesting to me to see how my colleagues viewed me. I simply didn't have the same status. I was a "Lady Bountiful," not a professional. The moment I went back on the payroll I was a professional again.' Today, Sarah donates a great deal of her money to charity, but she intends to continue working: 'It's the most meaningful sustenance I know. I'm a survivor. I don't even know the word "retirement".'"

In January 1979 *U.S. News & World Report* reported that Jody Tadder of Maryland discovered that her friends had been dropping out of the League of Women Voters to go to work. She had been personally jolted into the need for working back in 1974 when her husband was wounded by a prowler. "I realized that someday I might need to be the breadwinner. It could happen as fast as that." Mrs. Tadder, who was an officer in the League of Women Voters, enrolled in a Goucher College program to convert her volunteer experience into management training. "I wanted the challenge. I was depressed. There is a level in volunteer work when the satisfaction stops."[12]

But How Will I Spend the Rest of My Life?

Finally, there is the reality of the changing cycle of women's lives and their changing needs as their life patterns change. Even those women who embrace the traditional notion that a woman's true fulfillment comes as a wife and mother begin to realize that they become partially unemployed as their children grow up and leave home. Therefore, another noneconomic reason for wanting to work is to prepare for the time when the traditional wife–mother role is no longer a daily occupation. Some women say, "I don't have enough to do around the house to keep me busy," or "I know my children will leave home at some point and I don't want to be left with nothing else in my life after that."

Gail Sheehy in her "Happiness Report" confirms the problem of the empty nest: "Looking for jobs to replace the outlived purpose of mothering is particularly difficult for the middle-aged women of today. Their generation was never adequately prepared educationally or emotionally for the reality that paid employment becomes central to the self-esteem of middle-aged women . . . mobilizing their talents and pouring their energies into finding and doing paid work becomes one of their main methods of dealing with stress. This sudden and strong emphasis on work and achievement in the world brings with it exhilaration. . . . It is in this middle-aged group of women from 46 to 55 that the greatest number of people report establishing a firm sense of their own identities for the first time." [13]

Gloria Steinem wrote a fascinating article on why women work in the March 1979 issue of Ms. magazine. Part of that article consisted of interviews with a cross-section of women who commented on the meaning of work in their own lives. Jacqueline Kennedy Onassis, currently employed as an editor at Doubleday, talked about the assumption that women in our society were expected to find fulfillment in their lives as wives and mothers: "What has been sad for many women of my generation is that they weren't supposed to work if they had families. There they were, with the highest education, and what were they to do when the children were grown—watch the raindrops coming down the windowpane? Leave their fine minds unexercised? Of course, women should work if they want to. You have to be doing something you enjoy. That is a definition of happiness: 'complete use of one's faculties along lines leading to excellence in a life affording them scope.' It applies to women as well as to men. We can't all reach it, but we can try." [14]

Lindsy Van Gelder says in "Five Good Motives," which appears in the same issue of *Ms.:* "As a divorced mother supporting two children, Randy Baca spent more than twenty years working 'because I had to' in advertising and public relations in Phoenix, Arizona. Work was simply her way of life. Then two years ago, Randy married a radio executive with 'a very comfortable salary,' but she has chosen to continue in her post as executive director of the Arizona Small Business Association. 'I've worked for money much too long to stop. I'm also at the age where my children are grown and I'm realizing that now is when the fun really begins—now I can focus on getting things done. And I like the knowledge that nobody can do my job like I can. You know, if all of the wives who "don't have to work" stopped working, the economy would grind to a screeching halt."

Achievement

There is still another reason why women work. While this segment may represent a smaller number of women in the work force, theirs is a stong motivation and one that appears to be growing. It is the reason for work that motivates the most ambitious men in our society, the desire for professional achievement and personal fulfillment. This motivation is shared by career-oriented men and women. Such a serious commitment to career or profession has been held by only a few women until the last few years. There have always been career-oriented women in America, but until very recently they tended to be the exception rather than the rule. To the extent that those women were married (and many of them were), they were, of course, married to the more achieving men in our society.

A generation ago those women had to compensate for their eccentric desire to pursue a career outside of the accepted role of wife and mother. They had to "pay their dues" by attempting to be "supermoms." They were superwives, superhostesses, supermothers. They had to prove to their husbands and their neighbors that they could discharge all of the usual household responsibilities expected of any wife or mother in our society and could manage an outside career as well.

In recent years the desire for career gratification has been on the rise. Currently, about one in three working women in our society sees herself as career-oriented, according to the *Yankelovich Monitor*. [15] Our evidence indicates that career commitment is highly correlated with education. Again, this motivation for work goes far beyond the necessity of economic survival. This segment of working women do not scorn economic rewards. However, they tend to see money as evidence of achievement rather than as the only reason for seeking achievement. As one corporate executive said: "A company thinks of you what it pays you." This is further evidence that the economic motivation is deeply intertwined with symbolic meanings.

Lindsy Van Gelder reports on the symbolic value of the paycheck:

"Cary Ridder has a "rich kid" background (her family are part owners of the Knight-Ridder newspaper chain) and a trust fund income that she could live on if she chose to. Instead she works as a modestly salaried lobbyist for the Environmental Policy Institute in Washington, D.C. "In a society where you're valued by how much you make, you have much better self-esteem if you're paid. . . . I have to do the same things everybody else does to get my paycheck and my work is judged accordingly'."[16]

The Newspaper Advertising Bureau report comments that since 1971 the typical working woman has become younger and better educated. These characteristics are closely related to career orientation.

As younger women complete their schooling and enter the work force, there is every reason to believe the career orientation will continue to grow.

Notes

1. Gloria Steinem, "Special: Why Women Work," *Ms.* Magazine, March 1979, p. 45.

2. Robert Coles and Jane Hallowell Coles, "The Grass Isn't Greener, Just the Money," *New York Times,* April 10, 1979, from *Women of Crisis: Lives of Struggle and Hope* (New York: Delacorte, 1978).

3. Howard Rosen, "Research Debunks Myths about Women Who Work," *Arizona Review,* Third Quarter, 1979, p. 18.

4. *Ibid.,* p. 19

5. Evelyn Grant, "How Do You Feel about Working?" *Woman's Day,* October 11, 1979, p. 56

6. *Ibid.,* p. 54.

7. Gloria Steinem, p. 90.

8. *Women, Work, and the Markets of the 80's,* Newspaper Advertising Bureau Project, 1979.

9. *Roper Reports* (New York: The Roper Organization, February 1978).

10. *The Yankelovich Monitor* (annual) (New York: Yankelovich, Skelly, and White, 1972–1981).

11. Lindsy Van Gelder "Five Good Motives (Besides Money)," *Ms.* Magazine, March 1979, p. 52.

12. "Women at Work: Still Fighting 'Stereotyped Roles'," *US News and World Report,* January 15, 1979.

13. Gail Sheehy, "The Happiness Report," a 2-part article, *Redbook,* July 1979 and August 1979, Part 1, p. 6.

14. "Jacqueline Kennedy Onassis Talks About Working," *Ms.* Magazine, March 1979, pp. 50–51.

15. *Yankelovich Monitor.*

16. Lindsy Van Gelder, p. 92.

Chapter 3

Will It Continue?

Is the surge of women into the work force a temporary fad or a continuing trend? Scarcely a day goes by that I don't hear someone explaining how the biological clock will move all of those young female careerists of the baby boom generation out of the work place and back into the home. They reason that the basic urge of these young women to have children will overtake their temporary foray into the world of work. When it does, they will withdraw from the work force and fulfill their biological destinies.

Others earnestly discuss the potential confrontation between the women who have entered the work force and male breadwinners as we enter a recession and jobs become scarce. I hear predictions of a male backlash and of a female rejection of the new freedoms and new life styles.

Of course, no one can predict the future with total certainty but *all* the *indicators* I have seen *point to a continuation* of the *trend toward women's increasing participation in the labor force.* The most compelling evidence is the strong correlation between education and women's presence in the work force. The more education a woman has, the more likely she is to go to work. Two out of three of the best-educated women are in the work force, while fewer than one in four of the least well-educated women go to work.

As noted in Chapter 2, this suggests that economic necessity cannot be the only reason women go to work. One would assume that women with less than elementary school education are more in need of money and that women who have graduated from college or gone on to graduate school live in the most affluent households. For the most part better-educated women tend to marry the best-educated men, who in turn tend to be the highest achievers in our society. Conversely, the least well-educated women are less likely to have married men who can support them in comfort.

One reason for believing that the trend toward women entering or remaining in the work force will not be reversed is that more and more

Exhibit I

THE PROPORTION OF WOMEN AT EACH EDUCATIONAL LEVEL IN THE LABOR FORCE: 1979

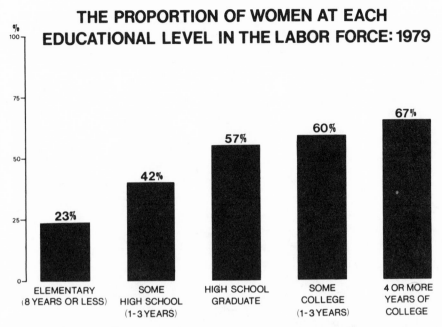

Base: All Women 16 Years and Over
Source: Bureau of Labor Statistics, Monthly Labor Review. July 1980

women are going to college. In 1950 three out of ten college students were female. By 1978 women constituted half of all students enrolled in colleges and universities in our country. Another reason that women can be expected to maintain a continued and ever stronger presence in the work force is that more of them are going on to graduate study than ever before.

Moreover, women are seeking graduate training in fields of study that used to be dominated by men. While still far from equal to men in earning degrees in law, medicine, architecture, or engineering, women's rate of growth in those fields has been phenomenal.

The clear correlation between education and women's presence in the work force, as well as the renewed dynamism of women's surge into advanced education in general and into graduate training in the professions in particular, all suggest that women are anticipating lifetime careers. Will women continue to enter and stay in the work force? There is no question that this trend will continue until it is no longer a debatable issue.

The pundits in Washington who forecast demographic trends underestimated how many women would be in the work force today be-

EXHIBIT **II**

GROWTH IN NUMBER OF DEGREES
EARNED BY WOMEN IN SELECTED FIELDS

PERCENT CHANGE 1965-1980

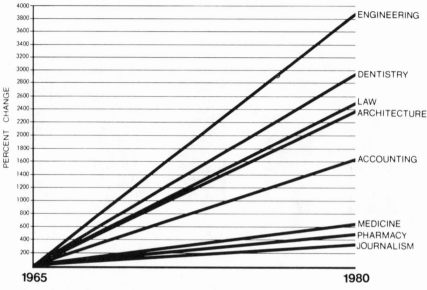

Source: Digest of Educational Statistics.
National Center for Educational Statistics

cause of their erroneous assumption that women with small children would leave work or not enter it. They had predicted that by 1980, 48.4 percent of all women in the United States sixteen years of age and older would be going to work.[1] That level of female participation in the work force was actually reached two years ahead of schedule (see Chapter 1, p. 9).

Therefore, the Bureau of Labor Statistics forecasts on the number of women who will work in the future are founded on an understated data base. Nonetheless, if we examine even this conservative estimate, we see that the forecasters expect 64.4 percent of the women between twenty and fifty-four years of age to be in the work force by 1990.

The 1980 Roper Public Opinion Poll conducted for Virginia Slims reports that the overwhelming majority of women and men anticipate that by the year 2000 "almost all women who can will be working." As for the more immediate future, the report states, "it seems very likely that during the eighties women will continue to enter the job market in increasing numbers.'' Its data show that the younger they are and the better educated they are, the more likely it is that women will enter or reenter the work force.

The same survey also confirms the role that education plays in motivating women to want to go to work. Roper says: "Education is the chief factor which differentiates between non-working women who intend to find jobs in the future and non-working women who prefer to remain at home."[2]

Changing Aspirations

Further evidence that women will continue to be active in the work force comes from a study sponsored by the National Commission on the Observance of International Woman's Year called *American Women Today and Tomorrow*. According to this study, "the trend among the young and the educated—and more of the young are educated—is toward an expanding concept of women's roles. The Expanding Outlook calls for a woman's job or career to be given as much emphasis and consideration as a man's." The report goes on to say that "the Expanding Outlook appears to be the wave of the future because it is the dominant outlook among key groups of women who are likely to be setting trends. These groups are comprised of women under thirty-five, women with post–high–school education, particularly college graduates, the non-marrieds (singles and divorced), and those who work in professional or technical occupations. It has a slight edge among clerical and sales workers and among labor union members. It holds the allegiance of significant minorities of all occupational groups including homemakers."[3]

One of the most dramatic findings of this report is that nine out of ten women under thirty-five years of age do not aspire to be "mainly a homemaker" for life. This traditional aspiration is held by only one in ten young women, although a greater proportion of older women still endorse the traditional role as the best way for women to live. But even among older women the perception that the ideal life style choice for women is to be mainly a homemaker is endorsed by only 30 percent of women between thirty-five and sixty-four years of age. Only 40 percent of women over sixty-five endorse this traditional view! This means that *the majority of women of all ages believe that women should participate in the work force in some combination with marriage and motherhood.*

It isn't that the younger women reject homemaking or marriage *per se*. They feel, rather, that women can and should expand into activities in the world outside their homes. The majority of women feel that the ideal life style choice would be to have children, stay home when the children are young, and combine a job or career with homemaking at other times in their lives. This point of view is held by just under half of all women. One in four women endorses the concept of having it all at once—that is, combining a job or career with homemaking and child care (if they have children) throughout their lives.

Of course, while many of these younger women aspire to either homemaking plus career or homemaking and career in some sequential pattern, many of them do not necessarily assume that they will marry and will raise families as their mothers did before them. Some may not marry at all, and many may live in a nontraditional life style arrangement that may not culminate in marriage. According to the *Yankelovich Monitor,* more than half of the American public think it is perfectly all right for a couple to live together without marriage if they love each other. [4] This new kind of household arrangement has a still higher level of endorsement from men and unmarried adults.

Others may decide against embarking on motherhood even if they should get married eventually. Whereas only a few years ago we might all have assumed that recently married couples were in a state of transition between the honeymoon and parenthood, there is a real possibility that many of them will not undertake the responsibility of bringing children into the world. Almost nine out of ten people in this country feel there is nothing wrong with a married couple's deciding not to have any children. The proportion holds true for both men and women.

The acceptance of childlessness as an option is a major attitudinal change which challenges traditional assumptions about society. This new attitude could have a major impact on the way people live and a direct relationship to whether women assume that they will work throughout their lifetimes, just as men have always done.

The notion that marriage and motherhood are not the only destiny for women in our society is reflected in the National Commission's study, where one in four of all married women interviewed were not certain that their marriages would last for their lifetimes. As the report points out, "this one-fourth of married women who are not absolutely certain that their marriages will last until death are theoretically looking at what has happened to others. Nearly one-fourth (twenty-two percent) of women between the ages of thirty-five and fifty-four who have ever been married have also been divorced. Many of them have remarried," and 18 percent of women have been widowed at some time.[5]

Young women are looking at the realities of life around them. Even though the ideal for most is to combine marriage and work, most of them also realize that there is nothing certain in this life. Therefore, it is not surprising that most of them assume they will be working for the better part of their lives.

Women's changing perceptions of their goals in life have implications for both their presence in the work force and the nature of their family and marital relationships. It is difficult to discuss the kind of work women seek and how they feel about that work without setting their attitudes toward work in the context of their personal life style goals. According to Roper, women today overwhelmingly continue to favor marriage as a way of life. As a matter of fact, 94 percent of all women interviewed in the Virginia Slims poll endorsed marriage. However, Roper says, they "are tending to perceive marriage as a responsibility to be shared between both partners through similar roles with husband and wife working to contribute earned income and with both husband and wife sharing homemaking and child-rearing responsibilities."[6]

The changing nature of homemaking and childrearing responsibilities will be discussed in future chapters. However, the attitude that marriage is something in which both husband and wife work to contribute earned income is really a revolutionary concept. When this is put in tandem with the further redefinition of women's role in relation to motherhood, we see that the change in women's lives is, in fact, a revolution. Roper says: "More than four out of five women (82%) in 1980 say that children are not an essential ingredient in a full and happy marriage. Therefore, motherhood, once an integral part of marriage, is no longer seen as an essential ingredient in marriage."[7]

We have noted earlier that one in four women do not expect their marriages to last a lifetime and that today's young women may not assume that they themselves will marry. Roper confirms this. He says that "in case of an unsuccessful marriage, more women today (62%) favor divorce as an acceptable solution than did so ten years ago (52%)."[8]

This reappraisal and redefinition of women's traditional role has a direct bearing on their present and potential involvement in the work force. The National Commission for the Observance of International Woman's Year report confirms that the majority of women seek a combination of marriage and work as an ideal goal. As we have noted, more of them would prefer to go in and out of the work force, alternating their family responsibilities and their working commitments. However, one in four hopes to combine job and homemaking throughout her lifetime. This point of view is endorsed to a greater extent by younger women. So it might turn out to be a pattern for the future.

The campus debates about marriage versus career that dominated our attention a generation ago would amaze today's young woman. They may marry later than their mothers and they may opt to delay having children (or have no children at all), but the question of whether or not to work is not even an issue!

Ironically, although Roper tells us that those women who still aspire to raise families consider twenty-four the ideal age for having babies, Gail Sheehy tells us that the happiest women are those who delayed having their children until a much later age. She says that "a striking number (slightly over half) of the women who came out on top of the overall satisfaction scale also waited at least until they were twenty-eight to have their first child or are still postponing parenthood or anticipate not having children at all." [9]

Since postponing motherhood to the age of twenty-eight or beyond is a rare but growing pattern among women nationwide (only about 11 percent do), the fact that fully half of the happiest women independently chose that path is an impressive finding.

Is the Biological Clock Ticking?

At the beginning of this chapter, I reported the prediction that the biological clock will catch up with the female careerists of the baby boom generation and that they will return to their traditional roles as wives and mothers. The foregoing data suggest that many of them may, in fact, eschew motherhood. Even those who do decide to raise families will probably have smaller families than their mothers did. And many of them will either continue to work or return to work as soon as their families are launched.

Professor Eli Ginzberg, for one, does not believe that the recent reduction in fertility is likely to be reversed. In rebuttal to Professor Richard Easterlin of the University of Pennsylvania, who suggests that the trends we have seen may not continue, Professor Ginzberg says: "I expect that we will continue to experience very low fertility." He continues: "Since women, like men, need a role and cannot be unengaged at home and not at work, I expect them to be tied more closely to the work place. . . . Secondly, of every five marriages that are now being consummated, two will eventually break up. It would be unthoughtful of women not to be concerned about their future, since we know that even if alimony were for real it would not be much of an answer. But most divorcees don't get it. If they do, it's very little and it does not come for very long. Just in self-defense, women have little option but to be concerned with work if two out of every five marriages will end in divorce."[10]

What About Male Backlash?

I also referred at the beginning of this chapter to the opinion of some ˙observers regarding a potential confrontation between the women who have entered the work force and male breadwinners as we enter a recession and jobs become scarce. Is this potential backlash real? Professor Ginzberg does not think so: "Let us remember that we are not dealing with a zero sum game. It does not follow that because an organization or a society helps women it necessarily must take things away from men. That's an error. As Mr. Brown suggested, if we can improve the productivity of the female part of the population, which is half the population, the total pie ought to get bigger and then men as well as women will be better off. I believe that."[11]

"Mr. Brown" is Charles L. Brown, board chairman of the American Telephone and Telegraph Company, who co-chaired a conference on "Women in the Work Force." At that same conference, John Macomber, president and chief executive officer of the Celanese Corporation, said that his organization retained a number of consultants to carry on a variety of studies relating to public responsibility issues. They did a specific study on the question of backlash. He terms backlash as the biggest "so what?" or nonsense question and adds that "there just isn't a problem except where a vociferous leader will organize some sort of position on it. It is a non-issue. It's a neat thing to talk about but it is not really there."[12]

On the other hand James Olson, vice-chairman of American Telephone and Telegraph, says that his company did "have a serious white male reaction to the function of the consent decree." He went on to say that "since we were utilizing the affirmative action override which in essence said that we had a deficiency in any one of the fifteen job categories in any protected class, it wasn't necessarily the best person who got promoted but somebody who was qualified. Obviously, we put no-

body in a job who wasn't qualified but there could be white males—
and there were white males—who maybe on the basis of who was the
best qualified didn't get the job. The reason was that we were trying to
make progress toward some interim goals which I think were right and
proper. I think we are getting close to the day when anybody is going to
have a fair chance at any job. Over time the situation will evolve into
what it should be. The best qualified person is going to have that opportunity."[13]

Was Your Mother a Role Model?

Another factor that supports my prediction that the trend will continue is the correlation of women's presence in the work force with the
occupational status of their mothers. Thirty-seven percent of the
women interviewed by Roper said that they had working mothers.[14]
Women who are currently employed are more likely to have had working mothers than women who do not go to work.

Having a working mother as a role model also seems to affect the
way working women feel about working and the potential working intentions of nonworking women. As noted in Chapter 2, two out of
three women with full-time jobs say they would rather go to work than
stay at home. Slightly more of these prefer-to-work women had working mothers than did the one in three who say they would rather stay
at home. Conversely, two out of three nonworking women say they
would prefer to stay at home rather than go to work. A higher proportion of those homemakers who opt for a job instead of staying home
are also the daughters of working mothers.

With more and more women in the work force and with the increasing presence of married women with children at work, it is inevitable that more and more people will grow up in households where the
mother goes to work. This demographic fact, in turn, may feed the
growing assumption that it is appropriate and inevitable for women to
be part of the work force.

A dramatic example of the power of a mother's example as a role
model was expressed by Eleanor Holmes Norton in a *Ms.* interview.
"In the black community the housewife lifestyle is almost unknown. In
my own childhood, everybody's mother worked—including the children whose parents were doctors or lawyers or other professionals.
Those were my role models. . . . I can't imagine not working at all. It
would be like being sick."[15]

Notes

1. *Monthly Labor Review,* Bureau of Labor Statistics, December 1976.
2. *The 1980 Virginia Slims American Women's Opinion Poll* (New York: The Roper Organization, 1980), p. 5.
3. Barbara Everitt Bryant *American Women Today and Tomorrow,* National Commission on the Observance of International Women's Year, (Washington D.C.: US Government Printing Office, 1977), p. 47.
4. *The Yankelovich Monitor* (annual), (New York: Yankelovich, Skelly and White, 1972–1981).
5. Barbara Everitt Bryant, p. 24.
6. *The 1980 Virginia Slims Poll,* p. 8.
7. *Ibid.,* p. 8.
8. *Ibid.,* p. 8.
9. Gail Sheehy, "The Happiness Report" (a 2-part article), *Redbook,* July 1979 and August 1979, Part 2, p. 8.
10. *Women in the Work Force Conference Report,* sponsored by American Telephone and Telegraph Co. and *Ladies' Home Journal,* New York, January 14–15, 1980, p. 3.
11. *Ibid.,* p. 4.
12. *Ibid.,* p. 16.
13. *Ibid.,* p. 17.
14. *Roper Reports,* The Roper Organization, New York, February 1978.
15. Lindsy Van Gelder, "Five Good Motives (Besides Money)," *Ms.* magazine, March 1979, p. 52.

Chapter 4

Women At Work

Having traced the surge of women entering the work force, analyzed what motivates them to go to work, explored the question as to whether this is a temporary or continuing phenomenon, let us now consider what the actual experience of working is like for those women who are currently in the work force. How do they feel about the work they do? What problems or satisfactions do they encounter in their jobs? What are their job-related hopes and aspirations for the future? In the early 1980s there is no single clear-cut picture of what women's work experience is like. The question might be whether the glass is half full or half empty.

Is the Glass Half Full?

Marshall Loeb, the managing editor of *Money* magazine, says that in the 1980s "the most important social development in our nation with tremendous impact on all our businesses will be the continuing rise to positions of power and influence of American women."[1] David Reisman reports having seen "an enormous widening of career opportunities" for women.[2] The Roper organization adds: "More women are working at fulltime jobs today than ever before and the trend appears to be one that is building in strength. Women are getting more career oriented and are seeking a broader selection of jobs than they ever did in the past. Increasingly, more women are intent on having fulltime careers and families and do not see any conflict in maintaining both. This trend is so strong that according to eighty-three percent of all the women interviewed it is very or fairly likely that by the year 2000 almost all women who are able will be working. More and more women, therefore, seem to be considering a career as another dimension along with that of marriage and family of a full and active life."[3]

Or Is It Half Empty?

On the other hand, the reality is that most working women find themselves in rather limited noncareer jobs with no discernible power or influence. According to the National Commission on Working Women, 80 percent of women in the work force are concentrated in lower-paying, lower-status jobs in service industries, clerical occupations, retail stores, factories, and plants. The commission's report points out that, for the most part, women in this 80 percent are "undervalued, underpaid, and underappreciated."[4]

The fact is that a woman earns about fifty-nine cents for every dol-

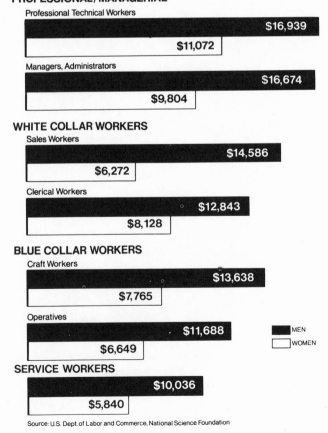

Exhibit I

OCCUPATION FOR OCCUPATION, WOMEN EARN LESS...

PROFESSIONAL/MANAGERIAL

Professional Technical Workers
- $16,939
- $11,072

Managers, Administrators
- $16,674
- $9,804

WHITE COLLAR WORKERS

Sales Workers
- $14,586
- $6,272

Clerical Workers
- $12,843
- $8,128

BLUE COLLAR WORKERS

Craft Workers
- $13,638
- $7,765

Operatives
- $11,688
- $6,649

MEN
WOMEN

SERVICE WORKERS
- $10,036
- $5,840

Source: U.S. Dept. of Labor and Commerce, National Science Foundation

TABLE 4-1.   ... But in Many Fields, They're Catching Up

These average salaries were offered to candidates for bachelors'
degrees in 1976, according to the National Science Foundation:

	WOMEN	MEN
Business		
Accounting	$12,252	$12,204
General business	$10,320	$10,512
Marketing	$ 9,768	$10,236
Humanities and Social Sciences		
Humanities	$ 8,916	$ 9,792
Social sciences	$ 9,240	$10,392
Engineering		
Aeronautical	$14,136	$13,824
Chemical	$15,396	$15,336
Civil	$13,836	$13,248
Electrical	$14,100	$13,848
Industrial	$13,968	$13,644
Mechanical	$14,712	$14,340
Metallurgical	$14,520	$14,544
Sciences		
Agricultural	$ 9,912	$10,272
Biological	$ 9,540	$ 9,840
Chemical	$12,624	$12,132
Computer science	$12,540	$12,420
Health professions	$ 9,900	$10,596
Mathematics	$11,784	$11,904
Other physical and earth		
sciences	$12,516	$12,636

SOURCE: U.S. Depts. of Labor and Commerce National Science Foundation.

lar a man earns. This is partly accounted for by the segregation of men
and women into male- and female-oriented fields and partly because
women have, in fact, been sporadic in their working lives.

An article on this subject in the *U.S. News & World Report* pointed
out that, occupation for occupation, women earn less than men.[5]

However, entry-level salaries in specific professional areas are
beginning to be equalized.

We might consider that in the 1970s women were concentrating on
gaining access to the world of work. They simply wanted in, and for the
most part, they came in. Women have flooded into the work force. The
majority of them want to stay there. Still, many working women have

real problems relating to the work that they do. In the 1980s it looks as though they are going to want more from their work.

According to Eli Ginzberg, the battleground for the 1980s could be the question of equality: "The 1980's will probably see the emergence of equal pay for comparable work quality. Not equal pay for equal work—that's easy—but for comparable work and that's tough."[6]

The Work Experience

It would be a mistake to consider women's working experience monolithically. There is really a two-tier situation. The 80 percent who make up the bulk of all working women in our country have specific kinds of problems and needs, and the 20 percent who are in professional or managerial jobs have other problems, other frustrations, and other needs.

The National Commission on Working Women conducted a survey on the working experiences of women. This study documents the problems and satisfactions of working women in general. It also contrasts the working experiences of the 80 percent of women in low-level, female ghetto jobs with those of professional and managerial women. What problems and satisfactions do women encounter in their work? The professionals obviously have more opportunities than "the 80 percent." On the other hand, both groups of working women share many common problems, and while they each have their frustrations, their problems occur for different reasons and appear to require different kinds of solutions.

TIME, MONEY, AND EDUCATION

The overriding concerns of both groups of working women are time and money. They feel that they don't have enough of either. The perception that their jobs "don't pay enough" is expressed more frequently by women in "the 80 percent" than by professional women. And the concern about not having time enough for leisure, while important for both, is slightly more of a problem for professional women than for their counterparts among "the 80 percent." Both segments of working women are equally concerned that they do not have enough time to continue their educations. Apparently, a sizable proportion of each group yearns for additional training and development.

While both professionals and "the 80 percent" experience limitations and frustrations in their jobs, these problems are far more onerous for the women in "the 80 percent" than for professional women.

BALANCING WORK AND FAMILY

The burden of juggling responsibilities of work and family life affects both segments of working women. Professional women are slightly more likely to say they need more help at home, and nonprofessional women are slightly more likely to report that their husbands don't want them to work.

CHILD CARE

Working women with children have special problems. A separate section of the National Commission's study focused on working mothers and issues relating to child care, "children too young for my peace of mind," and "problems with teenage children." While the patterns of their responses were similar, professional women were more outspoken on asking for child care.

DISCRIMINATION AND HARASSMENT

The perception that they are discriminated against at work because they are women is felt more acutely by the professional segment than by women in "the 80 percent." On the other hand, the problem of sexual harassment on the job was expressed equally by both groups. This problem occurs at a fairly low level.

ADVANCEMENT AND EARNINGS

Both segments want more opportunity for advancement and more money for their work. The chance for advancement was the greatest specific job-related problem for both segments. It was far more of a problem for "the 80 percent" than for professionals: 60 percent of "the 80 percent" said they had no chance to advance, as against 44 percent of professional women who felt that way.

The amount of money earned was the next greatest problem. The perception that their "salaries or wages were too low" was more of a problem for women in "the 80 percent" than for the professionals. Health benefits were also perceived as less adequate by women in "the 80 percent" segment.

WORK RELATED PROBLEMS

Three aspects of work situations or job-related conditions were problems for one in five working women or fewer. These were the way they were treated by their bosses, working conditions, and working hours.

Surprisingly few of either group complained about the work itself. It was far less a problem for the professionals than for "the 80 percent." Only 9 percent of professional women found their work a problem as compared to 19 percent of "the 80 percent" who have problems with their work.

Relations with co-workers do not appear to present too much of a problem for either segment. Only 7 percent of professionals and 9 percent of "the 80 percent" found that their relations with co-workers were a problem.

JOB SATISFACTION

In spite of this laundry list of work-related problems and frustrations at lack of opportunity, the majority of working women express satisfaction with their jobs. Professionals are particularly pleased with the work they do. Fifty percent of professionals "like their jobs very much," and 39 percent say they like their work "somewhat." Job satisfaction among "the 80 percent" varies with the nature of the work. Women with clerical and sales jobs like their work better than women employed in blue-collar jobs.

Only 13 percent of women doing professional kinds of work are dissatisfied with their jobs. Interestingly, there is no consistent relationship between educational level and the degree of job satisfaction or dissatisfaction among professional women.

However, give a girl some college education and she is less likely to be happy with a clerical job. More college-educated clericals say they are unhappy with their jobs than do those whose education ended with graduation from high school. Conversely, job dissatisfaction among blue-collar workers is lower among those who have graduated from college than among the least well-educated women in this segment.

The study documents the interrelationship of work and personal life in a woman's perspective about her work. Women who have never married are most dissatisfied with their jobs. This cuts across education and occupation. It holds true for the professionals as well as "the 80 percent." It doesn't matter whether she is college-educated or has not gone through high school. And even though the burdens of coping with job and family caused problems for the *mothers of dependent children,* these were the women who *were more likely to be satisfied with their jobs than the single women without family responsibilities.*

Working women without children are happier with their work than separated or divorced women. Divorced mothers in clerical jobs are slightly happier with the work they do than are the divorcees without family responsibilities. On the other hand, the divorced blue-collar mothers are more uphappy with their work than women in any other segment.

There is a strong association between a woman's job satisfaction and her overall satisfaction with her way of life. This pattern is consistent among women who work fulltime and those with part-time jobs.

The National Commission on Working Women's report said, "There is a very striking association between job satisfaction and way of life. Among those respondents who said they liked their jobs very much, only twenty-two percent reported either mild or serious dissatisfaction with their life. This proportion rose to thirty-five percent for those who like their job somewhat, fifty-two percent for those who dislike their job somewhat, and sixty-three percent for those who dislike their job very much."[7] This was a very dramatic finding indeed!

On closer examination of the life satisfaction question used to elicit this dramatic result, however, we discover that the wording of the question was as follows: "Generally, how satisfied are you with the way you are living now (that is, as far as money and what you are able to have is concerned)?" This might be a tautological question. Although satisfaction with money available is not necessarily interchangeable with job satisfaction, the written report gives the impression that working women's satisfaction with their way of life was a far broader and more encompassing attitude. We may speculate that those women who are happiest with their jobs are perhaps being better paid, although this is not necessarily always the case.

HOW NONWORKING WOMEN
FEEL ABOUT WORKING

According to the National Commission, three out of five nonworking women would go to work "if they were offered an interesting job." They were likely to anticipate far greater problems relating to that hypothetical job than were actually experienced by women out in the real world of work. Almost twice as many nonworking mothers were worried about needing child care or feared that their children would be too young for their peace of mind if they went to work as working mothers who really experienced those concerns.

Nonworking married mothers who anticipate that their husbands will not want them to go to work outnumber married women in the work force who report such resistance on the part of their husbands.

Again, a greater number of nonworking mothers worry that the job would be physically tiring than experience that problem in actuality. Almost twice as many nonworking mothers say they lack self-confidence to handle a job than do mothers who go to work. Even transportation is anticipated as more of a problem than it really is for the women who are in the work force.

The one problem that was anticipated to a lesser degree by the nonworking women than actually experienced by the working mothers was the problem of teenage children. Although it is not a major problem for women in the work force, it was underestimated somewhat by women who had not as yet gone to work.

Unmarried women are more concerned than married women with sex discrimination, sexual harassment, and personal confidence. In either case, while these are real problems for women in the work force, the level of anticipation of these problems expressed by the nonworking single women was not borne out by the actual experiences of those who go to work.

One of the conflicts between women's aspirations and the reality of the work experience is that most of them still want to combine careers, marriage, and family life. The majority of those prefer the option of going in and out of the work force rather than working continually. As was observed in Chapter 3 in the study done by the National Commission on the Observance of Women's Year, just about half of all women feel that the ideal life style would be to stay home when children are young and to combine job and homemaking at other times.[8] This, of course, is an option that unmarried women are not likely to have offered to them.

One of the problems about this in-and-out sequence of work and homemaking is that even if equal pay were available for equal work, the in-and-out pattern means that women don't reach the same levels of achievement as men and therefore may not make their way to the top earning levels as easily.

G. G. Michelson, a senior vice-president at R. & H. Macy, says, "It's not very difficult to explain that you have to stay in the pool if you're going to move ahead. The staying power in my generation was not dramatic."[9] The in-and-out pattern also means that many women are unsure of themselves when they do return to the work force. Therefore, they sense a need for job training or retraining and counseling.

Gail Sheehy presents both sides of this in-and-out pattern. On the one hand, as middle-aged women reenter the work force, the mere act of going to work focuses their energies and gives them a sense of purpose that helps compensate for the frustrations of the empty nest. She points out that women who have been able to take that leap achieve a wonderful "sense of accomplishment": "The middle-aged women who point the way to the younger women's futures are the only ones who rate accomplishment as their most important long range goal. Mobilizing their talents and pouring their energies into finding and doing paid work becomes one of their main methods of dealing with stress. This sudden and strong emphasis on work and achievement in the world brings with it exhilaration. Even though by now a great many of the middle-aged women are resigned to the belief that they will never achieve their original dream."[10]

On the other hand, the very fact that these women did not anticipate working in their middle years has left them unprepared. "Looking for jobs to replace the outlived purpose of mothering is particularly difficult for the middle-aged woman of today. Their generation was never adequately prepared educationally or emotionally for the reality that paid employment becomes central to the self-esteem of middle-aged women."[11] Many of the women who feel that they are trapped in limited jobs say "they didn't get sufficient training when they were young and now they really can't afford to take the cut in pay."[12] This becomes a circular problem. These middle-aged women did not get training when they were young because they never anticipated they would want to work when their families grew up.

Mary Ellen Verheyden-Hilliard says that the lack of preparation is sometimes ascribed to the "Cinderella Syndrome," the belief on the part of women that they will always be supported by men. "Somehow it seemed almost subversive to educate girls for financial independence. We often actively encourage them to plan for a life of dependency which will have disastrous results."[13]

Bernice Sandler, director of the Project on the Status and Education of Women sponsored by the Organization of American Colleges, notes that "for a long time women themselves did not seek long-term careers. In the 1950's a study found that only one out of twenty-five women in college intended to seek employment outside the home. Now those figures are largely reversed but society hasn't yet adjusted to meet the demand."[14]

All paths seem to lead back to preparation or education. And that in turn leads to expectations or anticipation of a life pattern quite different from that for which most women have been prepared.

The Female Ghetto

Both "the 80 percent" and the professional women tend to be concentrated in female work ghettos. For example, 40 percent of the professionals are teachers or nurses, the traditionally acceptable female professional occupations, and 65 percent of the clericals are secretaries.

Gail Sheehy tells us that the most unhappy women in her "Happiness Report" were living on one side of the female ghetto or the other, regardless of employment. The unhappiest women she interviewed were homemakers (30 percent) and secretaries (25 percent). She also tells us that it is these women who are least confident about changing anything in their lives. "Although they are least satisfied with their occupations, they are the least confident in the whole sample about making any change no matter how miserable they are."[15]

Alexis Herman, director of the Women's Bureau of the U.S. Department of Labor, termed occupational segregation the number one issue for working women in the 1980s. Of the 420 occupations listed in the Census Bureau's dictionary of occupational titles, she notes, women are concentrated in just twenty occupations. She defines a non-traditional job as "any job category where there is not visible and viable participation by women."

Occupational segregation seems to be a self-fulfilling prophecy. Joan Goodin, executive director of the National Commission on Working Women, said that since women have been concentrated in female-intensive occupations those jobs are considered second-class. They are held as unimportant and assigned low pay. In turn, society sees them as worthless and the women in them as less valuable than men. "The women have internalized that message and now we have a tremendous difference in terms of expectations between men and women."[16]

The perception that female-intensive job categories are second-class may bear some resemblance to Groucho Marx's classic remark that any club that would accept him as a member is one he wouldn't care to join. Apparently, any occupation that accepts women tends to become downgraded and therefore becomes a low-paying category.

Barbara Bergman, an economist at the University of Maryland, confirms the fact that when women enter a work category or an occupational category, the pay declines. She gave as an instance the drop in economic status of bank tellers in comparison with other banking occupations.

One Solution Is to Upgrade Traditional Jobs

Dina Beaumont of the Communications Workers of America said: "There is never going to be enough 'non-traditional' work to go around. We have to focus on the kind of work women are doing today and what its value is to society. That is the most radical notion that has been around in the last umpteen years."[17]

Much of the discussion at the Women in the Work Force Conference focused on the question of comparable pay for work of comparable worth. The question was raised as to why a woman who wants to be a good secretary or a good clerk should be penalized for her choice. A suggestion was made that perhaps the proper focus for action should be on securing better pay for traditional work as well as trying to encourage women to seek nontraditional careers.

Ellen Gurzinsky of the Amalgamated Clothing and Textile Workers Union said: "We have to look at job classification, the way work is distributed, what work is important to the functioning of the entire organization, then start paying women according to the service they provide."[18]

The Yearning for Learning

We have seen that both professional and nonprofessional women in the work force are concerned that they don't have enough opportunity for advancement and sense the need for greater training. The National Commission on Working Women reports that many women, both in "the 80 percent" and in the professional group, would like to continue their educations and feel the need for job counseling and advanced training in order to broaden their job opportunities.

Apparently, many women who are currently in the work force perceive additional education as one path out of boring, limited, or low-paying jobs, if not out of the female ghetto. However, the realities of the courses and counseling that are available to them may not serve as that magic path to upward mobility.

Harriet Rabb, assistant dean of the Columbia University Law School, warned that women tend to fall into what she calls an education trap by taking courses that have little relation to any job and that do not enhance chances for upward mobility. She recommends a system of risk-free job trials as a more productive alternative. If the woman does not succeed at her tryout, she can return to her former position. She suggested that labor unions can encourage this and other innovations, such as plantwide rather than departmental seniority systems, through the collective bargaining process. [19]

Escape from the Ghetto Starts Early

Jonathan Cole of the Center for the Social Sciences at Columbia University says, "To a large extent career patterns are determined at very early ages. The race is frequently run by the time women are past the teenage years." [20]

Bernice Sandler discusses the way women have traditionally been attracted to studies that steered them into jobs in the female ghetto. "For years women's roles have been stereotyped: on television, in the classroom, and in the family. Women are repeatedly portrayed as mothers with aprons on or they are shown primarily as nurses, librarians, waitresses, teachers, beauticians, and telephone operators. These are deep-rooted attitudes that take a long time to change. Little girls quickly get the message that women aren't supposed to work at certain kinds of jobs." [21]

Sandler describes the cultural lag among guidance counselors and in school textbooks which continue to reinforce these traditional stereotypes: "Guidance counselors should not automatically encourage girls to take, for example, home economics and business education courses. Institutions of learning have not made these kinds of shifts yet. Most textbooks and teaching materials continue to portray women exclusively in subservient jobs. They show women at home in the suburbs taking care of children and that is not the pattern that most women follow today, when more than half of the mothers of school-age children work. An eighth-grade arithmetic text is likely to show John building a bridge or dealing with stocks and bonds, while Mary is making cupcakes and measuring material to make a dress. It is a slow process to change because it takes several years to produce a textbook and several more to get financially strapped school systems to buy new materials."[22]

She goes on to say that women are often steered away from fields of study that would lead them to higher-paying jobs such as science and engineering: "One of these is something that has been identified as 'math anxiety' that seems to affect women more than men. It grows out of a culture that makes mathematical ability a masculine attribute that subtly discourages a woman from doing well in math and that soothes her by telling her that she really doesn't have a mathematical mind. Women tend to avoid dealing with math when they get this message. There is nothing genetically or sexually linked about this characteristic because girls are as adept at technical subjects as boys in the early grades. But somewhere around the fifth grade this begins to change. In subtle ways girls learn that math is not a very feminine ability, that boys won't like them if they are good in algebra, that technical skill doesn't hold many rewards for women. Sure enough, the girls' abilities and interests in math seem to disappear. Fewer than ten percent of the doctoral degrees in math, science, and engineering go to women and the result is that women are missing out on job opportunities because of their lack of scientific mathematical training."[23]

Her perspective was confirmed by the panel discussion on "Job Opportunities in the 1980's" conducted at the Women in the Work Force Conference. "Many participants agreed that more should be done to prepare individual women for career advancement. [They felt that] efforts should be made to inform young women and girls in school of the length of time they can expect to work as well as help them make realistic career plans. [They pointed out that] girls, in particular, need encouragement to pursue study in science and mathematics, areas important for careers in male-intensive, high technology industries. The panel recommended that broad-based programs involving business, education, and government should be developed to meet this need."[24]

Out of the Ghetto and into the
Executive Suite

John Macomber, the president and chief executive officer of the
Celanese Corporation, emphasized the importance of technical training for women who want to seek nontraditional careers: "One of the
problems that we in technology and science have had to cope with is the
dearth of women who have been able to claw their way through math
and physics and other such subjects who have the basic tools to succeed. Over the last ten or fifteen years women have been aggressive
about business schools, merchandising, and law schools."[25] He made
the point that these areas have always been accommodating to women,
as have been finance and publishing. He termed them "the word or
soft sciences." He went on to say; "Now, if you go over to the scientific
area which happens to be where an awful lot of people are employed in
this country, you do not find such a rosy picture. In fact, it's a terrible
picture but it's a lot better than it used to be. Ten years ago, less than
three percent of the women graduates in this country were chemical engineers: ninety-seven chemical engineers were men; three were women
every year. Now, when you're dealing with that kind of pool, and the
same applies to mechanical engineers, nuclear engineers, and so on, to
different degrees, you are dealing with a terrible problem. We haved
moved up to seventeen percent in five years. We've moved female
chemical engineers from a little less than three to about seventeen percent in five years. This is absolutely astounding! When it gets up to the
levels of twenty-five and thirty percent, then we will really be in a position to discuss women's staying power and technical competence."[26]

James Olson, vice-president of American Telephone and Telegraph, underscored the importance of technical training: "We are a
very technology oriented business and we are having trouble finding women who can be chief engineers. I think we need to work with
schools to make sure that young ladies still in high school recognize the
opportunities in the technically oriented fields and that universities are
making it easy to attract them. In general management I am convinced
that we will make significant progress if we give it total effort. But, it
isn't going to come overnight. If we work at the basics I think that the
numbers in reasonable time will take care of themselves."[27]

John Macomber of Celanese added: "In our kind of industry we
are dependent on technically trained people. Without basic training in
the sciences it is very unlikely that women are going to get into top

management positions. We plot the people going through the scientific schools, and by the way we start at grammar school because if we haven't gotten them by then, they're gone. We see a matter of twenty to twenty-five years before we get the kind of people coming into the system that we have in law today, in finance today, that we do not have in the hard sciences."[28]

David Reisman concurs on the importance for women to seek technical training. In an interview with the *New York Times* he is reported as urging women to expand out of what he calls "the talk trades" into science and technology.[29]

Is there room at the top? Eli Ginzberg made the point that if there is no more than a token woman in the top rank of a corporation, the Equal Employment Opportunity Commission is likely to conclude that the company is discriminating. Florence Skelly said, "The battleground for women has shifted from hiring to promotion." She added irreverently: "Let's get promoted and then we can worry about how they'll take it in the men's washroom."[30]

The Delicate Balance

Many of the participants at the conference agreed that women are still in a transitional period, are still ambivalent about careers, and have not fully resolved the conflict between jobs and families. "It's not a sin to have dual priorities," Ms. Skelly noted. Men, too, are "having difficulty striking a balance between work and personal life."[31]

Of course, it is clear that not every woman or every man, for that matter, has the determination and the drive to seek top achievement in corporate life. G. G. Michelson suggested, "Maybe a career doesn't develop in a straight line. Maybe we have to slow down career progress a little bit if your priority is for a well-integrated, balanced family. I think balance is the keynote."[32] She pointed out that one of the reasons there aren't more women at top management ranks is the in-and-out pattern whereby women move out of the work force to raise their families, then move back in. While this may represent an admirable sense of balance, it does not favor career advancement. On the other hand, it is her opinion that the young, career-oriented women of today are much more focused on lifetime careers: "There is very little doubt that these young women have the staying power. The numbers are such and the developments in the last ten years are such that there is no question that they are going to move ahead and have moved ahead to high levels of middle management and the beginning levels of upper management."[33]

George Ball, the president of E. F. Hutton, argues forcefully that there is no room in top management for an individual, male or female, who wants a balance between his work life and his personal life: "Quite frankly, if you're going to get to the very top of the business I don't think you can be a balanced individual. You've got to put in seventy or eighty hours a week. You've got to give up everything else. It's not a question of family or business. If you're going to be at the top of a corporation or organization of any sort, you are by definition an eccentric. You've got to make sacrifices. There is no room for balance if you're really going to devote yourself to running a major enterprise. You may be very smart, very well trained, very well schooled and have a tremendous amount of charisma, but so does everybody else you're competing against. Unless you can put in more raw hours and more intensity and more dedication than they can, you are not going to make it."[34]

The Obstacles

Even for those women who are sufficiently imbalanced and brilliant to make it to those levels, there are some external forces that have an impact on their performance as top managers. Mr. Olson told the story of a chief operating officer who is a woman, "a very capable woman who has some unique problems in trying to become a part of the so-called institution in that community. There are still service clubs not available to that individual . . . there are still some barriers existing out there."[35]

Mr. Ball relates an anecdote but with a slightly different outcome: "In foreign countries it is a problem most certainly. For example we have an arbitrage department in London run by a young lady two years out of school. Absolutely brilliant. She has four men working for her. And we were told by the members of the prestigious Merchants Association that one really doesn't have a woman in charge of a department like that. But she's making us a million dollars a year, so we told them to stick it in their ear. In the U.S. I think there is much less of a problem. Our lady brokers make just as much money as their male counterparts. They do it because they are just as good. They've got basically the same clients and can achieve the same results. I think most of the good investment counseling firms have women doing very senior portfolio management work and nobody pays much attention to the thing." [36]

According to the Roper Organization, sex discrimination is perceived by women as a real obstacle in climbing the organizational ladder: "A majority of women today (57%) claim that a woman who is aiming at an executive position in her company will meet with discrimination. A similar majority of women (55%) say that a woman who seeks a top government post has to confront the obstacle of the sex bias. More than half (52%) say that a woman wishing to establish a medical or legal practice or work in some other professional category meets with sex discrimination." [37] Even though these women feel that they are discriminated against in opportunities for obtaining top jobs in business, government, or the professions, about half or more feel that they have an equal chance for advancement with their male peers at work. Women are far less likely than men to feel that women have an equal chance to become executives.

About two-thirds of all working women and men say it makes no difference to them whether they work for a male or female boss. This represents an advancement since 1970, when just over half expressed this attitude. Women with the least and the most education are more likely to say that it makes no difference to them whether they work for a man or a woman. Just over one in four women say they would rather work for a man than for a woman.

The Opportunities

George Ball insists that talent is rewarded in his shop and that women and men have an equal opportunity to achieve the top assignments and the top salaries: "Wall Street is a very pragmatic place. Very good quantitative skills are being developed at the business schools and elsewhere by young men and women alike. They are able to enter the senior recompense levels of our firm and others very rapidly." [38]

Anne Hyde of Management Women, Inc., points out that women who want to achieve must be prepared to take risks: "I'm not sure that women truly understand what opportunity means. Rolling those dice. Taking that risk. Getting shot down. Knowing everybody is not going to like you." [39]

John Macomber suggests a four-part formula for success for those women who, as he says, "are willing to do the seventy hour work bit or are willing to lead semi-imbalanced lives":

- "One of them is proficiency. Really be very, very good at whatever you're doing . . . you just can't flow through by being pretty good.
- "Second is the ability to work through people . . . ninety percent of your problems are in working through people.
- "Third, management is an enormously creative process. Creativity in terms of running a business is something people need to think about right away.
- "Finally, they should always relate what they are doing to the strategy of the enterprise or their department, the strategy of what needs to be done. If one begins doing that at an early age it comes naturally when it really counts."[40]

Notes

1. Marshall Loeb, "America in the 80s: Ten Major Changes Ahead," speech given at Seagram Family Foundation, Scottsdale, Arizona, January 30, 1980.
2. Nan Robertson, "A Sociologist 'Emeritus' Who Is Far from Retired," *New York Times,* December 14, 1980.
3. *The 1980 Virginia Slims American Women's Opinion Poll* (New York: The Roper Organization, 1980), p. 34.
4. *National Survey of Working Women,* National Commission on Working Women, June 1979, p. ii.
5. "Working Women: Joys and Sorrows," *U.S. News & World Report,* January 15, 1979, p. 67.
6. *Women in the Work Force Conference Report,* sponsored by American Telephone and Telegraph Company and *Ladies' Home Journal,* New York, January 14–15, 1980, p. 4.
7. *National Survey of Working Women,* p. 12
8. Barbara Everitt Bryant, *American Women Today and Tomorrow* (Washington D.C.: Government Printing Office, for National Commission on the Observance of International Women's Year, 1977), p. 18.
9. *Women in the Work Force Conference Report,* p. 16.
10. Gail Sheehy, "The Happiness Report," *Redbook,* July 1979, p. 6.
11. *Ibid.*
12. *Ibid.,* p. 4.
13. "Working Women: Joys and Sorrows," p. 64.
14. "Women at Work: Still Fighting 'Stereotyped Roles'," *U.S. News & World Report,* January 15, 1979, p. 73.

15. Sheehy, "Happiness Report," p. 10.

16. *Women in the Work Force Conference Report,* p. 5.

17. *Ibid.*

18. *Ibid.*

19. *Ibid.*

20. *Ibid.,* p. 6

21. "Women at Work: Still Fighting 'Stereotyped Roles'," p. 73.

22. *Ibid.*

23. *Ibid.*

24. *Women in Work Force Conference Report,* p. 13.

25. *Ibid.,* p. 17.

26. *Ibid.*

27. *Ibid.,* p. 20.

28. *Ibid.*

29. Robertson, "A Sociologist 'Emeritus'."

30. *Women in the Work Force Conference Report,* p. 13.

31. *Ibid.*

32. *Ibid.,* p. 19.

33. *Ibid.,* p. 16.

34. *Ibid.,* p. 20.

35. *Ibid.,* p. 19.

36. *Ibid.,* p. 18.

37. *1980 Virginia Slims Poll,* p. 7.

38. *Women in the Work Force Conference Report,* p. 17.

39. *Ibid.,* p. 13.

40. *Ibid.,* p. 21.

II

Changing Markets

Chapter 5

Are Working Women
Different Kinds
of Consumers?

In Part I we tracked the quiet revolution and its most obvious manifestation: women's presence in the work force. We examined the reasons for this phenomenon and looked for evidence as to whether it will continue. We noted the strong correlation between education and women's presence in the work force. Finally, we looked at the actual work experience of women in the United States, the nature of their occupations, their levels of satisfaction with their work, their problems, and their aspirations.

In Part II we shall examine the marketing implications of the quiet revolution. I have participated in discussions about the changing role of women and its implications for advertising and marketing during most of the 1970s. At such discussions I am often asked a simple question that requires a rather complex answer. Many observers want to know how the changes in women's lives are reflected in advertising and marketing. Their question is reasonable. It seems logical that as advertisers and marketers become aware of these changes they would naturally apply them to their professional activities.

Although there have been some applications, and I shall refer to them, I am forced to admit at this point that the advertising and marketing communities have responded to the quiet revolution with great caution. It is true that marketing depends on understanding consumers, on developing products and services that meet consumer needs, and on communicating the benefits of those products to potential customers through advertising. Marketing by definition is based on information about consumers. We obtain that information from primary research of specific aspects of a market and analysis of the reams of secondary data that are available to all of us.

One would assume, therefore, that as news about the dramatic changes in women's lives became apparent, marketers and advertisers would tumble over each other in their efforts to reach this changing market. But this has not been the case. In an article entitled "What Every Marketer Should Know About Women" in the June 1978 *Harvard Business Review,* I suggested that outmoded assumptions about women may lead to marketing underachievement.

I pointed out a curious gap between the realities of social change and social trends and the picture of society reflected in most marketing plans and in the advertising that expresses those plans. I speculated that it is possible that the potential contribution of our highly sophisticated and specialized marketing tools is not fully realized because of a cultural lag in the social perspective of the very specialists who are charged with the marketing responsibility. And I suggested a solution. If the gap between what we know and what we do is in fact due to the perspective of marketing professionals rather than to their procedures, the solution lies in challenging the basic assumptions that underlie the application of marketing tools. Any practical-minded marketer can challenge the underlying assumptions on which past target definitions are based and, if necessary, bring his/her marketing procedures in step with present realities. I recommended the following procedure.

1. *Reexamine the Assumed Target.* First, examine the facts. The size and composition of particular groups or segments of consumers are available from the Census Bureau or the Bureau of Labor Statistics. Professional journals, the daily newspapers, and the popular press constantly carry reports on changing attitudes, values, and life styles. Many companies have access to continuing sources of public opinion poll data, which track social beliefs and attitudes. Does a review of both the hard and soft data suggest that some groups within our society are changing or represent departures from the monolithic norm?

2. *Evaluate the Market Potential of New Target Opportunity Groups.* We can learn whether these groups represent differing market opportunities through reanalysis of existing market data. An objective appraisal of the market behavior of these newly identified consumer groups can tell us whether they buy or use products differently from their neighbors and whether their media behavior is distinctive. An equally objective appraisal of their incidence or volume of product use can tell us the kind of value potential each group represents to a particular category or brand.

3. *Build Analytic Frame of New Perspective into Ongoing and Future Activities.* The reanalysis of existing data is possible only if the key demographic questions are built in as a matter of course. When they are not, or when new insights suggest the need for new questions, these should be included in all ongoing and future studies. (The New Demographic concept discussed in Chapter 7 is an example of this.) If some life cycle groups are underrepresented in some small sample studies such as copy tests, it may be necessary to set quotas or weight up the cells in order to represent each constituency in its true proportion.

4. *Explore the Attitudes/Needs of New Opportunity Groups.* It is classic research procedure to begin a study with a review of available data and to use qualitative exploration to generate hypotheses for ultimate quantification. Our procedure reverses this sequence. Hypotheses about potential targets are identified through a review of masses of data and verified through a reanalysis of existing data in order to determine whether their marketing and media behavior is unique. In order to understand why these redefined targets behave as they do, we need to return to qualitative exploration. The newly identified opportunity groups define the sample to be studied.

The difference is that we proceed from quantified evidence of marketing behavior to seek qualitative understanding of the reasons for that behavior. And the results are actionable, because we know the size of each group, exactly which products and brands they buy, and how much. And we know how to reach them through media. The qualitative stage helps us to identify the context within which each group of consumers uses products and gives us clues on how to talk to them in advertising.

5. *Redefine Marketing Targets.* If this kind of examination of data suggests that these newly identified opportunity segments represent viable markets, it should be possible to build this kind of perspective into future planning. No new tools or methodology is required. If a fresh examination of the facts suggests untapped opportunities, the kinds of marketing procedures that have worked so well in the past can be put to work to cultivate these redefined marketing targets.

I concluded that the first marketers who meet the challenge and close the gap between the realities of social change and their marketing procedures will reap the benefits of discovering new opportunity markets. The tools are available to all of us. We have nothing to lose but our assumptions.

This exploration of available attitudinal and demographic data is a continuing process. My perceptions and understanding of the changing women's market have also gone through a process of development and evolution. Each new piece in the jigsaw puzzle added another perspective on the implications of the change.

I must admit that in the beginning I took a fairly simple approach to the entire issue. I was as surprised as anyone else back in the early 1970s when I learned that there were almost as many women in the work force as were staying home keeping house. This simple demographic fact (which I term "Simple Demographic Fact Number One") boggled my mind. I began searching for more information about working women.

I should point out that my purpose in studying this phenomenon was pragmatic. It seemed to me that as women's lives changed they might, in fact, become very different kinds of consumers. I believed that any change in their consumer behavior would be relevant to the marketing planning and strategy development of advertisers and agencies. My intention was not to do a general sociological study of this fascinating phenomenon. I wanted to learn whether or not the changes in the women's market should lead to changed strategies and changed advertising.

After all, if it turned out that working women buy and use products and respond to media no differently from nonworking women, the entire exercise would not be useful to marketers. So the first question to answer was: *Are working women different kinds of consumers?* This seemed to be a straightforward question that could be answered quite simply.

As I began exploring the question, new insights about the women's market emerged. It became clear that the situation was not a simple one. Each new piece in the jigsaw puzzle started me off on a new series of questions. In this and succeeding chapters I shall share this odyssey of discovery with the reader. I shall describe my conceptual approach at each stage and show how my analysis of this unfolding saga evolved over time. The data reported in the following chapters were gathered during different stages in the development of this project and will not be updated. Most of the information in this chapter was gathered in 1972 and 1973. In succeeding years as new insights emerged, new analyses were conducted. These will be reported as they occurred.

In this chapter we ask, "Are working women different kinds of consumers?" Clearly this question must be answered if we are to learn whether advertisers and marketers should address the working woman market seriously or if, instead, the quiet revolution can be left to cocktail conversation. It's always fun to talk about women and change and what's happening in people's lives, but this kind of information becomes relevant to marketers only if it has bottom-line implications.

It seemed like a fairly simple question to answer. One would simply compare the purchase behavior and media behavior of working women to that of nonworking women. That would allow us to learn whether or not the way working women buy products or use media is different from the women's market overall.

In one of my company's earliest publications on this subject, we said: "If you are concerned with women as potential customers, women are, in marketing parlance, your target group. But it is increasingly difficult to take accurate aim at that target because it's moving. Women—the things they do, the things they want, the way they feel about themselves—are changing. We all know that. We read about it, we talk about it, but do we really focus on it in a marketing context?"[1]

In the early 1970s, when we first began examining the marketing potential of working women, one of the steps we took was to review current advertising at that time in order to learn whether marketers or advertisers were, in fact, addressing this segment of women. In the early 1970s working women were almost nonexistent in most advertising. If they were shown in ads and commercials at all, it was usually because they were props or minor players in a scene.

- For example, in travel advertising addressed to the business traveler one might have seen an airline stewardess serving drinks to the business traveler who, of course, was a man.
- Or one might have seen a reservations clerk behind the counter in an ad describing the advantages of one car rental service or another. The clerk was invariably female, and the business travelers queued up at the counter were invariably male.
- Or one might have seen a secretary in an office setting passing business papers or a cup of coffee to her boss. The ad would of course be addressed to the male business executive.

But working women as potential customers for the products advertised were really not to be seen in any of the ads we examined. That is why we titled the first presentation about the working women's market "The Invisible Consumer Market."

The more we looked at the invisible market of working women, the more we realized that it was not possible to study working women in isolation. In order to understand whether or not working women are different kinds of consumers, it is necessary to contrast them with nonworking women. And, of course, women's consumer behavior might

have certain general characteristics different from that of men. Therefore, even before we considered working women we needed to compare the total women's market with the total men's market. We did exactly that in the earliest analyses of this invisible consumer target.

Our first objective examination of the market and media behavior
of working women compared to that of nonworking women was done
through a computer analysis of Target Group Index (TGI) data. At
that time TGI was one of the principal services providing an annual
projectable study of consumer market and media behavior.

The information on the following pages is taken from that early
analysis.[2] It demonstrates that there are real differences between working women and their nonworking counterparts in their demographic
characteristics, in their market behavior, and in the way they use
media.

Women and Work—1972

Are working women really different from their stay-at-home
sisters? The following reviews the demographic and psychographic
characteristics and the product usage of women who work and women
who don't. This is a framework for identifying the ways in which they
are alike and the ways in which the single demographic characteristic of
employment distinguishes these two groups of women from each
other.

DEMOGRAPHICS

According to the census, in 1972, 44 percent of the adult women in
the United States worked full time or part time. Hence, a majority of
the adult women in our country were not in the work force.

Age

Almost all of the quantitative difference between the number of
working and nonworking women is accounted for by age differences.
Almost one in four nonworking women is over sixty-five years old. On
the other hand, women between eighteen and twenty-five years of age
are significantly more likely to have jobs than to stay at home. The
median age of working women is 38.5, while the median age of stay-at-
homes is 46.3.

Presence of Children by Age

Apparently the presence of children in the home is no deterrent to working. Almost an equal proportion of working and nonworking women have children under the age of eighteen. However, there appears to be a clear relationship between the likelihood of women to work and the ages of their youngest children. If the mother has children under two, she is more likely to be at home. Women's tendency to go to work increases with the age of their children.

Household Income

Working women tend to be more affluent than stay-at-homes. The median household income of working women is $10,020; that of nonworking women is $8,395. (Remember, this was 1972!) The nonworking women are more likely to be very poor or very rich. Working women are more likely than nonworking women to live in households at the upper-middle income level.

Education

The strong correlation between women's education and their presence in the work force is confirmed. Working women are more than twice as likely as nonworking women to have graduated from college, and they are more apt to have attended college. Nonworking women are far more likely than working women (or men) to have stopped their educations without graduating from high school.

Number in Household

There is not too much difference in family size between working and nonworking women. Nonworking women are slightly more likely to live in the smallest and the largest households. Working women are slightly more apt to live in three-to-four-person households.

Region

Women who work are slightly more likely to live near the action, in the largest metropolitan areas or suburban Standard Metropolitan Statistical Areas (SMSAs). Nonworking women, on the other hand, are somewhat more likely to be found in rural areas or non-SMSAs (under 35,000 population). The region in which a woman lives apparently has little effect on whether she goes to work or not. Working and nonworking women are found in consistent proportions in all census regions. Working women are slightly less likely to be found on the two coasts and slightly more likely to live in the North-Central region. An analysis of marketing regions confirms this, with the exception that working women are significantly above par in New England.

PSYCHOGRAPHICS

Self-Concept

Whether a woman works or not, she is likely to think of herself as awkward, kind, sociable, and tense in equal measures. If she does work, she is more likely to picture herself as dominating, efficient, stubborn, affectionate, brave, broad-minded, and intelligent. If she stays at home she is more likely to see herself as egocentric.

Buying Style

When it comes to shopping, working and nonworking women are equally cautious. Both are definitely style-conscious, but working women are more concerned about style than are the stay-at-homes.

Working women are more impulsive than nonworking women when they go shopping. On the other hand, they are more likely to plan their purchases in advance than do the women who stay at home.

Nonworking women are more apt to be economy-minded and concerned about ecology. They are slightly more likely to be both brand-loyal and experimental in buying products, and they are just slightly more persuasible than women who work.

MEDIA BEHAVIOR

Not all women are alike in their media habits. Working women and nonworking women spend their time differently.

- Nonworking women are far more likely than working women to be heavy viewers of television.
- For all other media, working women are somewhat more likely to be active listeners, readers, or observers than are nonworking

women. Working women are more likely to listen to radio, read magazines, read newspapers, and see outdoor advertising than are nonworking women.

Television

The television viewing habits of working women differ from those of nonworking women. Naturally, the women who stay at home are the heavier television viewers. The nonworking woman spends extra hours watching daytime television. The working woman does not have the opportunity to watch TV during the day. The largest percentage of the daytime audience is made up of those who remain at home.

Prime time and weekend daytime viewing differs greatly from weekday daytime. The same number of working and nonworking women watch TV in the evening and during the day on weekends. Working and nonworking women look at late night TV to an equal extent, except on weekends, when the working women tend to watch more.

Radio

Radio is a popular medium with working women. They listen to radio more than do nonworking women. A greater number of the women who work listen to radio from 3:00 P.M. through midnight than at other times of day.

Surprisingly, listening patterns throughout the day are fairly equal between the woman at work and the woman at home. Popular music and "Top 40" programs are the most common radio types for all women. However, more working women listen to radio stations of this sort than those who do not work. Modern country music and news programs are enjoyed equally by all women, regardless of employment status.

Magazines

With the availability of the TGI data, we are able to ascertain that women who work are substantially heavier readers of magazines than women who stay home during the day. An examination of magazines by magazine type—mass, class, and those with a special appeal to women—shows that in almost every case working women are heavier magazine readers than women at home.

One might expect the nonworking homemaker to be the one who reads magazines dealing with the home, but the working woman is even more likely to read publications on the home, especially *Better Homes and Gardens* and *American Home.* When it comes to mass and dual audience books like *Reader's Digest* or selective magazines like *Saturday Review* and *Psychology Today,* working women read relatively more than either housewives or men.

Although men dominate the audiences of business, news, and male publications, working women are far more likely than nonworking women to read these male interest magazines.

Newspapers

A greater number of working women than nonworking women read more than forty-six newspapers a month.

Analysis of each section of the daily and Sunday newspapers shows that the travel, business, and financial sections generate the same kind of interest among both groups. Working women read all other sections to a greater degree than their stay-at-home counterparts.

Outdoor Advertising

Although all women see less outdoor advertising than men, the working woman sees a much higher amount of available posters and bulletins than do the women who are at home during the daytime. When traveling to work, she has a greater opportunity to see posters than the nonworking woman. The quintile analysis shows that 6.2 percent of all working women travel 300 miles a week, as against 3.5 percent for nonworking women.

PURCHASE BEHAVIOR[3]

Some people have speculated that regardless of whether a woman works or not, we are all sisters under the skin when it comes to getting our clothes clean, putting food on the table, enjoying our recreation, or primping in front of our dressing table mirrors. Are there any real differences between working women and their stay-at-home sisters when they go marketing?

That should be an easy question to answer. A straightforward comparison of the purchase behavior of working women with that of nonworking women in a number of product categories should answer the question. Let's consider some examples.

Breakfast Cereal

Let's take a mass supermarket product like dry cereal. There is almost no difference in the extent to which working women and full-time housewives use cereal. Housewives are slightly more likely to purchase the presweetened and regular types, while working women are somewhat more likely to use the natural kind.

Coffee

What about another staple grocery product such as coffee? (Of course, these data predate the recent dramatic rise in coffee prices.) Apparently housewives are slightly more likely to use regular coffee and far more likely to buy instant coffee than are working women. On the other hand, the working woman is a better customer for freeze-dried coffee, the most expensive form of instant coffee.

Now let us examine some of the big-ticket products or services that are normally marketed to men.

Financial Activities

What impact does working have on women's financial activities? Working women are more likely than nonworking housewives to have savings accounts, regular checking accounts, and credit cards. The one area in which this pattern does not hold true is in ownership of securities other than government savings bonds. Working women are somewhat below the norm in owning securities.

Cars

One of the Detroit myths is that the only automotive decision women make is the color of the upholstery. Working women are somewhat more likely to have a driver's license, and they are slightly more likely to have two or more new cars in their garages. The housewife is likely to have shared in the car purchase decision. (All women are more likely than the total population to report this kind of sharing.) Both working women and housewives are below the norm in having selected a car on their own. However, it should be pointed out that the working woman is more likely than the full-time housewife to have bought her own car.

Travel

Is there any difference in the extent to which working and non-working women participate in travel activities? Working women are far more likely than nonworking women to buy luggage, to use travelers checks, to have traveled in the United States by plane, and to have stayed at a hotel.

This brief examination of five different product categories shows that working women do differ from housewives in some of their purchase behavior and that the pattern varies from one product category to another.

The Working Woman as Consumer

What we have learned about the market and media behavior of working and nonworking women answers the question as to whether working women as consumers are different from the women's market overall.

They most certainly are. Working women are younger, better educated, and more affluent than nonworking women. In most cases they are more active consumers of advertised products and services. They certainly have distinctive patterns of media behavior. This first examination of working women suggests that it is a market worth cultivating.

That answers the question, doesn't it?

The problem is that this kind of simplistic comparison of the consumer behavior of working and nonworking women implies that the situation is monolithic. It assumes that all working women are cut out of one pattern and that all nonworking women are cut out of another. Once we define the two patterns, we can determine not only how their behavior differs but also how to communicate to them in the market place.

But as we began to look beyond the surface, it quickly became clear that neither working women nor housewives represent monolithic groups, so this rather simplistic comparison might be concealing many differences on either side of the overall women's market.

Ironically, many marketers and advertisers still take this rather limited perspective when they study working women. I see many articles and reports that tell about the market and media behavior of "working women" as though they were all cut out of the same cloth. Clearly there must be something beyond the wholesale lumping together of all employed women if we are to understand the dynamics of this market and identify the opportunities that might be concealed by this monolithic perspective.

Notes

1. Rena Bartos, *The Moving Target,* J. Walter Thompson Company, 1974, p. 1
2. "Advertising to Women: The Impact of Employment and Life-Style on the Media Behavior of Women," JWT Special Markets Media Report, 1973 (photocopied).
3. "A Moving Target: The Influence of Women's Employment on Consumer Behavior" speech given by Rena Bartos to the American Marketing Association, January 28, 1977 (photocopied).

Chapter 6

The Concept of Life Cycle

The more we thought about the working woman's market, the more we realized that we might run the risk of creating new stereotypes about "the working woman" to replace the old stereotypes about housewives. It is my personal belief that the single prototypical housewife so dear to the hearts of advertising and marketing people during the 1950s and 1960s never existed. And there is certainly no single prototypical working woman.

One way to avoid creating new stereotypes is to close the reality gap between how women really are and how we show them in advertising. The most direct way to close that gap is to recognize their diversity. Neither housewives nor working women come out of the same mold. What's more, they never did. Women are wonderfully diverse regardless of occupation. They come in all ages and all degrees of sophistication, and they live in widely differing situations according to their stage in the life cycle.

The concept of life cycle is very simple. I term it "Simple Demographic Fact Number Two.": *Women change as consumers as they move through different stages of life.* The way they buy and use products and the way they read, watch, or listen to media are affected by whom they live with or whom they live without. Is there a man around the house? Are there any children at home? These two demographic facts are basic clues to the way both working and nonworking women behave in the market place.

The concept of life cycle seems so obvious, once one considers it, it is really amazing that it did not become a standard framework for marketing analysis many years ago. Nonetheless, all of us who are engaged in marketing to consumers have tended to take target definitions at face value. Over the years when I was involved in communications research, I remember asking my agency colleagues and our clients how to define the target group for a particular product or service. The point then was to ensure that our research projects were focused on the ultimate customers for the advertised product. If those products or

78

services were aimed at the women's market, invariably the target definition began with that classic phrase, "any housewife, eighteen to forty-nine."

I never challenged such definitions of the target at that time. In those more innocent days when I thought of a housewife I assumed that the lady was married. I had a mental picture of a woman wearing an apron in a suburban house with two children—the classic Dick, Jane, and Spot picture of the American family. It never occurred to me to ask how many of these women were not married or whether any of these housewives had no children living in their houses. It never occurred to me that maybe some of these "any housewives" had not yet started raising their families or that perhaps their children had grown up and left the nest.

The notion of life cycle came about fairly accidentally. In the early 1970s I had examined the published Census and Bureau of Labor Statistics (BLS) data about the women's market. I had read all of the available attitudinal information relating to working women and, as noted in Chapter 5, examined their actual market and media behavior through computer analysis of Target Group Index (TGI) data.

However, I wanted to go beyond this reanalysis of secondary data. I wanted to develop some insights about the special needs and interests of working women as distinct from nonworking women. This kind of understanding was needed in order to stimulate creative thinking about the marketing and advertising opportunities that might be developed to reach this untapped market. As a step in this exploration I decided to conduct some brainstorming discussions with working and professional women. The purpose was to develop some hypotheses that might in turn be built into a more formal study of this market.

One decision that had to be made early on was how to divide the working women who were going to participate in these groups. Should we mix senior and junior professionals together? Should we separate them by age? Then it occurred to me, after some introspection on the subject, that my own patterns of consumption had changed enormously at different stages in my own life cycle.

Clearly, a married couple and an unmarried career woman run very different kinds of households. Certainly, a household with children in it is very different from the household of a childless couple. And, of course, a household changes dramatically if and when the wife decides to return to professional life. There are all sorts of changes in schedule and in emphasis, ranging from the kind of entertaining she is able to do to the kinds of vacations she and her husband take together.

One of the inevitable differences in a woman's life after she goes to work is the crunch of time and changing priorities in the way her household is run. Then, of course, when children leave the nest to go to college or elsewhere, the family's patterns of living change once again. Clearly a household built around a family group has quite different patterns of behavior from those of a career couple.

After speculating about the options, I decided to invite women to the group discussions based on their situations in the life cycle.

- One group included married women who did not have children at home at the time, either because they had not begun to raise their families or because their children had grown up and left the nest.
- One group comprised working wives who were also working mothers. They had children under eighteen living in their homes.
- One group consisted of childless unmarried women, some single and some formerly married, either widowed or divorced.

The last group was included not to explore their personal emotional lives but to recognize the fact that unattached women without family responsibilities would no doubt have needs as consumers and ways of spending their money quite different from those of their married counterparts.

The group discussions were general and exploratory. The fascinating result was that each group responded very differently to the same general set of questions. It became clear that the presence of a husband does, of course, affect the way a woman lives, the kind of recreation she is involved in, the way she spends her vacations, and the way she spends her money. It also became clear that the presence of children alters the emphasis of the household enormously.

These insights were necessarily impressionistic, because they were based on small numbers of women. Therefore, in order to sharpen our understanding of the life cycle concept we applied it to a special computer analysis of market and media behavior. This was parallel to that described in Chapter 5, in which we examined how working and non-working women buy products and use media.

This time we grouped women into four life cycle groups:

- Those who were married with children at home
- Those who were married without any children at home, either because they had not started families or because they had empty nests, their children having grown up and left home
- Those who were not married—single, widowed, or divorced—with neither husband nor child at home

•Those who were not married but had children at home—the small but growing contingent of unmarried women who are bringing up children without benefit of a husband

We then divided each life cycle group into women who worked and women who did not work. The results of this analysis showed us that life cycle is extremely relevant to the consumer behavior of both non-working and working women. It is not enough to draw general comparisons between working women and nonworking women. That is painting with too broad a brush and conceals too many differences on either side of the equation.

If we really want to understand the impact of employment on the market and media behavior of working women, we should compare working women with their nonworking counterparts within life cycle stages. Our analysis showed that there were some situations in which their position in the life cycle was far more relevant to the kinds of products they bought or how they spent their time than whether they went to work or were full-time housewives. We could also see from this analysis how the realities of the paycheck changed women's behavior in the market place.

Since we had demonstrated that life cycle really is a relevant way to consider the women's market, we thought it was important to learn just how many women there were within each of the life cycle segments. This led us back to the Census and the BLS to learn just how many working women and nonworking women there were in each of the four life cycle groups.

Here we ran into the familiar frustration that one feels when one tries to match Census information from one report with that from another. The BLS gave us detailed information on the marital status and motherhood of working women. However, it showed comparable data only for "nonworking women."

Our earlier analysis of the occupational profile of all women (see Chapter 1) showed us that in addition to working women and housewives, there are two groups of women who are not part of the mainstream: the schoolgirls who are either too young to be keeping house or working, and the retired and disabled women who are either too old or too infirm to take on such responsibilities. The Census also reports on that mysterious group it labels "others" whose reasons for being out of the mainstream are not specified. In any case there was no way that we could isolate the life cycle situation of housewives as differentiated from the total of nonworking women.

Given this limitation, we developed a life cycle profile of all

American women without regard to their occupation. More women are living in an unmarried state with no children at home than are living in the traditional nuclear households with a husband and children.

EXHIBIT I

LIFE CYCLE PROFILE
OF AMERICAN WOMEN :1976

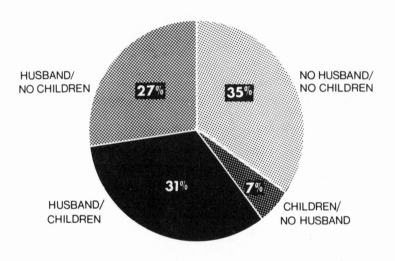

BUREAU OF LABOR STATISTICS   MARCH, 1976

Next, we wanted to compare the life cycle patterns of working women to those of housewives. Since we couldn't isolate housewives from other nonworking women, we developed life cycle profiles of working and nonworking women. This was frustrating, because *we knew that the "nonworking" group was cluttered with nonhousewives.*

Nevertheless, we could see that working women are to be found in all stages of the life cycle. This was real news to many of my professional colleagues, who were sure "working women" were young single girls employed as secretaries or receptionists for a few years before marrying and moving to the suburbs.

We explored the possibility of ordering some Census Bureau cross-tabulations to resolve this and other problems. We learned that the Census Bureau had conducted a mammoth study of 150,000 house-

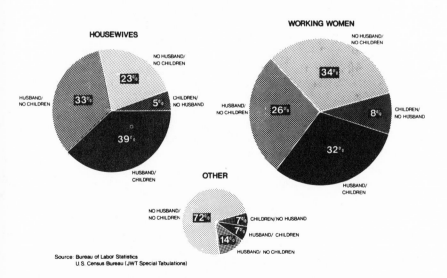

EXHIBIT II

LIFE CYCLE PROFILE OF AMERICAN WOMEN :1976

NON-WORKING WOMEN

WORKING WOMEN

SOURCE: BUREAU OF LABOR STATISTICS MARCH. 1977

EXHIBIT III

LIFE CYCLE PROFILE OF AMERICAN WOMEN: 1976

HOUSEWIVES

WORKING WOMEN

OTHER

Source: Bureau of Labor Statistics
U.S. Census Bureau (JWT Special Tabulations)

holds in 1976 and that the computer tape would be available for cross-tabulations early in 1978. At that point our company decided to invest in a fairly comprehensive cross-tabulation of the 1976 Survey of Income and Education.

At long last we were able to isolate those mysterious ladies in gray—the schoolgirls, the retired, and the disabled—from bona fide full-time housewives. That cross-tabulation enabled us to compare the life cycle profile of working women with the life cycle profile of full-time housewives. It resulted in a chart that was quite different from the earlier versions.

These data enabled us to analyze each life cycle segment realistically. As can be seen in the following, when we examined the market and media behavior of working and nonworking women within life cycle segments, we were able to get a much sharper picture of the differences.

EXHIBIT **IV**

HUSBAND/CHILDREN

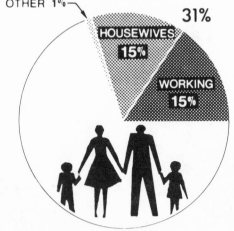

Source: Bureau of Labor Statistics
U.S. Census Bureau (JWT Special Tabulations)

While "married with children" equals "housewife" to many people when they visualize the "American woman," actually only 15 percent of the women in this country represented this traditional life style in 1976. At that time 31 percent of women in our country were at the "married with children" stage of the life cycle. However, as many of these wives and mothers were in the work force as stayed home to be full-time homemakers.

Following is a brief overview of the demographic profile, the psychographic characteristics, and the media behavior of both working and nonworking women in this life cycle group. Each of the other three life cycle groups will be described in a similar fashion. (All findings are based on data collected by TGI in 1972).

DEMOGRAPHICS[1]

Age

Most married women with children at home, whether they work or not, are concentrated between the ages of twenty-five and forty-nine. The younger the mother, the less likely she is to go to work. However, after thirty-five, proportionately more mothers work than stay at home. The median age for working mothers is 36.5, and that for nonworking mothers is 33.9

Presence of Children by Age

The higher age of working women is probably a reflection of the ages of their children. Women's participation in the labor force rises with the ages of their children. The mothers of teenagers are more likely to go to work than stay at home.

Household Income

Working mothers live in homes where the household income is higher than that of the nonworking mother. Apparently this is a reflection of that second paycheck in the household. The median household income for working mothers is $11,510, and for nonworking mothers it is $10,948.

Education

Married women with children under eighteen years of age tend to be somewhat slightly better educated than the female population as a whole. However, the working mothers in this group are far more likely than the full-time housewives to have graduated from college. The stay-at-homes are somewhat more likely than their working counterparts to have left school before finishing high school or to have considered their education complete upon graduation from high school.

Occupation

The occupational profile of working mothers follows that of all working women. They are somewhat less likely than childless married women or unmarried women to be in professional or managerial careers. They are slightly more likely to have jobs categorized as "other," and although very few women work in blue-collar jobs, more women of this life cycle group are found in "craftsman/foreman" jobs than of any other segment.

Number in Household

Apparently the size of the family is also a factor in whether or not a mother goes to work. A home with three or four people is more likely to have a working mother, while a home with five or more people generally has a mother who remains home during the day.

Region

Surprisingly, working mothers tend to live in less populated areas. TGI classifies these areas as non-SMSA and counties with population between 35,000 and 150,000. The nonworking mother is more inclined to live in suburbia. Equal numbers of working or nonworking mothers live in the central city.

Among this life cycle group the working mothers are somewhat above expectancy in the North Central and South marketing regions. They are more likely to be found in the East Central and Southeast, while nonworking mothers are more likely to live in the Southwest.

PSYCHOGRAPHICS

Self-Concept

The married woman with children, whether she works or not, is likely to think of herself as awkward, kind, trustworthy, sociable, affectionate, and creative. However, the mother who works is likely to see herself as dominating, broadminded, efficient, intelligent, and self-assured. The married woman with children at home who doesn't work sees herself as reserved and tense.

Buying Style

Working and nonworking mothers are remarkably similar in nearly all of their buying characteristics. However, the married working woman with children tends to be more impulsive, while the nonworking mother is a little more economy-minded.

Exhibit V

EXHIBIT V
HUSBAND/NO CHILDREN

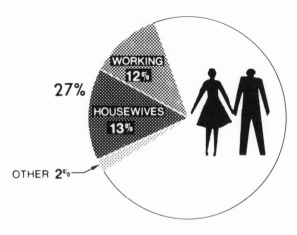

Source: Bureau of Labor Statistics
U.S. Census Bureau (JWT Special Tabulations)

Twenty-seven percent of all American women are married and have no children under eighteen living at home. They represent two stages in the life cycle. Some are young wives who have not yet started families or who may never do so. Others are middle-aged wives whose children are grown and gone from the home. Just under half the women in this group work, while slightly more than half stay home and keep house.

DEMOGRAPHICS

Age

An analysis of the age patterns of this segment reveals that most of the women in this life situation are in the "empty nest" years. This suggests that their children are past eighteen. They are far more likely than any other life cycle group to be over fifty years old.

However, at the youngest age level, these childless wives are twice as likely to be out at work as to be home keeping house. This suggests that these young women have not as yet embarked on family responsibilities. There is a substantial group among the stay-at-homes who are past retirement age. The median age for married working women without children is 48.4; it is 58.8 for those who stay at home.

Household Income

Working women with no children under eighteen are more affluent than their nonworking counterparts. The majority of those who work have household incomes between $10,000 to $25,000 a year. The nonworking married woman without children is less fortunate and generally lives in a home where the household income falls below $8,000. But a small portion of those women who do not work enjoy household incomes of over $25,000 each year. The median household income for married working women with no children is $10,955, as against $7,659 for their nonworking counterparts.

Education

A significantly higher proportion of married working women with no children are college-educated than of the stay-at-homes. Fewer of the nonworking married women without children at home have graduated from or attended college, and many did not graduate from high school.

Occupation

Married working women without children are more likely than any other life-cycle group to have professional or clerical/sales jobs. Nearly 30 percent stated they held a position classified as professional, technical, manager, or proprietor in 1973. They are somewhat less likely than the other segments to work in "other" occupations.

Region

A greater number of married working women without children are found in the largest metropolitan areas and suburban areas, while the nonworking woman without children is much more likely to be located in rural areas and in counties with population between 35,000 and 150,000. Women in this life cycle group who live in New England and the West Central regions are somewhat more likely to work than to stay at home.

PSYCHOGRAPHICS

Self-Concept

Whether the married woman without children works or not, she is likely to think of herself as kind, frank, awkward, intelligent, creative, reserved, and amicable. But if she goes to work, she is more likely to perceive herself as dominating, stubborn, affectionate, efficient, brave, and self-assured. If she doesn't go out to work, she is more likely to see herself as egocentric.

Buying Style

All married women without childern are fairly cautious and tend to buy brand-name items. The married working woman without children at home leans toward being an impulsive shopper. Like other women, she is very style-conscious. When she doesn't work, she is more likely to be a conformist when she goes marketing. But many see themselves also as experimenters. She tends to be concerned about ecology and is a slightly more persuasible customer.

EXHIBIT **VI**

NO HUSBAND/NO CHILDREN

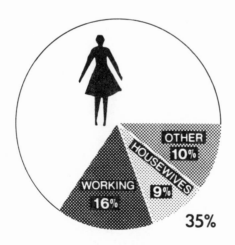

OTHER 10%

HOUSEWIVES 9%

WORKING 16%

35%

Source: Bureau of Labor Statistics
U.S. Census Bureau (JWT Special Tabulations)

There are more women in the country with neither husbands nor children (35 percent) than there are in the traditional group of married women with children under eighteen living at home. More women are marrying late. Many who do marry get divorced. And there are the widows. While the ratio of working women to housewives is roughly two to one, this group contains a sizable number of "all others"— schoolgirls, retired women, and "others".

DEMOGRAPHICS

Age

The majority of the unattached, separated, widowed, or divorced women without children at home are found to be either very young or over fifty years of age. Most of the unmarried young women (eighteen to twenty-four) can be found in the work force, along with those aged fifty to sixty-four. The older middle-aged unmarried women are far more likely than any other age group in this segment to be at work.

The nonworking unattached women are for the most part past retirement age. It can be speculated that many of these older women have outlived their husbands or may be single women who have retired from the work force. The median age for unattached working women without any children is 42.7; it is sixty-five for those not working.

Household Income

The household income level for this group of women is the lowest of all life cycle segments and substantially below that of men. We can see the low level of household income if we look at the medians. The median household income for those who work is $6,904 and for those at home, $3,280. The fact that many of the nonworking group are retired pulls down the household income level considerably.

Education

The education of many of the working women in this segment is impressive. At least 40 percent of those who work have spent some time in college, and more than 20 percent graduated from college. But among the women at home the educational level is rather low. The majority did not complete high school.

Occupation

The occupational profile of working women with no family responsibilities is consistent with that of the total female work force. They are slightly more likely than the married working women with children at home, and slightly less likely than childless married women, to have professional or managerial careers.

Number in Household

The majority of women in this life cycle group live in homes or apartments with one or two occupants per home. This is similar to the family size of married women without children at home. More nonworking single women live in these one- or two-person households; unmarried working women are more likely to live in larger households, with three or four persons per home. It is possible that these women are living with their parents.

Region

The working women in this life cycle group is more likely to live in the largest metropolitan areas, whereas the nonworking women are more apt to live in less populated areas (under 150,000 population). Compared with the total population, working women in this life cycle segment are somewhat more likely to be found in the Northeast, particularly in the New England and Mid-Atlantic marketing regions. They are somewhat less likely to cluster in the Southeast or Southwest.

PSYCHOGRAPHICS

Self-Concept

Single women with no children describe themselves as kind, self-assured, and reserved. The working women in this life cycle segment are more likely than the stay-at-homes to perceive themselves as dominating, stubborn, affectionate, funny, brave, creative, amicable, intelligent, and efficient. The nonworking women with no family responsibilities tends to rate herself as egocentric to a greater extent than her working counterpart.

Buying Style

Whether working or not, these women consider themselves ecologists. Among all women, they show the highest degree of interest in environmental problems.

Like other women, the single working woman with no children is style-conscious. She is concerned with how she looks and what she wears. When she goes shopping she takes along a shopping list that she prepared ahead of time. Then again, many in this segment also see themselves as impulsive, buying products on the spur of the moment.

Nonworking single women with no children are more likely to describe themselves as conformists, economy-minded, experimental, brand-loyal, and persuasible.

Eхнiвiт **VII**

CHILDREN / NO HUSBAND

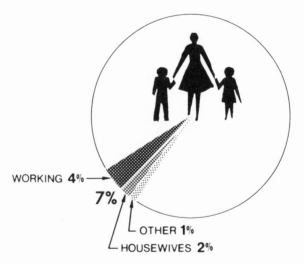

WORKING **4**%

7%

OTHER 1%

HOUSEWIVES **2**%

Source: Bureau of Labor Statistics
U.S. Census Bureau (JWT Special Tabulations)

An increasing number of divorcees and widows with children are heads of their own households, with full responsibility for how their families live and how they spend their money. We find 7 percent of American women in this segment. Twice as many of the women in this category go to work as stay home and keep house. While their number is small, this may be a growing market. Their needs and concerns are different from those of the single or formerly married women without responsibilities and also different from those of the married women with children who live with their husbands.

DEMOGRAPHICS

Age

Women in this life cycle group are young. More than one-third of the working and nonworking women are between the ages of eighteen and twenty-four. The median age of the single working mother is 29.6; it is 32.9 for the nonworking single mother.

Presence of Children by Age

Compared to married women with children, the age of the children seems to be less of an influence on whether or not a woman in this life cycle segment goes to work. Before their children reach their teens, mothers in this group are slightly more likely to stay at home. After their children become teenagers, these women are slightly more likely to go to work. Regardless of whether they go to work or not, these single mothers are less likely than married mothers to have very young children, and they are more likely to be mothers of teenagers.

Household Income

Women in this segment are fairly poor. Many live in homes where the household income is below $8,000. The nonworking woman is the least fortunate. Half of the stay-at-homes find themselves with less than $5,000 a year to live on, while one out of three working women lives at this low income level. If the unmarried mother goes to work, her median household income is $7,065, and if she stays at home it is $4,975.

Education

The educational levels reached by single mothers are mixed. There are fewer college graduates among this group than any other life cycle segment. However, their level of college attendance is relatively high.

The stay-at-homes are far more apt to have dropped out of school before graduating from high school. Working women, on the other hand, have a higher level of education than the ones who stay at home.

Occupation

The single working mother can be found in clerical or sales positions. The majority, however, fall into occupations classified as "other." They are less likely than any of the other life cycle segments to have professional or managerical jobs.

Number in Households

Women with children and without husbands are apt to live in larger households. This is as true of the working mother as the stay-at-home. This suggests that women in this life cycle group have gone home to mother or have doubled up with other families.

Region

Women in this life cycle segment are more likely to live in the largest metropolitan areas if they go to work and in rural counties with under 35,000 population if they stay at home. The woman who goes to work is above expectation in the extent to which she lives in the East Central marketing region. Working single mothers are more likely to live in suburban areas than in cities or rural communities. The nonworking single mothers are relatively more likely to be found in central city and non-SMSA localities.

PSYCHOGRAPHICS

Self-Concept

The single, separated, widowed, or divorced women with children describe themselves as awkward, affectionate, efficient, creative, amicable, refined, tense, and kind. If working, they see themselves as dominating, stubborn, and broad-minded. And if not working, they see themselves as reserved, brave, funny, and egocentric.

Buying Style

More than any other life cycle group, the single mother describes her shopping habits as impulsive and experimental. If she goes to work she is more likely to say she plans ahead when she goes shopping; if she stays at home she is more likely to describe herself as an ecologist and economy-minded when she goes to market.

Impact of Life Cycle in the Market Place

We have examined the demographic and psychographic characteristics of working and nonworking women in each of four life cycle situations. But the question for marketers is whether the factor of life cycle has an impact on their behavior in the market place.

Our hypothesis is simple. In order to really understand the impact working has on women as consumers, it is necessary to compare working women with nonworking women in the same life situation. We have done this, and we find that it is a much more discriminating way to tell whether working women are really different from their nonworking sisters in the market place.

Let us now reexamine the same product categories discussed in Chapter 5, this time going beyond the monolithic comparison of working women with nonworking women by also considering their situations in the life cycle.[2]

BREAKFAST CEREAL

We noticed in Chapter 5 that there wasn't much difference between working and nonworking women in the buying of cereal. But regardless of whether married women go to work or not, families with children at home are the heavy cereal users, particularly of the presweetened form. Working mothers are slightly more likely than their stay-at-home counterparts to buy natural cereal.

Among the unmarried women, that small group of mothers without husbands reaffirms that the use of presweetened cereal is linked to the presence of children. The working woman with no children or husband around the house is more likely to buy natural cereal.

COFFEE

All married women, with or without children, are slightly above par in their use of regular coffee. The heaviest user seems to be the childless housewife at home. Apparently, having a lot of time allows her to brew more coffee.

The nonworking mother and the childless working woman are the best customers for freeze-dried coffee. Apparently, having children around the house drives women to drink a lot of instant coffee, whether they go to work or not. Unmarried women seem to be much less likely than their married sisters to use any kind of coffee—regular, freeze-dried, or instant. Two exceptions are the single working woman's use of freeze-dried coffee and the fact that the stay-at-homes, with or without children, particularly the latter, are apt to buy instant coffee.

FINANCIAL ACTIVITIES

We noted earlier that working women are far more likely than nonworking women to be involved in financial activities, except for securities. Let's take a look at how this is affected by their stage in the life cycle.

The married nonworking housewife with children tops her working counterpart in having a savings account. On the other hand, the childless married woman who works is more likely to have her own savings account than her stay-at-home counterpart. The housewife with children at home is more likely to have a checking account than her childless neighbor. However, in each case their working sisters are more active checking account customers.

What about credit cards? All married women, particularly those with children, are above par in having such cards. However, if they go to work they are even more likely to say, "Charge it."

Earlier we saw that working women are less likely to own securities. Now we find that there is a real difference between the married women with children and those without. Childless couples apparently have more funds available for investment.

How do unmarried women compare with married women in terms of money? Most of their financial activities are below the norm. The one exception is that unmarried childless women are likely to have savings accounts.

CARS

The married woman with no children under eighteen at home is least likely of the four groups to have a driver's license. Working mothers and working and nonworking childless married women are the most likely to have two or more new cars in their garages.

All married women are distinctly above par in the extent to which they report sharing in the purchase decision. But whether they have children at home or not, the working wives seem to have a greater voice in that decision. Conversely, all married women with and without children are far below the norm in buying cars on their own. But in each case the working woman is slightly more likely to buy her own car than her nonworking neighbor.

Unmarried women are less involved in almost every aspect of car ownership than married women, with one dramatic exception. Unmarried working women, both those with children and particularly those without, are clearly above the norm in the extent to which they have selected and paid for their own cars.

TRAVEL

We saw earlier that working women are far more likely to engage in travel than their stay-at-home neighbors. What we did not show is whether there is any difference in terms of their life situations. We now find that working married women without children at home are by far the best customers for travel among all married women.

When we look at the unmarried side of the coin, we see that the combination of no children and an available paycheck appears to be a passport to women's travel activity.

Thus we see that if we really want to learn how working women differ from nonworking women as consumers, we should compare their marketing behavior within life cycle segments. This is a game that any number can play, because the information is available to all of us. It just requires some straightforward cross-tabs to decide how these targets differ from each other, how they are alike, and where to reach them.

Simple Demographic Fact Number Two shows:

- Women change as consumers as they move through different stages in life.

- The presence (or absence) of a husband or children are keys to her marketing behavior.
- The way to understand how working affects women as consumers is to compare working to nonworking women within life cycles.

Notes

1. "Advertising to Women: The Impact of Employment and Life-Style on the Media Behavior of Women," JWT Special Markets Media Report, 1973 (photocopied).
2. "A Moving Target: The Influence of Women's Employment on Consumer Behavior," speech given by Rena Bartos to The American Marketing Association, January 28, 1977 (photocopied).

Chapter 7

Meet the New Demographics

We have asked whether the fact that women go to work changes them as consumers. In Chapter 5 we compared the demographic and psychographic profiles of working women and nonworking women, as well as their patterns of media and market behavior. Our understanding of the impact of employment on consumer behavior of women was sharpened when, in Chapter 6, we added the perspective of life cycle. We considered not just whether a woman goes to work or stays at home but also whether she is married or not and whether there are children in her household. By placing our comparison of the market and media behavior of working and nonworking women within life cycle, we gained new insight into the market potential of working women.

Since the changing role of women in our society is so dynamic and open-ended, we shall never have the final answers. There is a constant flow of new information on the subject. Sometimes that information does not have any immediate marketing applications. It may become a fascinating parenthetical observation in the course of a discussion about the impact of working women on the market place and then turn into grist for luncheon or cocktail party conversation.

In a way this is like detective work. At some point in our study of a subject such as working women, we think we have all the answers. Then a fascinating new clue emerges, leading us to ask new kinds of questions. Two items reported by the *Yankelovich Monitor* gave us that kind of clue.[1]

In the course of examining perceptions of and attitudes toward the phenomenon of working women, the *Monitor* asked two questions, one of the working women and the other of the housewives in their sample.

Why Working Women Are Not All Alike

In 1971 the *Monitor* began asking working women whether they think the work they do is "just a job" or a "career." This was not intended to elicit a definition of their specific job assignments but rather was an effort to learn how these working women felt about the work they did. In other words, it was an attitudinal question, not a job definition.

At the time we first encountered this question the ratio of working women was roughly about 70 percent "job" to 30 percent "career." Only three in ten working women regarded themselves as career oriented at that time. The proportion of working women who perceived themselves as career-oriented rose to a ratio of one in three in the mid-1970s, then dipped back to the three-in-ten proportion in 1978. We speculate that the slight decrease in career perceptions in 1978 was a reflection of the large number of housewives who flooded into the work force about that time and were far more likely to be in the "just a job" category than career-oriented.

A generation ago there were only a handful of women who carved out careers because they were really motivated to do so. Today, according to Yankelovich, about four in ten women who work are strongly committed to careers. These women are motivated by the work itself. They equate working with an opportunity for self-realization, self-expression, and personal fulfillment.

EXHIBIT I

ATTITUDES OF
WORKING WOMEN TOWARD WORK: TRENDS

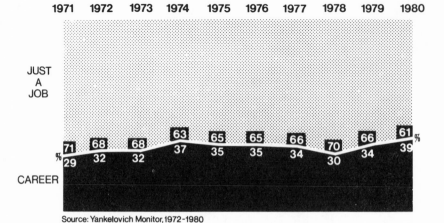

Source: Yankelovich Monitor, 1972-1980

Meanwhile, Back at the Ranch House . . .

But what about the 35 percent of all adult women who are at home keeping house? Apparently, not all housewives are equally committed to the housewife role. In 1971 the *Yankelovich Monitor* began asking housewives if they ever planned to work (or go back to work). Answers to this kind of question in an interview situation obviously are not necessarily predictive of behavior. We really didn't know whether or not these women would, in fact, rush downtown with résumés in hand. However, it did seem clear that housewives who said yes to this question had a very different mind set or predisposition from those housewives who said they preferred to stay at home.

Thinking back to all of the target marketing plans that are addressed to the mythical target of "any housewife, eighteen to forty-nine," we wondered whether the housewife who said she would like to go to work was not a different kind of target from the housewife who said she had no intention of working and preferred to stay at home.

When we first came across this question in the early 1970s, approximately half of the housewives interviewed said they planned to work sometime in the future. In recent years the proportion of plan-to-work housewives has dropped off somewhat. Currently, roughly one in three full-time housewives say they would like to go to work. At first glance it would seem that this might signal a return to the hearth and that the flood of wives into the work force might, in fact, begin to be reversed.

When we first came across this question, we realized that it was not a prediction of behavior but a predisposition. However, it was a clue.

• We began to wonder whether all housewives really are cut out of the same mold. The question of whether a housewife might want to go to work might indicate that she had value systems and attitudes different from those of her stay-at-home neighbor. Therefore, she might be a very different kind of consumer from the full-time homemaker who has no intention of going to work.

• We also wondered whether working women who were career-oriented were different in other ways from their co-workers who considered the work they do just a job.

Both of these questions are extremely relevant to marketing and advertising. All of our marketing activities and the advertising strategies that result from those activities are built on specific definitions of the "target group" to which the advertising is directed. If the assumed targets "any housewife, eighteen to forty-nine" and "any working

Exhibit II

ATTITUDES OF
HOUSEWIVES TOWARD WORK: TRENDS

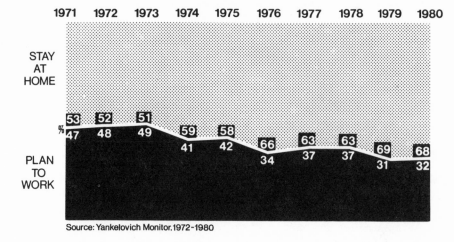

Source: Yankelovich Monitor.1972-1980

woman'' each contain distinctly different segments of women, then we need to rethink and redefine the way we approach the woman's market. Those redefinitions, in turn, could lead to different marketing opportunities and very different advertising strategies.

However, this kind of fundamental redefinition of target groups cannot be done on the basis of impressions or intuition. Marketing decision-makers understandably need strong factual evidence if they are to change their procedures.

At this stage we had nothing but a hunch. In earlier stages of our inquiry we were able to verify this kind of hunch or hypothesis by reanalysis of existing data.

• In Chapter 5 we asked whether working women and nonworking women are different kinds of consumers. We were able to reanalyze a large body of market and media data in the Target Group Index in order to answer this question. We saw that they do differ from each other in their market and media behavior.

• In Chapter 6 we pursued a hunch that situation in the life cycle might affect the way working and nonworking women buy products and use media. Again, we were able to verify this hypothesis by a reanalysis of available market and media data. We saw that studying working and nonworking women within the framework of life cycle gave us a much more discriminating way to define the women's market.

Linking Clues of Change to Marketing Actions

The challenge of the new clues suggested by the *Monitor* questions is that there was no way we could verify our speculations that these questions might identify very distinct segments within both the housewives' and working women's markets. In order to link our hunches about this new perspective to marketing actions, we needed to build these questions into our data base. This is a real-world example of how a marketer can link clues of change to ongoing marketing procedures.

As a first step we asked the Yankelovich people to do a special analysis for us that compared the responses of these four groups of women to a number of social value questions studied by the *Monitor* service. When we received the results of that analysis, we were startled to learn that at that time, at least, plan-to-work housewives had much more in common with the two types of working women than with their stay-at-home neighbors. *As a matter of fact, the stay-at-home housewives were really out of step with the majority of other women.*

Exhibit III, which visualizes the attitudinal differences between stay-at-home housewives and the other three groups of women, was developed at the time this analysis was first done. It is based on the 1974 *Yankelovich Monitor* report. The insight it provided raised some very disquieting questions:

- We wondered whether we had been building our marketing strategies and directing our advertising to only a limited segment of the female audience.
- We also wondered whether we had been applying our sophisticated marketing tools to just a limited corner of the market.

I began to worry about all of the research studies that had been done of the so-called woman's market. I wondered what types of women influenced the marketing decisions that resulted from those studies. The problem was that until now there was no way to find out. We had no way of knowing which of the housewives in our audiences or in our research studies are the stay-at-home variety and which ones are those who say they "plan to work." And even if we had been innovative enough at that time to talk to working women, it had not occurred to us

Exhibit III

ATTITUDES TOWARD WORK:
HOUSEWIVES AND WORKING WOMEN
1973

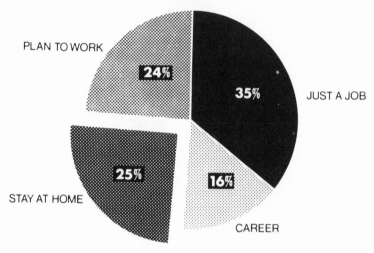

Source: Yankelovich Monitor, 1974
Bureau of Labor Statistics, 1974

to differentiate between the "just a job" and the career-minded segments of the working woman market.

At this point all we had were some intriguing speculations. We had no hard evidence as to whether these different groups of women actually behaved differently in the market place. And since the marketing and advertising concern here was whether or not we should reconsider the way we define our marketing targets, we needed to know if plan-to-work housewives were any different from the stay-at-homes when they went out to buy products. We needed to know how career women and "just a job" working women compare as consumers. For each group it was important to answer some questions: Who buys more? What brands? What products? Do they watch the same TV programs? What do they read? These are crucial marketing questions, and they deserve factual answers. The problem was that at that time we had no hard evidence that could answer those questions.

The real challenge in trying to make a connection between fascinating clues such as those we identified in the *Yankelovich Monitor* and real-world marketing actions is to know whether these groups of consumers are really different in their marketing behavior. This is how the "New Demographics" were born. As subscribers to an annual marketing and media study called the Target Group Index (TGI),* we requested that they add this pair of questions to their questionnaires. The plan-to-work question was to be asked of all housewives in their sample, and the career/job question of all working women whom they interviewed.

The questions were simple. We just had not thought of asking them before. They were added to the 1975 TGI questionnaire and have been included ever since. As a result of that simple step, we discovered that we did, in fact, have a new way of defining the woman's market. The conventional labels "housewives" and "working women" subdivide into four distinct segments of women. We call those segments the "New Demographics."

Meet the New Demographics

Here I would like to introduce you to four types of women that you might not have considered before:

- The stay-at-home housewife
- The plan-to-work housewife
- The "just a job" working woman
- The career-oriented working woman

Ever since 1975 we have been able to forge a link between our speculations about these four segments of women and their actual behavior in the market place. We have learned how they differ from each other demographically and psychographically, as well as in their media and marketing behavior.

We have learned some new facts about the New Demographics. First, how many of them are there? In the Exhibit IV we project the proportion of the four New Demographic segments in the *Yankelovich Monitor* to the Bureau of Labor Statistics report of the actual numbers of housewives and working women in the real world.

---

*The parent organization of the Target Group Index, Axiom Market Research Bureau, joined forces with the Simmons Market Research operation in 1979. The amalgamated company, Simmons Market Research Bureau, continued the New Demographic questions. They are currently also being asked by the Magazine Research Institute, Inc., and the Print Measurement Bureau (Canada).

EXHIBIT IV

SIZE OF THE SEGMENTS

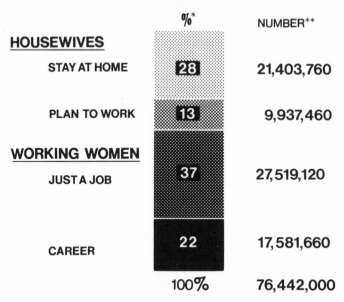

BASE: ALL WOMEN 16 AND OVER WHO ARE IN LABOR FORCE OR KEEPING HOUSE
* SOURCE: YANKELOVICH MONITOR, 1981
** BUREAU OF LABOR STATISTICS JAN. 1981

This new way of analyzing the woman's market was so dramatic that we decided to play a retrospective game and apply the proportions of the New Demographic groups reported by Yankelovich each year to the BLS ratio of working to nonworking women in each of those years. Exhibit V is a review of the ratio of working women to housewives during the 1970s. This trend chart starts in 1971, because that is the year Yankelovich began asking the New Demographic questions. These are the crucial years when the ratio of working women to housewives crossed over from equality to majority.

As we look at the movement of the four New Demographic groups during those years, we see that the watershed year was 1974. In that year the proportion of plan-to-work housewives began to diminish, and the proportion of working women accelerated rapidly.

We had originally wanted to separate plan-to-work from stay-at-home housewives, because we suspected they might be different types of marketing targets. It never occurred to us that their answers to the plan-to-work question would anticipate their actual behavior! In each

Exhibit V

RATIO OF WORKING WOMEN TO HOUSEWIVES: TRENDS: 1971-1980

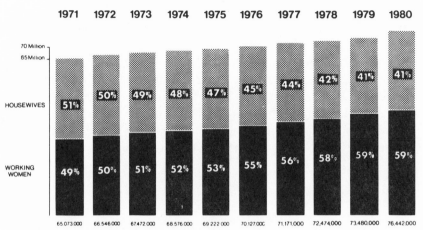

Base: All women 16 and over in the labor force or keeping house
Source: Bureau of Labor Statistics, Employment and Earnings, Jan., 1972-1981

Exhibit VI

THE NEW DEMOGRAPHICS: TRENDS: 1971-1980

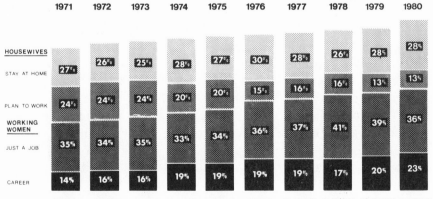

BASE   ALL WOMEN 16 AND OVER IN THE LABOR FORCE OR KEEPING HOUSE

SOURCE   BUREAU OF LABOR STATISTICS. EMPLOYMENT AND EARNINGS. JAN. 1972 – 1981
YANKELOVICH MONITOR. 1972 – 1981

succeeding year the proportion of plan-to-work housewives has diminished (Exhibit VI). They have put their intentions into practice. They joined the ranks of working women as they departed from their homemaker roles. And as they did so, the number of "just a job" working women expanded rapidly.

Demographics

What is the evidence that this new typology does represent four distinct segments of women? I said earlier that by incorporating these questions in TGI since 1975 we have been able to forge a link between our speculations about the four segments and their actual behavior in the market place. Certainly, their demographic differences underscore the need to treat them as distinctly different segments.

EDUCATION

We have always known that education is a key to women working. There is a high correlation between women's education and their likelihood to be in the work force. However, this analysis also reveals that education is strongly related to career orientation: 55 percent of all career-oriented women have either attended or graduated from college.
  • The educational profile of plan-to-work housewives is very similar to that of "just a job" working women. They are just slightly more likely to have graduated from college and to have completed their high school educations than "just a job" women, but the differences between the two groups are minor. As we noted earlier, there seems to be an active movement of plan-to-work housewives into the "just a job" working segment.
  • Plan-to-work housewives are relatively better educated than their stay-at-home neighbors. As a matter of fact, the stay-at-home housewives are less likely than any other group to have gone to college and more likely than any other segment to have left school before completing high school.

AGE

Another key demographic variable is age.
  • Stay-at-home housewives are by far the oldest of all the groups of

women. Just over half of them are over fifty years of age. Their median age is fifty.

• Plan-to-work housewives, on the other hand, are the youngest of the New Demographics, with a median age of thirty-two. They are far more likely than any other segment of women to be below middle age. The largest number of them are between twenty-five and thirty-four years of age.

• There is less difference in age between the "just a job" and career women. They each have a median age of thirty-six. However, a higher ratio of "just a job" women are in the very young years between eighteen to twenty-four. Career women, on the other hand, are slightly more likely to be between twenty-five and thirty-four than their "just a job" counterparts.

• As a matter of fact, "just a job" women cluster at two ends of the age spectrum, under twenty-five and over fifty, while career women are squarely in the middle between twenty-five and forty-nine.

MARITAL STATUS

As might be expected, the greatest number of full-time housewives are married. But there are still a portion of stay-at-home and plan-to-work housewives who are without husbands. Of course, these might be widows or divorcees.

Three out of five of both types of working women are currently married. This belies the outdated assumption that women who have never married or whose marriages have dissolved are the only ones to go to work.

HAVE CHILDREN UNDER EIGHTEEN

A crucial demographic determinant as to whether or not a housewife goes to work seems to be the presence of children. Plan-to-work housewives are far more likely than any other group to have children under eighteen years of age in their households. Half or just under half of all the other groups are also mothers of children under eighteen.

AGE OF CHILDREN

The plan-to-work housewives not only are more likely to have children under eighteen in their households, they are most likely to be the mothers of very young children, those at the infant stage—under two years of age—or preschool toddlers between two and five years old.

Working women in each segment have children at all age levels but they are less likely than either group of housewives to have very young children at home.

HOUSEHOLD INCOME

Career women live in the most affluent households of the four segments of women. They are far more likely to be in households with $25,000 or more annual household income as well as in the next lower income bracket between $15,000 and $25,000.

It is not surprising that career women live in the most affluent households, as they themselves earn more money than their "job" counterparts. And the 60 percent of them who are married tend to be married to the most achieving men. Therefore, their joint household incomes would be higher than those of any other group.

It is clear that the motivation to work expressed by plan-to-work housewives isn't only an economic one. They are slightly more affluent, overall, than their stay-at-home neighbors. Their household incomes are slightly higher than those of "just a job" working women as well.

REGION

There are not too many differences among the four New Demographic segments on the basis of region. We note that career women are slightly more likely than any of the other three segments to be found on the West Coast.

We also note that stay-at-home housewives are slightly more likely to live in the South. Probably the greatest single regional difference is among working women in the North Central area. A higher proportion of working women in that region term themselves job-oriented rather than career-oriented.

OCCUPATION

We said earlier that the job/career question is a matter not of job definition but of attitude. However, it is not surprising that a much higher proportion of career-oriented women than job-oriented women are found in professional/managerial occupations. Again, "job" women are more likely than career-oriented women to be in clerical sales occupations or in that catchall category known as "other."

It should be noted that career-oriented women are found in all occupational categories. This attitude toward their work is not identical with the occupational definitions discussed in Chapter 4. In that chapter we differentiated between the 80 percent of women who are in clerical or service jobs and the 20 percent who are in professional or managerial occupations.

Psychographics

We have seen that the four New Demographics have very distinctive demographic profiles. Their psychographic profiles are equally distinctive.

HOW THEY SEE THEMSELVES[2]

• Career women have stronger self-images than any other segment of women. They are more likely than the others to describe themselves as trustworthy, kind, refined, broad-minded, efficient, intelligent, and frank. They are the only ones who think of themselves as self-assured, although even their level of self-assurance is not imposing. Their most outstanding differentiation from the norm is the extent to which they see themselves as amicable. They are also more likely than any other group to describe themselves as creative.

• "Just a job" working women tend to be close to the norm. However, they are a faint echo of their career counterparts in describing themselves as trustworthy, kind, refined, stubborn, broad-minded, and affectionate. More than any other group, they admit to a sense of humor. They are slightly above career women in this perception. This is one case where "just a job" women have a stronger self-image than career women.

• Plan-to-work housewives are more tense and stubborn than any other segment of women. They also describe themselves as sociable, affectionate, and awkward. They echo the career women in feeling that they are creative.

• Stay-at-home housewives are not at all likely to think of themselves as brave or stubborn. They are mildly likely to see themselves as kind and sociable. They are least likely of any of the other segments of women to think of themselves as assertive. They are far below the norm in thinking of themselves as brave, stubborn, dominating, intelligent, frank, or broad-minded. They are least likely to have a sense of humor, and they have particularly low egos. On the positive side, they are mildly likely to think of themselves as trustworthy, kind, and sociable. They are not nearly as tense as their plan-to-work neighbors, or as "just a job" working women, for that matter. However, they are more tense than career women.

BUYING STYLE

Career women are more likely than the others to plan ahead when they go marketing or shopping. Plan-to-work housewives and "just a job" working women plan ahead more than do stay-at-home housewives. Both types of housewives are more economy-minded than working women. Plan-to-work housewives are most concerned about economy. There is real difference between the two segments of working women. The "just a job" women are more concerned than career women about the money they spend.

Career women and stay-at-home housewives resemble each other in being cautious shoppers and brand-loyal to a greater extent than the other groups. "Just a job" working women are least likely to be brand-loyal and most likely to be experimental when they go shopping. This group is obviously responsive to new products and to competitive promotions. This is particularly significant to marketers, because they are the largest segment of women in our population at present.

All women are likely to be more style-conscious than men, but there is a noticeable hierarchy of involvement with style as one moves across the spectrum from stay-at-home housewives, who are mildly concerned with style, to career women, for whom it is a strong interest. The stay-at-homes are the only segment of the four who are above the norm in admitting that they are persuasible. On the other hand, they are less likely than their plan-to-work neighbors to be impulse buyers. The two working women segments are frankly more likely to make impulsive purchases.

All women are slightly below the norm in perceiving themselves as conformist. However, plan-to-work housewives are most likely to reject the conformist typology.

On the surface there appears to be a conflict in the fact that career women are more likely than the others to be cautious and plan ahead in their purchase decisions but nevertheless admit to being impulse buyers. My judgment is that this is a matter of the nature of the purchase and the level of product decision involved. They do plan ahead in making big-ticket purchases such as cars or travel. On the other hand, since they have more money available, they are in a position to make an impulsive buying decision when something catches their fancy.

Purchase Behavior[3]

In Chapter 5 we examined the purchase behavior of working and nonworking women in relation to five product categories. In Chapter 6 we placed our examination of the market behavior of working and nonworking women within the framework of the life cycle, as applied to the same five product categories. Although Part III will study the market behavior of the New Demographic segments in more depth, at this point we shall continue our examination of the purchase behavior of working and nonworking women. In this instance we place them within the context of the New Demographic typology. We will observe how the four New Demographic segments relate to the five product categories discussed previously.

BREAKFAST CEREAL

"Just a job" working women are slightly better customers for cereal than anyone else. The plan-to-work housewives are the only ones above par in the use of regular cereal, and they are the principal users of the presweetened type. Of course, this is accounted for by all the small children they have at home.

Earlier we saw that working women are more likely than nonworking women to buy natural cereal. But it is really the career-oriented woman who is the chief user. She is echoed in this by the plan-to-work housewife. So we see that not all working women and not all housewives are alike in their purchase patterns of this mass product.

COFFEE

The stay-at-home housewife is the only one above the norm in use of regular ground coffee, the traditional form of coffee. The career woman is the best customer for freeze-dried coffee. Again, she is echoed by the plan-to-work housewife. While both types of house-wives are more likely to use instant coffee than are working women, the plan-to-work housewife is twice as active in this market as her stay-at-home neighbor.

FINANCIAL ACTIVITIES

The career-oriented working woman dominates financial ac-tivities. She is more likely than any other group to have a savings ac-count, to maintain a regular checking account, to have any credit cards, or to have investments. Among the housewives, it is the one who plans to work who does all of these things, but to a far lesser degree than the career woman.

The "just a job" working woman is just about at par in everything but investments, where she is well below the norm. The stay-at-home housewife is far less involved in financial activity than any of the other groups.

The contrast in the investment behavior of career women and the "just a job" working women is dramatic evidence of the need to go beyond the monolithic grouping of working women. Not all working women represent the same kind of market potential!

CARS

Who is most likely to drive? The career woman again, followed by the plan-to-work housewife. But when it comes to having more than one car at home bought new, although the career woman is the most likely customer, a substantial proportion of stay-at-home housewives also report well-stocked garages. We can speculate that this skewing reflects income, but at two different ends of the life style spectrum.

Looking at purchase decision, we see that, as usual, all women are above the norm in having shared that decision. The two housewife groups are more likely to have done so. The plan-to-work housewife took the most active part in the shared decision.

Again, while all women are below par in their having made the deci-sion themselves, there is a dramatic difference in this regard between the working women and the nonworking women. The career woman is the most likely of the four groups to have bought a car herself.

TRAVEL

We noted earlier that the absence of children and presence of a paycheck favor women's travel activities, but now we can see that the career-oriented working woman is really the prime customer for travel. The plan-to-work housewife has bought some luggage, but she doesn't seem to have taken many trips as yet!

This brief review of the demographic and psychographic profiles of the four New Demographic groups demonstrates their diversity. We have seen that they have quite distinctive patterns of purchase behavior. Later chapters will document their market place behavior in more depth and will also study the way they respond to and use media.

The evidence thus far suggests that the New Demographics typology is a highly discriminating way to segment the working woman and the housewife markets. It takes us beyond the monolithic cookie cutter approach to the women's market. It should help us to avoid creating new stereotypes.

Notes

1. *The Yankelovich Monitor* (annual) (New York: Yankelovich, Skelly, and White), 1972–1981.
2. Dr. Timothy Joyce, creator of the Target Group Index system, describes the development of the self-concept analysis as follows: "Webster's English Dictionary was scanned to identify self-descriptive adjectives. We chose about 500 of these and gave 700 respondents self-administered questionnaires in which they rated themselves on each of these adjectives. Through a factor analysis, we identified twenty psychographic factors, each of which is composed of several descriptive adjectives."
3. From "A Moving Target: The Influence of Women's Employment on Consumer Behavior," speech given by Rena Bartos to the American Marketing Association, January 28, 1977 (photocopied).

Chapter 8

Understanding the
New Demographics

We have seen that the New Demographic segmentation is far more discriminating than the crude division of women on the basis of whether or not they are employed. There is ample evidence that grouping women on both their New Demographic and their life cycle characteristics enables us to pinpoint precisely how much market potential each group has for a particular product or service. Further, our media and demographic information enables us to determine just who they are, where they are, and how to reach them.

Even with this new dimension in target group analysis, there was a gap in our understanding. In order to develop effective communications to women in these New Demographic/life cycle groups, we needed to know how they felt about themselves and about the activities in their lives in which our clients' products and services might be used.

Knowing what they watch, read, and listen to, and what products and brands they buy still left us with much we didn't know about them.

- We didn't know what they look for in products and what motivates their brand decisions.
- We didn't know whether there are some universals common to all groups.
- We didn't know whether those universals are different from the generalizations about "what women want" that we have articulated from past studies of the women's market.

In order to gain some insights into these unanswered questions, we undertook an exploratory study of the attitudes of the four New Demographic groups of women. [1] We wanted to go beyond the facts of what they buy and use to explore the attitudinal context within which they approach keeping house, personal grooming and cosmetics, recreation, vacations, travel, driving cars, and financial activities. The

116

objective was to identify the special perspective of each of these New Demographic groups toward these areas of activity and to define the life style context within which they approach the mundane activities of keeping house, serving meals, and buying clothes.

This sequence of quantitative analysis followed by qualitative exploration reverses the classic research procedure. The usual sequence is to use qualitative exploration to develop hypotheses for ultimate quantification. We, on the other hand, developed some speculations about the dynamics of the women's market through a review of masses of data. We verified the utility of these speculations about life cycle and employment through reanalysis of existing data.

When we identified the New Demographic concept, our hypothesis could not be confirmed or denied through reanalysis of existing data, because the attitudinal questions on which they are based had not been asked before. Therefore, we added the New Demographic questions to a standardized study of market and media behavior in order to extend our redefinition of the market.

We then reanalyzed our market and media data from the perspective of the New Demographics. As has been demonstrated in Chapter 7 and will be documented in Part III, segmenting the women's market on the basis of the New Demographic typology was very discriminating. However, there was still a gap in our understanding. In order to understand why the New Demographic/life cycle segments behave as they do, we needed to return to qualitative exploration. The New Demographic typology defined the samples to be studied.

This approach proceeds from quantified evidence of marketing behavior to seek qualitative understanding of the reasons for that behavior. The results are actionable because we know the size of each group, exactly which products and brands it buys, and how much. And because we know what women in each life cycle/New Demographic segment read, watch, and listen to, we are able to identify just how to reach each group through the media.

In Part III we shall discuss the market place behavior of the New Demographics. As we examine how the New Demographic segments buy and use a number of products and services, we shall tap into both the factual analysis of their purchase patterns obtained from marketing data and the attitudinal insights provided by the qualitative study described previously. Before proceeding to an examination of their media and market behavior, let us consider how the four New Demographic segments feel about themselves and their attitudes toward their own lives.

Stay-at-Home Housewives

Even though these women, by definition, have no intention of going to work, they may have worked at some time in their lives. Some of them are likely to have worked for some years before marriage and children; others may have worked even after they had children. Even though they have no desire to change the patterns of their lives, some of them suggest that they see their lives as fairly limited. One Chicago housewife said when asked how she spent her free time: "I never thought Mothers' Club meetings would be my big out!"

But they also see themselves as "more than just a housewife." Housework is just one of the things they do, just one part of the job. If there are children at home, their lives are largely focused on their families. They see themselves as "household engineers," coordinating their children's activities, scheduling their own activities around those of their children, providing meals to suit the children's schedules, supervising their lives, arranging a family life. They feel it is important for them to be there when the children come home from school and to provide real family meals on weekends. While they may be able to swing getaway weekends with their husbands, their vacation time is usually a family affair, at least until the children are old enough to strike out on their own.

"'Household engineer' just sounds more interesting to me, really ... 'housewife' sounds like you just stay at home and do nothing but housework. . . . I hate to cook and I hate to clean. You have to raise your children and there's things to do . . . the shopping and looking for prices . . . and there's the plumbing."

An Atlanta housewife explained her active schedule as follows: "I'm just constantly going all the time. I would like to stay home just one day and be bored stiff like everybody says I'm going to be because I'm a housewife. But you know it's constant, you're running down to school—my daughter's in cheerleading, she's going to be a Bluebird, etcetera. . . . I do have more time to get my housework done now that the kids are in school."

This sense of being needed at home explains why some of these homemakers don't want to go to work: "No, I don't think I would like to go back to work on a full-time basis. I think I have a full-time job just getting my son to do his homework. I don't think I could handle that when I got home from a full day of work."

When they say "I'm a full-time homemaker," they include such responsibilities as maintaining the home, which may mean plumbing, repairs, or making their own draperies, as well as marketing with know-how, keeping track of family expenditures, and entertaining. "You more or less correlate all parts of your household. You take care of the cooking and cleaning, but you also manage the family activities."

They also make time for outside activities that are personally rewarding. These outside interests are a lifeline to making them feel creative and accomplished, a way to renew themselves. They say that such diverse activities as handicrafts, sports, classes, dancing, singing, reading, bowling, volleyball, hockey, gardening, tennis, lunching with friends, and volunteer work help them to break away from the daily routines of family and household responsibilities.

Younger women with small children either make special efforts and arrangements to acquire this time or simply enjoy their knitting while looking after a child at play outdoors. Once the children are in school they can make time for themselves more easily.

The older women, especially if living alone, feel the need to make special efforts to get out and keep busy so as not to "stagnate or get depressed," even if they don't actually have interests and activities that come naturally.

A hint of geographic differences emerged from this particular sampling of women regarding how they spent their free time:

- New York women spoke of physical and cultural activities such as crafts, reading, singing, bowling, hockey, gardening, and the PTA.
- Chicago women described more sedentary activities. They talked about "relaxing," playing cards, knitting, and mothers' clubs.
- Women in Atlanta were deeply engaged in social and church activities, sororities, and volunteer organizations.
- The respondents in Los Angeles were sun- and sports-oriented or else enjoyed sewing, weaving, or painting. Several had no children.

Stay-at-homes see themselves as having the need for these self-fulfilling activities and the right to them. If they are now fully engaged with family responsibilities, they look forward to the time when they may do more for themselves. If the children are grown, they feel free to indulge their hobbies and interests. And although they may recognize that they are not as well organized or efficient as they assume working women must be, they appreciate "not being under the nine-to-five pressure. They enjoy being "my own boss." Their description of the details of their lives suggests a kind of professionalization of housewifery. One Chicago housewife said, "I think you can call yourself a family manager position . . . but don't try it because the pay is low." Another said: "You are kind of like social counselor, recreational counselor, educator, nurse, teacher, chauffeur . . . you come under many titles."

This is not to say that all of these housewives are gung-ho about their roles or that they feel their lives are as rewarding as they wish. Some long for more time for themselves, for self-fulfillment, or just to get away from it all. Some feel that the time will come when they might like to work to prove themselves or that they might be willing to work to earn a little money, but they speak of part-time work or work near to home, because they cannot conceive of relinquishing their roles at home. They may envy the working woman's grooming and wardrobe, her stimulating life and independence, but they see her as having neglected her children and sacrificing homemaking, entertaining, and the creative and relaxing aspects of the life of the woman at home.

The attitudes and self-perceptions of these women suggest that the stereotypes of the housewife who lives for a highly polished home or the housewife who can never master the mess probably do not apply to most middle-class women today. Some may have higher standards than others, and some may be able to manage the job better, but they do see beyond it. They see themselves as living in a world with wider horizons and other rewards. Remember, however, that not everyone wants or needs "wider horizons."

Plan-to-Work Housewives

Some of the plan-to-work housewives find that being a homemaker is personally rewarding. They are committed to their roles as housewives, but they also want to earn money. Their intentions of going to work are prompted by economics rather than restlessness: "I feel special because I'm home. . . . I'm there when they're home . . . but I have split feelings. I think of the things we could have if I earned money."

Others feel that if they do return to work they will limit themselves to part-time jobs. Their primary orientation is to home and family. They want to earn money, but they still feel that they are needed at home: "I worked as a secretary for seven years before I was married and just a short time after I was married. And I do plan to go back part time in the near future simply because I think my children have reached that state that I can work and to be perfectly honest I seem to be constantly running and doing things anyway. It would be nice to have a salary to go with it but still strictly part time for a couple of years. My youngest is in the sixth grade and I still feel I need to be home."

However, some plan-to-work housewives find less gratification in the housewife role. They yearn for the personal rewards of working. Some want to work because of the sense of accomplishment and achievement that comes in having completed a job. As one woman puts it: "When you work, you do a job and it's finished."

Others say that they enjoyed their jobs when they were in the workforce and feel that going back to work would be stimulating: "Well, I worked when I got out of school and worked for an insurance company, and then I worked for a staff of five attorneys which stimulated my interests. And I worked later for a man that started his own business, and I really enjoyed it. I feel that after a while you've done all you can do at home, and I'd love to go back to work."

Still others talk about work in terms of personal fulfillment and identity: "I will go back. I was a financial developer for a not-for-profit corporation, and I did enjoy it. It's personal fulfillment rather than the money. Obviously, at a not-for-profit organization you're not going to make . . ." "I'm looking for self-identity."

The yearnings of the plan-to-work housewives are expressed by the comments of two women who find that stay-at-home life tends to be boring. Although they take pride in their housewifely skills, they feel that the more time they have at home the less likely they are to use that time productively. They have a sense of diminished accomplishment or organization, and they long for the recognition that comes with going to work: "I found that when I did work a couple of years ago, I did get a lot of things done that normally are still sitting there now. . . . I like other activities but they get boring after a while. Like they said, the money is nice. But also I would want to know if I could do it again— that somebody would think that I would help their company in some way, for my own personal reasons. If I could go out and do something and somebody would want me—"

"I happen to love to cook and I used to love to clean. But I don't take pride in it any more. And when my kids were smaller, I was much better organized. I find now that the more time that I have alone I'm not as organized as I was before. Besides the fact it's costing me a lot of money to keep myself occupied outside the house, and nothing is really accomplished. I know that if I go to work I'll come home really excited about what I've done. And I used to be very happy after something was accomplished in the house. I don't have that kind of glory any more."

Some of these women feel that they are not as efficient at their housework as they would be if they were working. "My sister is working and she is more organized that I am." "A woman's work is never done." However, many of them handle their housework with dispatch. They get it done early and get on with the business of the day. This includes attention to marketing and meals and the care and attention that children require. It also includes doing things for their own personal gratification and future career development. Their activities are not so much a means of escaping from daily routines as for the personal rewards. They really like their outside activities. They are committed to them. However, they are somehow more executive about the activities they pursue than their stay-at-home neighbors.

Their sense of self is expressed in several ways. They want to look neat and clean for their own self-pride. They don't like to look "housewifey." They want to learn, to "keep up." They like to think their time is all their own, to organize as they wish. They may even be reluctant to give up their personal pursuits to go to work.

The plan-to-work housewives whose husbands hold the purse strings tightly are not reconciled to the subservience implied in that relationship. They fantasize about what their lives will be like if they go to work. They speculate on how they will manage the household and how they will dress. They don't seek just the "matching handbag" approach to fashion but talk about whether their styles will be "casual" and what the "dress code" will be.

They do not feel that if they go to work they will be sacrificing their children's welfare. They expect to wait until they feel the children don't need them at home all day before starting work. Their children will then profit from their incomes; they will be able to do more for their children, enabling them to travel more and become more independent. The children of working mothers, they point out, have more room to develop because they are not subject to the tyranny of a mother who lives exclusively for them.

On the whole, plan-to-work mothers are proud of their commitment to homemaking at present or in the past. They may intend to keep it up or to neglect some aspects of it when they go to work. Different women anticipate different ways of coping with the change. Some plan to maintain the same standards at home by being more efficient or "catching up" at night. Some expect to maintain control of their

households either by themselves or with paid help. Others expect to en-
list more help from their families.

Some plan-to-work housewives feel that their standards will
change when they return to work. They say that they will "overlook"
or will feature quick broiled meals during the week. Still others feel that
their houses will be cleaner when they go to work because their time will
be more organized.

This limited exploration into the attitudes of plan-to-work housewives suggests some intriguing questions to be explored in the future. It
would be interesting to know how the identity-minded and income-
minded women compare—which ones anticipate family cooperation
and which ones expect to go it alone. Do they differ with regard to their
standards of housekeeping? Which ones expect to relinquish entertaining and their own outside activities?

"Just a Job" Working Women

These women may not be terribly involved with their jobs, but almost all of them do enjoy the fact of going to work. Only one or two
said they were working out of stark necessity and would prefer to be
home. One of the two finds the routine of going to work too confining.
She articulates about the time squeeze that is common to most working
women: "Well, I'd love not to work, but I've never tried it. I would like
to do more volunteer work. I have a big thing about helping other people and children. I'm so regimented at my work, you know, you go to
do this during the day and then you have to do this at night, because
you've only got so many hours . . . like shopping is either at night or on
the weekend."

A more common attitude among the "just a job" working women
was the feeling that going to work is socially stimulating. They say it
puts them in touch with other people. Staying at home would be too
limiting and too boring: "I enjoy working because I like the contact. I
feel I produce more than the other things [hobbies, volunteer
activities], and I certainly don't mean to belittle any of them, but
they're just not my thing. I would like a full-time salary with part-time
work."

"I wouldn't be a housewife. I mean there's no reason for me to stay
home. There are no children. I would go crazy sitting in the house."

A husband's involvement in the working decision as well as a renewed self-image was reported by one woman. She said that both she and her husband felt that going to work would help her to get a new perspective about her life which, in turn, was expressed in the switch from slopping around in tee-shirts and jeans to feeling attractive at least part of the time. "One reason I went back to work was because both my husband and I thought that I needed a different outlook, a change of pace, because I was running around in jeans and tennis shoes and Scholl sandals and sloppy tee-shirts. Now I like that look sometimes, but not all the time."

A new sense of sharing and partnership comes with the very fact of having gone to work. One woman said that her husband helps more with the housework since she has gone back to work because she is contributing to the family's income: "My husband helps and I feel that he *should* now that I help with the income so much."

Some of these "just a job" working women have changed their attitudes toward household tasks. They have a changed sense of priorities: "Since I have worked full time and again part time, I react differently to housework, because I found out that it really doesn't have to get done. It's not that important."

Others say that they achieve the same results as they did when they were full-time housewives, but schedule their housework differently. The difference is that working women don't mind picking up around the house now that they're working, or that they have to do the cleaning in the evenings or on weekends: "My house is not as clean as it used to be, but I've got a big house and a lot of people and I have a schedule. Like Sunday I cook for most of the week. . . . I bought a crock pot."

Some think they have neater, cleaner homes than the women at home who are entrapped in a disorderly life because of children: "The house looks just as good as it always has."

Some of these working wives appear to regret the skimmed-over housework and lack of time to cook for their families. Others regret insufficient time for social and self-improving activities: "My house is never clean. It's organized but I usually have one day off in the week. On Saturdays I can't get anything done in the way of house cleaning as it seems I always have to take the girls somewhere. My husband likes a really clean house, and when we first married, for the first ten years, I kept a really nice house. Then, I had a maid for three years and that ruined me."

These "just a job" working women enjoy traveling. Their main travel motivations appear to be the attainment of a "getaway" feeling and the experience of luxury. They don't seem to be notably independent in planning their holidays or in coping with the problems of traveling. As a matter of fact, one of their motivations for working is to be able to feel pampered and luxuriant on their vacations: "Mostly, I like a luxurious type vacation. I like to go to Hilton Head and places like that and I visit relatives. I have a sister in California." "The cruise to the islands was very nice. The waiters on the boat were terrific. I mean all you had to do was take out a cigarette and they were lighting it for you immediately. The service on the cruise itself was superior. We had a good time."

Career-oriented Working Women

Going to work provides a certain measure of self-esteem for "just a job" working women. This is based primarily on their financial productivity. Working wives in that category share the income-producing role with their husbands.

On the other hand, career women feel that going to work makes them more interesting as people and rescues them from the dullness of being bridge-playing housewives: "I think that when a woman is occupied outside the home she is more attractive to her mate because you're not with the same humdrum things. She has something to enlighten someone else with . . . a lot of housewives are just plain out dull because they don't do anything with themselves." "Did you ever play bridge with that group? Each one trying to outtell the other one on something they had at home . . . boring. . . . I'm me. Maybe I don't have anything, but I enjoy what I do."

These women talked about the sense of independence and personal worth that comes with going to work: "I definitely feel a far greater sense of independence and personal worth now that I'm working, and the money angle is part of it, in a sense. I was married to a man who made a great deal of money who would tell me that I would be nothing if it weren't for him, that I was incapable of being anything because I was nothing but a woman. And I don't feel that any more. Working is part of what makes you feel that way."

They may or may not maintain high standards of housekeeping, but they are usually not troubled by it. The younger unmarried career women may simply assign it a low priority. For example, they say that they make beds if company is coming. The somewhat older career wives have more exacting standards. Nevertheless, they schedule their housework to fit their own personal or family needs: "Saturday is my day. Everyone fends for himself. On Sunday I do laundry and cooking for the week." "I can be very lax and I can get very energetic. It depends on what's going on with the family."

Some career women do their housework on weeknights in order to be free on the weekends. Others prefer an unencumbered week and do it on the weekend. In either case they are suiting their own preferences and exercising their own control.

They also exercise their own control of the situation in setting priorities for what gets done in their homes. Some prefer cooking while skimming over the cleaning. Some cook only for company but keep a meticulous house. In either case they feel that working imposes a discipline to get things done.

The older women, especially if they have exacting standards and no tradition of help from their husbands, may exert this discipline to the extent of cutting into their own free time. However, these women are conscious of that sacrifice. They seem to be the exception among career women.

There are other ways in which career women demonstrate that housekeeping, though an important aspect of their lives, is not the central theme. They may delegate a certain number of household chores to their husbands or children. However, unlike the "just a job" wives, they seem not to derive particular pleasure from the "togetherness" of that sharing of responsibility.

In some cases they feel that the children should not be asked to sacrifice *their* time to household chores. Career-oriented working mothers do not feel that they neglect their children. If the children are young, these career mothers manage a "hot breakfast for them," and "Mommy makes french toast on Saturday." They make time to be with their children. They gear vacations for their children's pleasure, even though the children's desires may not coincide with their personal preferences.

Some career women may see housework as a challenge or enjoy it because it is *not* an obligation. Older career women may do their housework in a thorough and systematic way. But at least one younger woman "does it under cover and doesn't mention it."

Their range of practices in financial matters is much like that of other married women. But when career women handle the mechanics of financial record-keeping, they seem to derive pleasure not so much from the doing of it but rather from getting it done or knowing where the money is going. As in other households there is general agreement about how the money is to be spent. However, career wives may also feel that both they and their husbands are free to act independently: "Some decisions are left to him, some to me." "He can buy his cameras, I can rent a piano." They also feel free to use their own money to buy the kind of car they personally want, without consulting their spouses.

Unmarried career women, like "just a job" single women, take pride in their competence in managing their money and their interest in making investments. Some are proud of how much they are earning and are informed about pension plans, treasury bills, and so on.

In telling about their vacations and travel activities, career women also sound more executive than the other working women. Unmarried career women manage their travels by flying, because they don't like to drive alone. They stay at good hotels that provide security. And if a career woman travels with her mother, it's to show her something new, not just to have her company.

Some unmarried career women choose to travel on tours, because they provide company at meals. At the same time, traveling on tours allows them to make travel plans without depending on their friends as travel companions.

A number of these career women take pride in planning vacations and organizing them. Some career wives do all the planning. Career women have more money and travel more, but they aren't careless with their money. They stay at luxury places but travel with economy. Many have had the experience of traveling when they were young, though at that time they traveled on a real scale of economy.

They enjoy business travel because it means that "you don't have to watch the pennies." They don't say, as one "just a job" woman said, that "it spoils me for vacations I can afford!"

Their views about grooming seem to have a different emphasis from those of the "just a job" women. They are less concerned about mere conformity to dress codes and more concerned with their own personal images. We can speculate that they take the dress code and fashion for granted.

In their approach to fashion they are deeply aware that the way they dress and present themselves to the world is not only an important element in their professional images but a reflection of their own self-esteem. They say the way they dress is to "project professionalism," "project a rising young image," "to elicit respect—that is why my dresses are conservative," or "to suit me, out of respect and love for myself."

Note

1. Rena Bartos, *Understanding the New Demographics,* J. Walter Thompson Co., 1977 (photocopied). Subsequent quotes throughout chapter are taken from this qualitative research report.

III

Changing Audiences—
Changing Consumers

Chapter 9

Women and Media

We have seen that the four types of women we describe as the New Demographics vary strongly in their demographic characteristics, their buying styles, and their self-perceptions. The challenge to the marketer who wishes to reach them through advertising is to learn how they use media. What do they read? What do they watch? What do they listen to? Do the four segments of women really have different patterns of media behavior?

Since advertising, by definition, is carried to consumers through the channels of mass media, a marketer might very well ask whether the nuances of difference among the four groups are not washed out by the universal nature of mass communications.

In this chapter I shall attempt to examine how the four New Demographic groups respond to various types of media. Patterns of media use reported here are based on custom analyses of Target Group Index (TGI) data. I shall use the quintile concept in this analysis.

It is customary for analysts of media behavior to divide the audiences of each medium into quintiles or equal fifths, ranging from the heaviest viewers or users of that medium down to the lightest. In analyzing the patterns of media behavior of any segment within the population, we can thus compare its distribution of light to heavy media usage to that of the total population, so that we can observe whether that segment is heavier or lighter in its usage of a particular medium. This provides the basis for comparing the patterns of media behavior of women to those of men, for example, or the differences, if any, in the way the various segments within the women's market respond to media.

Before we consider how the New Demographics compare among themselves in the ways they use media, let us put their media behavior in perspective. Are there any patterns of media use that are characteristic of all women and different from those of men? Let us take an overall look at how the total universe of women differs from the total universe of men in the ways they respond to media.

In the following we shall examine only the heaviest users of each medium (or top quintile) in order to see whether women differ from men in the degree to which they are strong supporters of each medium.

• Women seem to be more responsive to and involved with television than are men.

• Overall, women are far more likely than men to watch television during the day. This is not too surprising since women as a group are more likely to be available to view daytime television programs. More of them are likely to be at home during the day.

• However, even though both men and women should be available to watch television during the evening, women are more likely than men to look at television during the prime time evening hours.

• While both sexes are found in the audiences of the major print media, there are differences between them. Women are more likely than men to be heavy readers of magazines.

• Men, on the other hand, are far more likely than women to be heavy readers of newspapers.

• Men, as a group, are more likely than women to be away from home during the day. Similarly, men are more likely to travel by car; they rack up many more miles on their speedometers than do women drivers. Therefore, not surprisingly, men are far more likely than women to be heavy viewers of outdoor advertising.

This overview shows that there are clear differences in the patterns of media behavior of men and of women. However, when we consider the media behavior of the four New Demographic segments within the women's market, it becomes equally clear that there are real differences in the way that each of the four segments of women approaches media. While it is true that the mass media reach all types of women, it is equally true that the differences in the media behavior of the four New Demographics demonstrates that the women's market is not a monolithic mass.

How The New Demographics Use Media[1]

Before examining each medium in detail, let us compare the heaviest users of each medium among the four New Demographic groups. This overview is parallel to the male/female comparison described previously.

• The sharpest differences among the New Demographics occur in relation to daytime TV. Not surprisingly, both types of housewives are far more likely to watch TV during the day than are women who work. However, more than half of the plan-to-work segment of housewives are very heavy viewers of TV, and career women are far less likely than "just a job" working women to be found among the heaviest viewers of daytime TV.

• Although all groups should be available to watch TV during the evening, among the New Demographics, plan-to-work housewives are the greatest fans of prime time TV. Stay-at-home housewives are above the norm in heavy viewership of prime time TV, followed by "just a job" working women.

• The two working segments are particularly responsive to radio, followed closely by plan-to-work housewives. Stay-at-home housewives are least likely to be heavy radio listeners.

• Career women outdistance all other segments in heavy reading of magazines. They are echoed in this by plan-to-work housewives, but at a lower level of intensity.

• Career women also outdistance the other segments in their likelihood to read newspapers. They are the only female segment above the norm in being heavy readers of newspapers.

• Both types of working women are far more likely to be heavy viewers of outdoor advertising than are housewives. While plan-to-work housewives are below the norm in seeing outdoor billboards, they are more likely to do so than their stay-at-home counterparts.

PRIME TIME TV

We have seen that women as a group are more likely than men to watch TV in the evening hours. Even though all segments of women are presumably available to view TV between 7:00 P.M. and 11:00 P.M., it is the housewives who are particularly heavy viewers of television in the evening. Therefore, it is housewives rather than working women who account for the female portion of the prime time television audience.

DAYTIME TV

What about daytime TV? We have always known that full-time housewives are the heart and soul of the daytime TV audience. Back in 1975, when this kind of data first became available to us, I was sure that plan-to-work housewives would be out of the house, on the golf course, at the PTA meeting, or engaged in some other form of away-from-home activity. I was sure that when we could identify which housewives were the stay-at-home variety and which ones identified themselves as wanting to go to work, the stay-at-home housewives would turn out to be the heroines of the daytime TV audience.

Much to our surprise, we discovered that while it is true that house-wives overall account for the most intense viewing of TV during the day, it is the plan-to-work housewives who are the core of the daytime TV audience! They have their sets turned on far more than do their stay-at-home neighbors. Not surprisingly, working women are far less available to watch TV during the day. Career women are least likely to watch television during the daytime hours.

RADIO

We have always known that working women tend to listen more to radio than do housewives. However, there are real differences in the radio listening patterns of the two types of housewives. The stay-at-homes are less likely than the other segments of women to switch on their radios. Plan-to-work housewives have their radios turned on far more than their stay-at-home neighbors. This is consistent with every-thing we have seen about this very intriguing segment of consumers. They seem to be more active users of all media and more active con-sumers in general. Actually, this is not too surprising when we consider that they are the youngest of the four segments of women. Besides, they are better educated than the housewives who say they prefer to stay at home rather than go to work.

There have been some interesting changes among the working women's listening audience. In the few years that we have been study-ing patterns of radio listening among the two types of working women we have seen some shifts. Our earliest data suggested that career women were more likely than the "just a job" working women to turn on their radios. However, as more and more young housewives have flooded into the work force, especially into the "just a job" segment, the patterns of radio listening of "just a job" women have changed. Our current data suggest that working women who think of their work as "a job" have not only caught up with career women in radio listen-ing, but they are, in fact, slightly ahead of career women in the extent to which they turn on their radios.

MAGAZINES

We have always known that the habit of reading correlates closely with educational level. Therefore, it is no surprise that career-minded working women are the most likely of the four segments to be heavy readers of magazines. We had anticipated that levels of magazine reading might be a continuum, with stay-at-home housewives least likely to read magazines and career women most likely to do so. However, plan-to-work housewives are second to career women in the extent to which they read magazines. There is far more similarity in the reading patterns of plan-to-work housewives and career women than there is between the behavior of the "just a job" working women and the working women who identify themselves as career-oriented.

This is dramatic confirmation of the fact that *the two types of working women are truly different segments of consumers.* The advertiser who lumps them together as the "working woman audience" could be making a grave mistake. As we shall see, they are very different in their patterns of market behavior. And there are real nuances of difference in the way they respond to media.

There is no question that a highly effective path to the career women market is through magazines. Career women are, in fact, the heaviest readers of magazines of all segments of the population, including men.

NEWSPAPERS

The relationship of reading and education carries over to the way the New Demographic segments respond to newspapers. Therefore, it is no surprise that career women are the most likely of all segments of women to be heavy readers of newspapers. Overall, we observed earlier, men are more likely than women to be newspaper readers. However, career women are not only the most likely of all segments of women to be heavy readers of newspapers, they are also more likely to read newspapers than are the total universe of men.

There is a true continuum of newspaper readership across the New Demographics segments. The spectrum starts with the stay-at-home housewives, who are the least likely to read newspapers, and continues across to the career women, who are the heaviest readers of newspapers among all segments of women. This is one medium in which the "just a job" working women are more active than either type of housewife.

OUTDOOR ADVERTISING

We have seen that men are far more likely than women to be exposed to outdoor advertising on billboards. Among women, working women, both job and career types, are far more likely than either of the housewife groups to be in a position to see outdoor advertising. Career women have more exposure to outdoor billboards and posters than their "just a job" counterparts.

When we examine which particular kinds of career women are most likely to see outdoor advertising, we see that marriage does make a difference. Career wives are apparently less likely to be out in their cars and passing highway signs than are unmarried career women, both those with children at home and those without. Also, unmarried childless working women who consider their work "just a job" are far more likely to see outdoor advertising than either working wives or working mothers in the "just a job" category. With no husband and no child around the house, working women use their cars more. Therefore, they see more outdoor advertising. Not surprisingly, they also see more of this kind of advertising than either stay-at-home or plan-to-work housewives who share their husbandless and childless situation in the life cycle.

Are Their Media Tastes a Clue to Their Interests?

This brief overview of the extent to which different segments of women use each of the media does not give us any insight as to what they are like as people.

To understand how their New Demographic typology as well as their situations in the life cycle affect their personal tastes and interests, we need to know not just how much they watch TV, listen to radio, or read magazines and newspapers, but what they choose to watch or read or listen to. Hence, we shall now examine the kinds of programs they select and the kinds of magazines they read.

In the following discussion it must be kept in mind that I comment only on those programs or media vehicles in which a particular segment of women is significantly above the norm of the total population. The mere fact that one group is not mentioned does not mean it is not in the audience of that medium. It means that they are about average compared to the population as a whole. It is terribly important to keep this in mind. As people discuss light and heavy usage of a medium, they tend to assume an all-or-nothing situation. In fact, media usage is far more of a continuum than an either/or kind of pattern. All segments are represented among all audiences of all media. In the following discussion I comment only on those kinds of vehicles in which a particular segment is sharply different from the norm.

Please note also that many of the specific programs included in this discussion may not be still on the air by the time you read this book. Programs are identified in order to provide some understanding of the nature of these women's tastes and interests. Even though a particular program is not currently broadcast, the character of that program can help us understand something about the interests of its viewers.

Stay-at-Home Housewives

PRIME TIME TV

Although stay-at-home housewives are more likely to watch prime time TV than either of the working women groups, they tend to be about average in their selection of the various types of programs they watch, with only one or two exceptions. They are particularly responsive to general drama programs. They tend to watch general dramatic programs more than the norm, and they also tend to watch a great many programs of this type.

It is clear that if there are children in their homes, they choose TV programs differently from their childless neighbors. The presence of children in the homes of stay-at-home housewives increases the likelihood that they will tune in to situation comedies, movies, and police/detective dramas. They are also more likely than the average to watch advice and self-help programs.

While stay-at-home housewives overall are not likely to differ from the total population in the time at which they look at TV in the evening, those who have children at home are likely to watch more programs at both the family hour and the adult hour time slots.

During early fringe viewing time, the stay-at-homes are more likely than any other segment of the population to look at news programs. They are also attracted to game shows during this time period. If they are married and childless, they are particularly responsive to both news programs and game shows. Both segments of unmarried stay-at-homes watch both types of programs. However, those with children at home are especially enthusiastic about game shows. The latter group also tends to look at movies in late fringe time more than any other segment of stay-at-home housewives.

Women in general are less likely to be interested in watching sports programs on TV. Stay-at-home housewives are no exception. Their viewing of sports programs is clearly below the average.

Although they are present in the audiences of every major program, the individual programs to which they are particularly responsive are "Donny and Marie," "All in the Family," "Barnaby Jones," "The Waltons," and "Little House on the Prairie." In the fringe hour they like to watch "Dinah," "Mike Douglas," and "Merv Griffin." They are strong supporters of morning news programs, the "Today" show, "Good Morning America," "CBS Midday News," and "CBS Evening News."

DAYTIME TV

They are likely to be above average in their viewing of all types of daytime TV programs. They are active members of the audiences for situation comedies, talk shows, and game shows, as well as for "general drama" (soap opera) and news programs during the day.

Stay-at-home housewives with children in their homes are more likely to be tuned in to situation comedies, game shows, and soap operas, while childless stay-at-home housewives are more likely to watch talk shows and news programs during the day.

It should be noted that these nuances of difference are at a fairly high level of viewing. All stay-at-home housewives are far above the norm in watching all categories of daytime programs. But there are differences in the programs they choose to watch, depending upon whether or not there are children in their households.

RADIO

The responsiveness of stay-at-home housewives to talk shows is confirmed when we see the kind of radio stations they tend to listen to. They are particularly likely to listen to telephone talk programs and general talk programs. Those without children at home are also likely to tune in to soft music, semiclassical, and all-news stations. Stay-at-home housewives with children in their homes tune in to country music stations.

We have seen that stay-at-home housewives are just about average when it comes to magazine reading. They tend to be about average compared to all women in their readership of the service and shelter magazines. They are far less likely than women as a whole to read such women's magazines as *Cosmopolitan, Ms., Playgirl,* or *Essence. Work Basket* is the only service magazine in which they are in any way above the norm in readership. *Southern Living* is the only home magazine they are slightly more likely to read. They are about on a par or slightly below par for all women in the extent to which they read any of the other types of magazines. They are somewhat more likely to read *Photoplay* than any other segment of women. They are just under the norm in reading the *McFadden* and *True Story* kinds of magazine. They are far less likely than other women to read the fashion magazines or *Bride's* magazine. However, they are particularly responsive to the *Christian Science Monitor.*

Among the dual-audience magazines, stay-at-homes are especially apt to read *Reader's Digest* and somewhat likely to read *Town and Country.* There are women among the audiences of the general men's, business, sports, and science magazines. There are even a certain proportion of stay-at-home housewives who read these types of publications, but stay-at-home housewives are far below the norm of the total population in reading any of the men's publications.

Plan-to-Work Housewives

We have seen that plan-to-work housewives are very enthusiastic users of almost every medium. They are numbered among the heaviest viewers of prime time TV. It is not surprising, then, that they are tuned in to every category of evening program far more than any other segment of women. They are most likely to watch situation comedies and more likely than any other segment to watch a great number of this type. They are more likely than stay-at-home housewives or either type of working woman to watch general drama programs in the evening. They are very likely to watch a number of those programs. They are far more responsive to variety shows, movies, police drama, and advice/self-help programs than any other group.

There is more enthusiasm for variety shows and advice programs among the married plan-to-work housewives with children at home than those with no children around the house. The presence of children also has a strong effect on the viewing behavior of unmarried plan-to-work housewives. Among this small group, those who have children at home are tuned in to every category of program to a greater extent than their childless counterparts. This is particularly true of situation comedies, movies, police and detective drama, and advice programs.

Since plan-to-work housewives are such heavy viewers of prime time TV, it is not surprising that they are more likely than any other group to view a large number of programs both during the family hour and during the so-called adult hour. They are particularly responsive to movies both during early fringe and late fringe viewing time. They also stay up and watch late-night talk shows more than any other group of women. Along with their stay-at-home neighbors they are strong fans of game shows during the early fringe time slots.

There is almost no single program in which plan-to-work housewives do not represent a disproportionate part of the audience. The only programs in which they are not above par are "Monday Night Football," "Carter Country," "Hawaii Five-O," "The Jeffersons," "Sixty Minutes," and "Merv Griffin."

DAYTIME TV

It should be noted that if any particular program is not mentioned it is because stay-at-home housewives are above the norm in watching it. They are such universal members of the TV audience that the only exceptions that bear comment are those in which they are merely at par rather than above it.

They tend to watch their news during the day. They are active viewers of "CBS Morning News," the "Today" show, "Good Morning, America," and "CBS Midday News." However, they are just at par and below in their viewership of these programs. Since plan-to-work housewives are the strongest supporters of daytime TV, it is not surprising that they are more likely to watch every category of program—situation comedies, talk shows, general drama, and news—more than any other segment of women.

RADIO

While plan-to-work housewives have their television sets going fairly constantly during the day, they also seem to have their radios turned on, particularly between ten in the morning and three in the afternoon. Although they are not above the norm in radio listening between three and seven o'clock, they listen to the radio during those late afternoon and early evening hours far more intensely than their stay-at-home neighbors.

Along with the stay-at-homes they do tune in to the talk stations, both telephone call-in and general talk programs. They also like to listen to music. They are particularly responsive to stations that play the top hits, the "gold" hits, and pop music. Married plan-to-work housewives without children at home also tune in to the classical and semi-classical programs. Unmarried plan-to-work housewives with children at home tune in to country music and black radio stations.

MAGAZINES

We have seen that the plan-to-work housewives are second only to career women in their readership of magazines. Not surprisingly, they are especially responsive to all the women's magazines, both the traditional and less traditional types. They are twice as likely as stay-at-home housewives to read *Cosmopolitan*. While the stay-at-homes were just at par in their readership of the general service and home magazines, plan-to-work housewives are particularly responsive to *Family Circle, Good Housekeeping, Woman's Day, Parent's Magazine,* and *Redbook*. They are strong supporters of some of the shelter magazines, particularly *Better Homes and Gardens* and *House and Garden*. And they are the only group other than career women who are above the norm in reading *Gourmet* magazine.

They are twice as likely as any other segment to read the *McFadden* group, and they are the most active readers of *True Story*. They are more likely than the stay-at-homes to read the fashion magazines: *Glamour, Harper's Bazaar, Mademoiselle,* and *Vogue*. However, their levels of readership for these magazines are below those of the two working groups.

Among dual-audience publications, plan-to-work housewives are likely to read *Reader's Digest, Star,* and *TV Guide.* Among the dual-audience selective magazines, they are above par in reading *Atlantic Monthly, Money* magazine, *The Saturday Review,* and *The Smithsonian.*

"Just a Job" Working Women

PRIME TIME TV

"Just a job" women, it should be remembered, represent the largest segment of all women in the population. Some 36 percent of all active women may be classified as belonging to the "just a job" segment. They are fairly average in the extent to which they watch TV during the prime time evening hours. They are found among the audiences of all types of programs and show no special involvement with one particular type of program as compared to another. They are just slightly more likely to be responsive to dramatic shows and situation comedies than other types of programs.

However, when we look at their situations in the life cycle, we see that "just a job" working wives with children at home are particularly likely to be tuned in to dramatic shows. If there are children but no man around their houses, they are somewhat above the norm in watching a great number of situation comedies. However, in both cases their support for these program types is far below that of the plan-to-work housewife.

"Just a job" working women are particularly responsive to a number of specific programs. However, in almost every case their involvement with these programs is far below the level of the plan-to-work housewives. For example, they are above the norm in watching "Eight is Enough," "All in the Family," "Happy Days," "Laverne and Shirley," "Love Boat," and "What's Happening?" They are more responsive than either of the housewife groups to "Barney Miller." They also enjoy watching "Maude" and "Rhoda."

Childless "just a job" women, both married and not, are responsive to "Alice." The childless married women particularly enjoy "Barnaby Jones" and "Maude," while the childless unmarried like "Rhoda." The only fringe-time TV program to which they are especially responsive is "Dinah." This segment is least likely of all groups of women to look at news programs either during the day or during the evening hours.

DAYTIME TV

Since they are less likely to be heavy viewers of daytime TV than either of the housewife groups, it is not surprising that the "just a job" working women are below the norm in the audiences for the major types of daytime TV programs. The one exception, although at a far lower level than for either of the housewife groups, is that they are somewhat responsive to soap operas.

RADIO

We have seen that "just a job" working women tend to be heavier radio listeners than any other group of women. The greatest support for this activity comes from unmarried women in this segment, both those with children at home and those without. The "just-a-jobbers" with neither husband nor child in their homes tend to listen to their radios primarily during the evening. However, if they are unmarried and have children at home, they have their radios going during the day as well. "Just a job" women in this life cycle group are tuned in to their radios between seven o'clock and midnight as well as during the after-midnight hours. They have their radios going at all time slots over the weekend except for the very early hours, 6:00 A.M. to 10:00 A.M.

The kinds of stations that they listen to are a clue to their tastes. They are especially responsive to progressive rock, stations that play the top hits, stations that play the "gold" hits, and popular music.

Among the married women in this segment, those with children at home are far more likely to have their sets tuned in to the music stations, the top hits, the "gold" hits, and pop, as well as country music and black stations. Those without children listen to soft music stations and telephone talk shows and are heavy supporters of the all-news stations.

The unmarried women in this segment reflect the tastes of their married neighbors to some degree. The presence of children means that they are particularly supportive of stations that play top hits, "gold" hits, and pop music. They are also very likely to tune in to progressive rock and black programs. The absence of children has them listening to progressive rock, top hits, and pop music.

MAGAZINES

"Just a job" working women rank third in the degree to which they read magazines, behind career women and the plan-to-work housewives. Working wives without children at home are most likely to be magazine readers. They are shown above the norm in support of almost every woman's magazine, although not nearly to the extent that career women are. They are active readers of *Cosmopolitan, Ms.,* and *Essence.* However, they fall below career women and plan-to-work housewives in their support of all the women's service magazines: *Family Circle, Good Housekeeping, McCall's, Redbook,* and *Woman's Day.*

They are equal to plan-to-work housewives in readership of the *Ladies' Home Journal.* They just top them in reading *Work Basket* and just behind them in reading *Family Health.* They are more responsive to *Apartment Life* (now *Metropolitan Home*) than are the plan-to-work housewives, but, again, to a lesser extent than career women. Although they are active readers of other shelter magazines, they are less involved with this type of magazine than either plan-to-work housewives or career women. This is true for *Better Homes and Gardens, House Beautiful,* and *House and Garden.*

They are active readers of the romance group of magazines— *McFadden, Photoplay,* and *True Story*—but they are not nearly as likely to read the McFadden magazines as are the plan-to-work housewives.

They are more responsive to fashion publications than the housewives but less so than the career women. This is true for *Glamour, Harper's Bazaar, Mademoiselle,* and *Vogue.* They are more likely than any other group to read *Bride's* magazine. Along with plan-to-work housewives and career women, they read the *National Enquirer.*

Among dual-audience magazines they are particularly strong readers of *People* magazine, *Ebony, Town and Country,* and *Jet.* As might be expected, they are below par in their participation in the audiences of any of the standard men's magazines, business, sports, or science. The only exception to this occurs among the childless, unmarried "just a job" working women. They happen to be more likely to read *Workbench* and *The National Lampoon* than any other segment of women.

Career Women

PRIME TIME TV

We have seen that career women are less likely to watch TV during the evening than any other segment of women. Therefore, it is not surprising that they are not especially committed to any particular program category in prime time TV.

Unmarried career women with children at home tend to watch late fringe movies somewhat more than the average, but not nearly to the same extent as their housewife counterparts. Unmarried childless career women also tune in to movies during early fringe time, but only half as often as do the stay-at-home housewives in this life cycle group.

All women are less likely than men to be responsive to sports on TV. That is why it is noteworthy to mention that career women are the one group of women interested in watching tennis on TV. Their presence in the audience for TV tennis is even greater than that of men. Unmarried career women are particularly enthusiastic about tennis. This is true of both childless career women and, especially, those who do have children at home. Parenthetically, we might note that childless, unmarried plan-to-work housewives also like to watch tennis on TV.

In trying to identify the particular programs that get the attention of career women in the evening, the situation is almost the reverse of that among the plan-to-work housewives. Among the plan-to-work housewives one might only mention as exceptions those programs in which they are not a major part of the audience. However, with career women precisely the opposite is true. There are only one or two programs to which career women are particularly responsive. In most cases, their support is not nearly as active as that of the housewife segments.

Overall, career women are likely to enjoy watching "Rhoda." If they are married and have children at home, they are also likely to be tuned in to "Donny and Marie," "Eight is Enough," "Happy Days," "Laverne and Shirley," "Operation Petticoat," "Three's Company," "Welcome Back, Kotter," and "What's Happening?" In almost every case they are far less likely to view these programs to the same extent as the plan-to-work housewives.

The influence of children on TV viewing is fairly dramatic when we examine the program selections of unmarried career women with children at home. They are also tuned in to a litany of programs including the "Friday Night Movie," "Sunday Night Movie," "Barney

Miller," "Charlie's Angels," and all of the previously mentioned group.

Unmarried childless career women are responsive to "All in the Family." Married career women with children at home like to watch "One Day at a Time." Their childless counterparts are particularly responsive to "Rhoda" and "Sixty Minutes." The latter are the only group of career women above par in watching "Little House on the Prairie." Career wives with children at home watch the late news and "ABC Movie," while childless career wives are tuned in to the "Tonight Show." The unmarried career mothers also watch late news and the "ABC Movie." Their childless counterparts particularly enjoy the "Tonight Show" and also watch "Merv Griffin."

The only segments of career women who are active viewers of general news programs are the childless career wives who watch the "NBC Evening News," and the childless unmarried career women, who watch the "Today" show.

DAYTIME TV

Career women are very limited in their involvement with daytime TV. This is reflected in their relatively low level of response to the various categories of daytime TV programs. There is no particular program type that involves them. Among career women only the unmarried childless segment tune in to daytime talk shows more than the general population.

RADIO

We have seen that radio is a good medium for career women. Unmarried career women are particularly strong radio fans. The heaviest radio listeners among all life cycle New Demographic segments are unmarried career mothers. Their childless counterparts are also enthusiastic about radio. In general, career women are most likely to listen to radio during drive time, between 6:00 A.M. and 10:00 A.M. However, the unmarried segment of career women have their radios turned on during the late afternoon and evening hours as well. This seems to be more of a life cycle characteristic than a New Demographic one. All unmarried segments but the stay-at-home have their radios going at all hours including past midnight.

Career women are especially responsive to all types of music stations with the exception of country music. They are somewhat less responsive to progressive rock music than to top hits, "gold" hits, pop music, soft music, classical, and semiclassical stations. The career wives and mothers follow this pattern. Childless career wives enjoy popular music, soft music, classical, and semiclassical programs. However, they also tune in to all-news stations as well. Career mothers with no husbands at home add progressive rock to their list. They are particularly supportive of stations that play top hits. They also tune in to telephone talk shows. The husbandless, childless career women also support progressive rock as well as the whole spectrum of popular, soft, and classical music stations.

MAGAZINES

We saw earlier that career women are the heaviest magazine readers of all segments of women. As a matter of fact, since men as a group are less likely than women to read magazines, career women are probably the single most active segment of magazine readers. Their selection of magazines is testimony to their broad range of interests. As might be expected, they respond to the magazines relating to the "traditional women's interests" such as homemaking, gracious living, fashion, and home decorating, and those in the broader range of general interests.

They are strong supporters of every category of women's magazines, including the traditional "big three" service publications: *Good Housekeeping, Ladies' Home Journal,* and *McCall's;* the store books: *Woman's Day* and *Family Circle,* along with the whole range of shelter magazines; those dealing with gracious living; and all sorts of fashion magazines, both the high-fashion world of *Vogue* and *Harper's Bazaar* and the "young fashion" of *Mademoiselle* and *Glamour.*

Among dual-audience publications they are far more likely than the total population (which, of course, includes men) to be readers of the general mass publications, selective publications, news publications, travel magazines, and black publications.

The only conclusion that one can reach after examining the list of publications that career women support is that people who read read. For example, they are far more likely than any of the other women's segments to read such diverse publications as *Cosmopolitan* and *Ms.* They are more likely than the others to read the traditional women's magazines such as *Ladies' Home Journal, McCall's,* and *Good Housekeeping.* They are above par in their support of *Family Circle* and

Woman's Day. It should be noted that the plan-to-work housewife comes close to their levels of readership for the two store books and for *Good Housekeeping.* The only general woman's publication in which they are topped by another segment of women is *Parent's* magazine, which gets its highest level of readership from plan-to-work housewives.

Career women are also more likely than "just a job" working women to support *Glamour* and *Mademoiselle.* Their readership of *Bride's* magazine is slightly behind that of the "just a job" working women. Along with the stay-at-home housewives, they support the *Christian Science Monitor.* They are the strongest supporters of the *National Geographic* magazine of all segments in the population, including men. Along with the "just a job" working women, they are the strongest supporters of *People* magazine. Career women are far more likely to read that publication than their "job" counterparts. They top all segments of the population in reading the *Reader's Digest.* However, they are not as likely as the plan-to-work housewives to read either *Star* or *TV Guide.*

We see their real strength when we examine general selective publications. They are above par in readership of every selective magazine on the list with the exception of *Rolling Stone.* They are the most active audience for *Atlantic Monthly, Ebony, Money, Natural History, New Yorker, Psychology Today, Saturday Review, Scientific American, The Smithsonian,* and *Town and Country.*

They are the most enthusiastic audience for *Newsweek* and *Time.* Their support for these is at a higher level than that of men overall. Conversely, men are more likely than any of the women's segments to read *U.S. News & World Report,* although career women are the most active audience for that publication among women.

Career women are far more likely than any segment of the population to read the travel publications: *East/West, Travel & Leisure.* As might be expected, they do not equal men's readership of a list of specific men's interest publications including business, sports, and science magazines. However, they are more likely than any other group of women to read *Esquire, Penthouse,* or *Playboy.* They are clearly more likely than any other group of women to read a variety of business publications. They are above the norm of the total population in their support of *Fortune* magazine, *The Wall Street Journal,* and *Business Week.* Career wives without children at home are far more likely than any other segment of career women or women in general to read *The Wall Street Journal, Business Week,* or *Fortune.*

Implications for the 1980s[2]

As we enter the 1980s industry pundits have sounded two themes: the revolution in media technology that will result in demassification of media, and the swift social changes that have impacted on the demography and life styles of American consumers. While forecasts on the timetable and the extent of demassification are still murky, there is no doubt that social change has altered the landscape of consumer markets in general, and the women's market in particular.

This brief overview of their media behavior shows how the various segments within the women's market find their own patterns among the choices currently available among the mass media.

The revolution in media technology promises new, exciting potential for advertisers. In the 1980s we shall move from the homogenized, broad-stroke channels of mass media to an array of segmented communication opportunities, which have been labeled "demassification." At long last we will be able to match the marketing segments that we identify through analysis of social change to new, increasingly discriminating media channels.

The days when the media planner listened politely to some abstract definition of marketing segments and then proceeded to force it all into the cookie-cutter pattern of "any housewife, eighteen to forty-nine" are gone. The two most overworked words in marketing are "challenge" and "opportunity." And yet I can think of no other way to describe the media potential of the 1980s. We have heard a great deal about the media revolution and demassification. At long last we shall be able to link our media to the marketing opportunities offered by the many segments in the consumer market place that lurk behind the cookie cutters.

Notes

1. Based on special JWT analyses of TGI and Simmons Market Research Bureau data.
2. Taken from an article by Rena Bartos "Beyond the Cookie Cutters" in *Marketing and Media Decisions,* 15th anniversary issue, 1981.

Chapter 10

Women and Homemaking

The bottom-line question for marketers is if or how the changes in women's lives have impacted on their behavior in the market place. How does the fact that a women goes to work change the way she buys and uses products? Is there really a difference in the marketing behavior of traditional-minded housewives who say they prefer to stay at home and plan-to-work housewives who give lip service to wanting to go to work outside the home? Do they really buy and use products differently? Why is it necessary to separate working women who say their work is "just a job" from career-oriented working women when we consider the working women's market? And what is the role of life cycle in all this?

To answer these questions and to gain some insight on how changing demographics and changing aspirations have impacted on women as consumers, the following chapters will examine the market place behavior of these types of women within a broad range of product categories.[1]

- This chapter and Chapter 11 will deal with products relating to homemaking and fashion, which are considered to be traditional women's markets.
- Chapters 12, 13, and 14 will deal with the "big ticket" categories that have been traditionally marketed to men: cars, travel, and finance.

For each specific category we shall examine the objective facts of purchase behavior and frequency of use, as well as attitudes toward the area of behavior in which this product or service is used. Both behavior and attitudes will be considered from a New Demographic perspective as well as from the viewpoint of stage in the life cycle.

The traditional marketing view of women has been that they have the prime responsibility for all the household functions: those that relate to food, marketing for the family's food and groceries, menu planning, cooking, preparation, serving, and entertaining; those related to keeping the house clean and orderly and seeing that the family's laundry is done; and those related to the purchase and maintenance of home furnishings, home appliances, and decorating the house, which serves as a background for all of these home-oriented activities. Therefore, traditional marketing plans have usually designated the marketing target for the products that fit within this range of homemaking activities as that mythical "any homemaker, eighteen to forty-nine."

As we begin to examine the realities, we see that most women are not the isolated consumers described by that classic target definition. Most women, even the traditional stay-at-home housewives, do not go about all of these traditional home-related tasks and activities in splendid isolation, unless they happen to live alone. Those who are married and those who have children at home perform these functions in a family context. Their husbands and their children are involved in many of the home-related chores and many of the purchase decisions relating to those chores.

When we first begin exploring the concepts of life cycle and the New Demographics, we speculated that perhaps the *husbands of working wives might turn out to be an unexpected marketing target* simply because there is more available income in the two-paycheck household. Since two-income families are particularly good customers for a broad range of products and services, we speculated that husbands of working wives are, therefore, particularly desirable consumers. Yet *until very recently no study of the men's market ever identified which men are married to full-time homemakers and which are married to working wives.*

Another aspect of this new perspective is that husbands, and sometimes children, seem to be increasingly involved in the traditional female realms of marketing, cooking, cleaning, and laundry. As a framework for understanding how to address the potential buyers and users of products and services that fit into this broad category of home-related activities, we need to understand women's fundamental attitudes toward housework and homemaking and the dynamics of their families' participation in these chores.

It is not simply a matter of whether a woman does or does not enjoy cooking or finds ironing an unpleasant task. It is more a question of understanding her personal priorities and the role that home-related activities play in the overall context of her concerns, involvements, and commitments. A casual observer might not see too much difference in the objective activity of homemaking among the various segments of women. After all, whether a woman is a career woman or a committed stay-at-home housewife, somehow the house is cleaned, the laundry is done, and food gets on the table.

The clue to communicating with women in the various New Demographic segments and at various stages of the life cycle is to understand where housekeeping fits into their own personal scheme of things. If the home and its related chores and responsibilities represent the total boundary of her interests, she operates within one kind of context. If the home is a welcome refuge to which she returns after a full and active day engaged in other pursuits, she functions in another kind of context.

The framework within which women live their lives probably links directly to the way in which they buy and use products and the total atmosphere of their homes. For example, the traditional complaint that "woman's work is never done" is something that we hear only from stay-at-home housewives. Many stay-at-home housewives have rather limited horizons, so their housework looms as a never-ending task. They say such things as: "My destiny is childraising and homemaking." "Don't say 'just a housewife.' It's a full-time job." "You deserve a night out now and then; you appreciate your kids more." They seem to feel that housework is overwhelming and endless: "You never finish. Never." "You do the same thing every day."

For the more active and outward bound plan-to-work housewives, housework appears to be somewhat of a challenge, something they dispose of in order to get on to more interesting activities. These women turn to products and appliances to help them streamline the operation instead of making the activity of housekeeping a never-ending job that is an end in itself. They say that housework is "no big deal." "My child leaves for kindergarten, I pick up, I clean, and then I sit there with absolutely nothing to do." "How much can you clean a house? How many days a week can you wash a wash?" "When my children aren't home, it doesn't take long to clean a house." "There are so many things that save you time; housework isn't as hard as it used to be years ago."

But they feel that there must be something more to life than just keeping house. "There's more to life than just cleaning a house and raising children. You love doing those things, but you want to have something else to look forward to." "I'd like to go to work because I like to be around people. I like the stimulation. You would feel like you're doing something with your life." "I'd like to go to work because I'd like to get away from dishes, diapers, and baby crying." Plan-to-work housewives are outward bound and involved in their communities. "It's a great feeling to get out and do something other than being in the house." "I've been president of the PTA." "You're happier when you're involved outside of the house. I was elected chairlady."

Of course, the two groups of working women have similar needs to place their home-related chores in context as essential to the way they and their families live, but not as the total focus of their attention and the total boundary of their lives.

"Just a job" working women place the human priorities first. They're neither overwhelmed by housework nor compulsive about it. "On Saturday and Sunday, I clean house. I have to. But when it's time to cook, I say, 'Let's go out to eat.'" "If the family says 'Let's go to a show,'—you go. If they feel like going on a picnic, you go on a picnic." "If I want to go somewhere, I leave it. I'd always be ready to go."

Some career women tell us that their perceptions of housework changed when they went to work. Their priorities are different. They put less emphasis on household perfection, and they appear to be enjoying their home environments more. "I used to be a fanatic housewife. My guests were afraid to dirty an ashtray." "I live in my house now. I'm learning to enjoy my children more, and my husband and my surroundings."

Then, of course, as we consider both full-time homemakers and working women in relation to household chores, we have to challenge some of the assumptions we might bring to that examination. When I first began discussing this subject with my colleagues and with other professional associates a few years ago, most people said, "Well of course, working women want convenience products." "The traditional housewife takes great pride in the way she does things; so therefore, she won't want to take short cuts because the products that streamline her chores, in a way, demean her personal contribution to the end result."

It's easy to make generalizations of this sort, but the realities don't always bear them out. It is true that working women seek convenience. The one universal fact that might be observed about the difference between the life styles of women who work and the life styles of those who don't is the pressure of time. There simply aren't enough hours in the day for a working woman to do everything that she might have done as a full-time homemaker. Therefore, she has to consider tradeoffs.

So, yes, time is a problem, and yes, working women do seek convenience. But there are many ways to achieve convenience. We must not assume that in seeking convenience, working women will automatically turn to such solutions as TV dinners. As a matter of fact, many women seem to equate true convenience with better management of their time and the efficient employment of products and appliances that streamline the job. Rather than turn to the TV dinner, working women may turn to their microwave ovens to get dinner on the table in a fraction of the usual time, without sacrificing their standards of quality.

As a matter of fact, career-oriented working women are far more likely than any other segment of women to have purchased household appliances designed to save time or streamline the cooking process. They are more likely than any other segment to have bought an electric crock pot, a microwave oven, or an electric toaster oven. They are also more likely to have availed themselves of the convenience of an automatic dishwasher or a garbage disposer. They are fairly consistently seconded in their purchase of these convenience products by plan-to-work housewives.

"Just a job" working women are slightly more likely to buy electric crock pots than are plan-to-work housewives, but career women are three times as likely as job women to be in the market for crock pots. Stay-at-home housewives are less likely to use the time-saving appliances. However, they are strong supporters of separate home freezers. They are better customers for freezers than any other segment of women. Although stay-at-homes lag behind career women and plan-to-work housewives in having automatic dishwashers and garbage disposals, they are better customers for these products than "just a job" working women.

As a matter of fact, many plan-to-work housewives also have an organized approach to housework. They have their houses under control. This attitude appears to be linked not so much to whether they do or do not work for a paycheck as to the fact that they have activities and interests beyond the narrow horizons of their own homes. "When I'm busy, I get more done." "If I plan everything out, it's great. You really take more pride in your work." "I plan my week. I'm in organization work. When I can plan if I want to go out for lunch with the girls, or if I want company over, I don't get bottled up when I don't have time for this. I can stretch the hours."

"Just a job" working women frankly turn to products to streamline their housework. "I used to soak play clothes overnight. Now I put Spray 'n' Wash in the washer." "Thank heavens for perma-pressed clothes all the way. I don't think my iron's been out in a year."

Another way that women in all the New Demographic segments

stretch their time is by cooking ahead and freezing food. Every woman has her own individual pattern of food preparation. In fact, some of these ways cut across the New Demographic typology. But, in essence, the more that time matters, and the more that she is concerned with the quality of the food that she eats and serves, the more likely she is to avail herself of the concept of cooking ahead—preparing food in large batches and freezing meals for future use.

Some women use the crock pot as a solution. They put the ingredients in early in the day, before they leave for work or for their outside activities, and then they have a meal to serve the family at night. The streamlining of chores and planning ahead are equally true of plan-to-work housewives and working women. Some of the plan-to-work housewives say: "When I'm cooking, I make a a double amount and freeze ahead." "The days that I have outside activities, I get up early; I start supper; I just have to warm it up when I come in."

Similarly, "just a job" working women talk about organizing their cooking chores and planning ahead. "I cook the day before and re-heat." "I cook for two or three days and freeze ahead." On the other hand, sometimes they trade off time and money by buying steaks or more expensive cuts of meat because they can be broiled quickly. "You cook differently when you work."

One example of what I mean by the importance of context is documented by the purchase and usage patterns of women in relation to the simple chores of furniture waxing and polishing and rug shampooing. One might assume that these home maintenance or home grooming tasks are the special province of the traditional house-proud housewife and might be the kind of thing that working women, particularly career women, would find boring.

Much to our surprise when we examine the facts of their purchase patterns, we see that these types of products are used fairly universally, that every segment of women is in the market for them. However, career women and plan-to-work housewives are above the norm in the extent to which they buy them. Also, much to our surprise, although self-designated stay-at-home housewives use these products, they are less likely to use rug shampoo, for example, as frequently as do career women. The very active and energetic plan-to-work housewives are far heavier users of all these household products than their stay-at-home neighbors.

The category of paper products also reflects some New Demographic differences. Use of paper towels and toilet tissue is almost universal. More than eight out of ten homemakers buy paper napkins and facial tissues. In spite of the almost universal nature of these products, career women are slightly more likely than the other segments of women to buy and use paper towels, paper napkins, and facial tissues. They are clearly more likely than the others to use disposable cloths as well as paper towels. As in many other categories, they are echoed in this pattern by the plan-to-work housewives. "Just a job" working women are just over the norm in using this combination of products, and stay-at-homes are slightly below the norm in using both paper towels and disposable cloths.

The difference in the context with which the various segments of women approach these tasks is that stay-at-home housewives talk about the chore of housekeeping in terms of "woman's work is never done." They seem to feel that housework is overwhelming and endless. "You never finish. Never." "You do the same thing every day." Their standards of excellence are not very high. They say things like: "If it looks dirty, I clean it." "People don't notice if it's clean, but they notice if it's dirty." "You can tell if it's just today's or yesterday's mess. Toys on the floor is not like having a dirty sink." "As long as it's clean on top, and it's not vile, I don't have to make my life worthwhile because my cabinets are clean." They admit that they are more motivated to clean when the results will be noticed. "I think you clean more when you know someone is coming over." They somehow assume that women who go to work are more competent at housewifery because they manage their time efficiently. "It's easier to clean when you're working."

On the other hand, some career women find some household chores to be a welcome change of pace, almost like a man puttering in a workshop or in his garden as a way of unwinding after the pressures of the office. Some career women say they get more done when they go to work. They have a "can do" attitude toward household chores. They feel that housework gives contrast with the pressures of their work; it serves as an energy-releaser. These women are organized and plan ahead. Not surprisingly, they look for products that help them do the job, but they insist that the products they use must provide real convenience.

In part, these differences in approach to housecleaning relate to the standard of expectation that each type of woman has for the kind of home she runs and how well it is groomed and maintained. As we observed earlier, career women tend to be better educated and live in more affluent households than any other segment of women. They appear to have a level of expectation that assumes they will live in an orderly and well-maintained home. They seem not to regard it as an impossible goal to achieve. These women take pride in their homes. "I take pride in the place I live." "No matter where you live, it reflects back on you and your family and your appearance." As we shall see in discussing women's attitudes toward fashion and grooming, career women are particularly concerned with the image that they project. Therefore, it is not surprising that they see their home settings as an extension of that personal image.

Plan-to-work housewives have similarly high levels of expectation. They care about their homes. They appear to have higher standards of household order than some of the stay-at-home housewives. "When it's neat and clean, you're proud of your home." "I'm kind of particular. When people drop in, I just don't like things to lie around." "Your bed should be made and your dishes cleaned, no spotted floors, everything picked up, no papers all over." They seem to expect to maintain the same standards of home care if and when they go to work. "If I went to work, I'd be even more proud of my home." "...the contrast with work. I'd be glad to be home." "I would have more social life when I work. I'd care how my house looked." "It would be more of a challenge to accomplish a nice, clean, spotless house and do a good job at work."

The "just a job" working women, on the other hand, have a varied approach to housework. Some do a little every day; others have a weekly schedule. Most are quite flexible as to how and when housework gets done. It clearly is not their top priority. "I always used to do housework on Friday. I would never go anywhere. Now I go. If it's done, it's done. If not, next Monday, or whatever day is convenient." "I used to shop once a week. Now, en route, a little at a time." "You get it done somehow, but you're not going to kill yourself." "I wash every night. I don't wait to leave it for the weekend."

Another major change that has cut across all life cycle and New Demographic segments is the fact that *"women's work" is no longer exclusively women's work.* All segments of women but the stay-at-home housewives refer to the fact that their husbands and children participate in household chores to some degree or other. This has been a fascinating development. The plan-to-work housewives, as well as both segments of working women, expect their children to participate in household tasks. In many cases the children have a voice in the selection of the products they use. These comments were made by plan-to-work housewives: "My children do all the furniture, so they wanted Gloss 'n' Toss. So I bought it. After all, they are doing it." "When children clean, they take better care of things, and put things away better." "I made my sons do housework. It's good for them to know how to do everything—iron, sew, clean house."

The "just a job" working mothers say that their children's cooperation is a real help. "If I get stuck at work late, she'll make dinner." "My oldest daughter took over. I'm just a boarder." "My daughter likes to be in the kitchen. She does floors for me a lot now." "I tell my daughter to wash the floor. She does it on her knees. She says, 'Why don't you get a mop?' I say, 'No way!'"

And these working mothers think it's good for their children to help with these chores: "I am working. They can just as easily take over." "It's good for the kids if they take on a little more."

Some career mothers feel that their children's cooperation helps break through cultural stereotypes about what is "men's work" and what is "women's work." They report that their children help with the housework. One woman said that her sons did all the chores and did not think it was unmasculine or sissy for boys to be helping out. Some career women feel that giving children responsibilities helps them to mature. Others note that since their children are involved in using the products to accomplish these tasks, they have definite opinions on which ones are easy to use. These career mothers give their children a voice in selecting the products, since it is the child, not the parent, who will be using it.

We have a good deal of impressionistic testimony about the extent to which husbands do or do not help with household tasks. The career women we talked to testified to the new attitudes of partnership and sharing. "If your husband is achievement-oriented, he accepts his wife as being career-minded." "If you have mutual respect for your careers, the issues of housework and meals become very much shared." "The lawyer I worked for did all the shopping because his wife worked. One did one thing, and one the other. It's a beautiful relationship. Whoever has the free time; it's give and take, back and forth."

The "just a job" working women also talked about getting help from their husbands. "You have to have cooperation from your husband if you go to work." "My husband helps me quite a bit." "Of course I leave marketing to my husband because he works nights." "If I am working late, and he is not, he'll sort the laundry and start the laundry for me." And they appreciate this kind of husbandly help when it occurs. "My husband surprised me. He washed the blankets and the clothing. It was a big help. Oh, thank God! You know it. I don't expect it all the time, but I appreciate it when he does." "My husband is nicer since I work."

The plan-to-work housewives report that their husbands are helping with the housework now. They believe that their husbands would help even more if and when they go to work. "There's more communication—better relationship—between husband and wife when they share." "We're more involved in each other's interests." "Husbands are more ready to participate."

Of course, these comments were based on a rather limited sample of New Demographic segments in the course of our qualitative exploration. A number of more objective indicators of husbands' participation in marketing and household chores has come in from various sources. *Time* magazine issued a report headed "The Changing Roles of Men and Women on Brand Selection." It cited Simmons Market Research Bureau data that say men are responsible for 40 percent of all supermarket shopping. Men account for approximately one-third of brand choices when they shop for products they use personally, such as headache remedies, vitamins, mouthwash, toothpaste, shampoo, and similar products. The *Time* report concludes that "men do indeed play a significant role in brand decisions . . . with male share of influence increasing consistently with education."[2]

We were also delighted to learn that the *Yankelovich Monitor* quantified the degree to which husbands participate in household tasks.[3] In their annual trend study both husbands and wives were asked to what extent husbands have participated in a list of household chores: marketing, helping with dishes, cooking, vacuuming furniture and rugs, laundry, cleaning the bathroom, cleaning the stove, mopping floors, and ironing. This question has been asked consistently ever since 1974. In 1976 "helping with children" was added to the list.

Our impressionistic data suggested that the husbands of stay-at-home housewives were not particularly cooperative in helping around the house. The interesting reality is that husbands of full-time homemakers claim to have participated in every one of the household chores asked about. However, the men who are married to working women report a much higher level of involvement with every single one of the household responsibilities mentioned.[4]

The task of marketing for food and groceries seems to be a chore that husbands and wives share fairly universally. This does not mean that in every household the husband goes to market as often as the wife. For example, looking at five-year average of household activities, we see that seven out of ten husbands of full-time homemakers report participating in the marketing task, as against almost eight out of ten of the husbands of working wives.

The next most frequently reported activity is helping with the dishes. Here husbands of working women are far more likely than the husbands of full-time homemakers to say that they do the dishes or help their wives with them. Husbands also cooperate with the cooking or do part of the cooking. More than half of the husbands in the two-paycheck households say that they help with the cooking and help with the dishes. In the homes of the full-time housewives, about four out of ten husbands are likely to report helping with the preparation and cleaning up of meals. A similar pattern occurs when we analyze the extent to which husbands report helping to care for children. Husbands of working wives are slightly more likely to say that they help with the children than are husbands of full-time homemakers.

As we get to some of the less popular chores—vacuuming, laundry, bathroom cleaning, and so on—the differences in participation levels of the husbands of working wives and the husbands of homemakers become sharper. More than twice as many husbands whose wives go to work report that they help with vacuuming or laundry than do the husbands of the full-time housewives. One in three working wives is lucky enough to have a husband who helps with the bathroom-cleaning and stove-cleaning. Roughly one in four full-time homemakers gets this kind of help from her spouse. Twice as many husbands of working wives as husbands of full-time homemakers say that they help with mopping the floors.

The most disliked household task seems to be ironing. This really separates the men from the boys. Athough their participation in this particular chore is at a very low level, three times as many two-paycheck husbands say that they do some ironing as married men whose wives do not go out of the home to work.

The fascinating and surprising thing about this report is that while we might have suspected some degree of participation from men whose wives are in the work force, the husbands of full-time homemakers turned out to be quite involved in a number of household tasks as well, even though the less attractive chores get their participation at a somewhat low level. We don't know whether these husbands really participate to the extent that they claim to, or whether they think that they should make such claims because they ought to. Even if they don't really participate in household activities to the extent that they report, the fact that they feel that they should do so reflects an enormous change in the attitudes of most men and most women toward the responsibilities of the two sexes.

An interesting example of this basic change in attitude is illustrated by a picture I often show when I speak on this subject. It is a photograph of Gerald Ford in his shirtsleeves at the kitchen sink. It happens to be from a 1974 issue of *Vogue* magazine. [5] This particular picture and magazine issue might be seen as a marvelous symbol of social change all by themselves. The magazine itself is a high-fashion publication. In previous years it concentrated on beautiful women in very expensive clothes against very elegant settings. The implication was that the lady was so elegant that she probably didn't know where the kitchen was and/or she had hordes of servants somewhere in the background to take care of all those mundane details. This particular issue of the magazine reflected changing life styles in the United States in the trend toward a servantless society. It featured several prominent people in their home settings and talked about how these people entertain and live.

The picture of Gerald Ford was the lead illustration. I found it particularly intriguing. This happened to be at the stage in his career when he was Vice President, before he had become President, and he seemed totally relaxed and at ease in this domestic setting. He was obviously perfectly pleased to have this picture taken.

If we think back not too many years, someone of his stature who epitomized conventional middle American attitudes toward life would probably have found it highly embarrassing to admit that he helped his wife with the dishes, let alone to have the illustrated record of the fact emblazoned from coast to coast. I used to say that if he did help Betty with the dishes twenty years ago, he probably would have pulled down the shades so that his neighbors might not see him. But this totally masculine, very straight-arrow middle American found himself perfectly at ease in this very visible testimony of his sharing of household chores. That, I think, is a true symbol of change. Remember, Betty Ford is not a professional women. She is a full-time homemaker. And yet we see that the attitudes of sharing and participation seem to have spilled over from the households of the working women to the households of many of the women who do not go to work.

When we listen to the wives' side of the story, we note that both working and full-time homemakers report less help from their husbands than the husbands claim to give. The one exception to this is in the area of child care. Plan-to-work housewives are twice as likely as stay-at-home housewives to report that their husbands help in caring for children.

On the other hand, husbands seem to help with the dishes more in the homes of stay-at-home homemakers, while the husbands of plan-to-work housewives do a little more cooking and vacuuming. The differences here are not too great.

For the remaining chores, the two types of housewives report almost similar levels of participation by their husbands. The only noteworthy thing about their report is that in each case the husbands themselves claim that they help far more than their wives say that they really do.

On the other side of the coin, those husbands of working women who reported participation in all household chores to a greater extent than did the husbands of full-time homemakers also claimed that they helped their wives far more than the wives admitted. While the working wives do report that their husbands help, they apparently do not do so nearly as much as the husbands think they do. The differences here are that the men married to "just a job" working women tend to help more with marketing and with children than do the husbands of career women.

Career women report that their husbands help with all of the remaining chores—cooking, vacuuming, laundry, bathroom cleaning, stove cleaning, mopping floors, and ironing—to a greater extent than claimed by the "just a job" working women. In every case the husbands think they help far more than their wives say they do! Obviously, the amount of help is in the eye of the beholder. We are reporting the perceptions of these husbands and wives, not an objective observation of their true behavior.

No matter whose word we take, there is obviously a great deal of partnership and sharing between husbands and wives among all segments of the New Demographics. This is reflected in growing participation of husbands in the full spectrum of household chores. The quiet revolution seems to be shaking up traditional ways of defining household responsibilities. And these changing patterns suggest that we reexamine our assumption that the only target for home-oriented products and services is "any housewife, eighteen to forty-nine." The targets really are on the move.

Notes

1. Unless otherwise specified, the qualitative and quantitative data reported in this and the following chapters (10–14) were taken from "Understanding the New Demographics" and special JWT analyses of Target Group Index, respectively.

2. *Changing Roles of Men and Women on Brand Selection,* Time Inc., 1980.
3. *The Yankelovich Monitor* (annual) (New York: Yankelovich, Skelly, and White, 1972–1981).
4. Special JWT analyses of Yankelovich data.
5. *Vogue,* June 24, 1974, p. 70.

Chapter 11

Women and Fashion

The changing context of women's lives is reflected in their changing self-images and how they aspire to look. These changes have direct impact on how they approach those universal feminine concerns of grooming and fashion.

I can think of no other area of behavior in which underlying assumptions about what women want may be so outdated. Only a few years ago fashion and all that it encompassed (clothes, accessories, furs, jewelry, cosmetics, hairdressing, and fragrance) was marketed in a fairly monolithic way. The underlying assumption behind all fashion and cosmetic marketing was that women's main goal in life was to make themselves as attractive as possible in order to get or keep a man. Consequently, in presenting fashion and grooming products the emphasis was on all-out glamour.

Of course, there was tacit recognition that women don't spend all of their time at parties, on dates, or in a social spotlight. Housewives had to cope with household chores and marketing, and for those day in, day out situations they wore simple little housedresses. Women who went to work wore simple frocks to the office while they planned for the effects they were going to create on Saturday night.

A few years ago I participated in a seminar in Brussels on the image of women in advertising. One of the participants was a man responsible for marketing a major brand of cosmetics and fragrances throughout Europe. He espoused the traditional point of view that since the only reason women use cosmetics is to attract a man, sex appeal is the only way to sell cosmetics.

The discussion took place early in the morning in a room full of professionals, a high proportion of whom were women. I made the point that while the people in that room, both men and women, of course want to be attractive to the opposite sex, there are other reasons why people get themselves together and select the clothes they wear and go through the ritual of grooming. I pointed out that everyone in that room that morning was dressed appropriately for a professional meeting, that everyone was well groomed and no one was trying to be overtly seductive or romantic in the way they presented themselves.

An article on the fragrance market in *Marketing Communications* says that "fragrance marketing and the women's movement may seem like strange bedfellows at first glance, but they have been influencing each other since early in the decade when Charlie strode assertively on to the scene and almost immediately became the country's bestselling fragrance. If Charlie was developed partially in response to the women's movement, she in turn helped to popularize the image of an independent woman. The strategies of many recent fragrance introductions are clearly designed to keep pace with, or even a half step ahead of, women's evolving self-concept."[1]

A vice-president of Revlon articulated this change in strategic emphasis: "Ten years ago fragrance was much more of a special occasion usage situation. Therefore, it was much more directly related to romance and love than it is today. One of the successes of fragrance marketing in the last few years is that we have gotten women out of the idea that if they are staying around the house, or going to the office, they don't need fragrance. We have established the concept of a wardrobe of fragrances for different occasions or moods. The women's movement idea of doing things for your own satisfaction and gratification, rather than just to attract a man, contributed to the achievement of the marketing goal. It contributed in another way, too. Now fifty percent or more of women are working and earning an income. This is helpful when you are trying to get across the notion that fragrance is part of a basic ritual of grooming."[2]

Another expert commented on the changed context of fragrance marketing. She said, "In 1970 fragrances were being marketed to connote 'raw sex'."[3] She observed that now many of these brands have been repositioned into feelings, mood, romance, and product quality areas. She went on to say that "the new opportunity area is 'ego sense'. The term encompasses the ideas of self-satisfaction and self-esteem. . . . Women's perception of self is growing beyond femininity in itself as a goal. Also women are moving away from looking to other people for clues to behavior. They have begun to regard themselves as authorities. This trend contributes to the potential importance of the 'ego sense' sub category."

These comments are a far cry from the perception of my European colleague that women's only motivation in buying cosmetics, fragrances, and fashion is to attract or keep a man. How are these changing motivations for the use of fashion and cosmetics expressed in the market place? Starting with a straightforward comparison of working women to nonworking women, women who work are more likely to use cosmetics, hair products, personal care items, and over-the-counter drugs than are women who do not go to work. They are particularly likely to be heavy users of cosmetics. In addition, women who work are likely to buy more clothes. They are better customers than their stay-at-home counterparts for dresses, blouses, and skirts.

An analysis that categorizes working women on the basis of their occupational levels reinforces the value of professional managerial women to the fashion and cosmetic industries. This report tells us that career women are highly style-conscious and that women in blue-collar industries and full-time homemakers are not particularly concerned with style. According to these data career women are simply the best customers for dresses, skirts, leather boots and shoes, and precious jewelry. They are more likely to buy and use up many different kinds of cosmetics and toiletries, including lipstick, lip gloss, hair setting lotion, and quality perfumes. They watch their weight and are thus the best customers for low-calorie soft drinks. They are also health conscious and, therefore, most likely to use vitamins.

Applying the New Demographic perspective to this general pattern, these are some nuances of difference among the four segments:[4]

While it is true that stay-at-home housewives are least likely to be good customers for fashion or cosmetics, the plan-to-work housewives, who are the youngest group of all active women, are very responsive to cosmetics and to weight control products such as yogurt and diet soft drinks.

There are real differences between career-oriented women and women who consider their work just a job. Career women are far more likely than job women to be concerned with their weight. Therefore, they are more likely to be responsive to yogurt and diet soft drinks. Both types of working women, job and career, use up their cosmetics and fragrances with more frequency than do the stay-at-home or plan-to-work housewives, simply because they do go out of the house more often. On the other hand, when we examine how much they spend on cosmetics and toiletries, career-oriented working women are almost twice as valuable customers as their "just a job" counterparts. They also use fragrances far more frequently than women who think their work is just a job.

Women who earn their own paychecks are more likely to spend money on luxuries such as jewelry or furs than are full-time homemakers. Career women are particularly likely to buy fine jewelry or to have bought diamond rings for themselves. On the other hand, "just a job" working women are somewhat more likely to have bought furs. Actually, one of their motivations for going to work is to be able to indulge in some of the luxuries that were not possible when they were full-time housewives.

Aside from the differences in the way they buy or use these types of products, are there any differences in the way the New Demographic segments approach the whole area of personal grooming? In order to answer this question, we conducted an in-depth exploration of the attitudes of the four New Demographic groups toward clothes, cosmetics, and personal grooming. Their responses tell us that their self-perceptions and attitudes toward their own lives are also reflected in their present patterns of grooming and how they aspire to look.

When *stay-at-home housewives* talk about grooming they focus on clothes rather than makeup and cosmetics. They don't seem to go much beyond combing their hair, putting on lipstick, and using makeup when they go out. They are self-conscious about what they wear. It may be "old ugly stuff you wouldn't wear anywhere else" or a nightgown until the house is cleaned. "I can't wait to be finished and dress, but I do my hair first thing because there's always a chance I'll have to drive them to school". "My mother taught me to dress immediately; to be neat and combed." "I want to look attractive all the time—it's important to feel good about yourself; you work better".

They frankly admit that the way they dress at home for housekeeping activities or the way they look on an "ordinary day" ranges from "presentable" to "lousy." "You're kidding. The cruddiest. That's it." "What I wear during the day is not all that bad. I mean, I'll wear something that if I have to go out, it's presentable. If it gets scuzzy by the afternoon, I take it off and throw on a new top or a clean pair of jeans or something."

These women make a clear distinction between how they look at home and how they dress away from home. "Now, I have three categories of clothing: one is schlocky, ickyish—that would be for the home, for tidying up, or if I'm cleaning; the other type is for when I go somewhere, and yet another if we go out on the weekend." Their at-home wardrobes are very limited and seem to be built around blue jeans. "People don't know me if I'm not in my sweatshirt." "Well, my wardrobe is so extensive that I have two pairs of super good jeans. Those are my going out jeans. The other ones have got patches, you know."

Some freshen up when their husbands come home—and some

don't! "I change my top and put on makeup for my husband for when he comes from work." "My mother always tells me I should be dressed in something nice rather than my sweatshirt when my husband comes home at night and I think that if he did what I did all day long, he's lucky that I'm in a sweatshirt and got a meal prepared for him."

In their minds, women who work set the standard for grooming. "If I worked, I'd buy a beautiful white suit. I would." Some are wistful about how well groomed or attractive other women look. However, this seems to be a standard to which they don't aspire themselves. "Yet, you'll go into some people's houses and the girls are dressed very nice and I think 'oh, if I could only be like that,' but I know my day isn't going to be easy."

Even if they do their best to look well at all times, they recognize that they are in a different league from working women, who have more money for clothes, who have to look their best every day, who wear "coordinated" clothes and carry matching handbags, who wear "in" clothes, and who can afford to give away out-of-style clothing and to wear clothes that are sent to the cleaner, rather than wash-and-wear. They also feel that working women know what's in, whereas housewives can't be sure, since they are not often "downtown" to see it.

Most of the housewives who say they *plan to work* want to "look good" all the time. The "housewife syndrome" is not for them; one young housewife articulated the relationship between her own self-esteem and the way she looks. "I went through one year when my children were very young where I wasn't myself. I seemed to fall into like a housewife's syndrome, of no makeup—I wouldn't say sloppy, but it wasn't me, and towards the end of that year, I looked in the mirror and I said I don't like myself any more. What's happened to me? This isn't the girl that went to work and used to dress—I somehow brought myself out of it. In the morning it's like second nature to me—before I'll make a bed I'll put some makeup on, comb my hair and look like a human being, and then I'll make the bed—my feeling now is the house can wait."

Some say they dress for the outer world. They want to look good to others: "I'm in jeans and an old shirt to clean the house and then about two in the afternoon I clean myself up and then that's when I go to the store; in fact I don't even like to go to the store if I don't have my hair fixed and makeup on. Invariably the Avon woman will come knocking on the door at 10 o'clock in the morning when you have your hair in rollers and not a bit of makeup."

Some say their grooming is for themselves. They feel good and they work better if they know they look good. "I'm very different. I like to look neat just for me." "If I'm really going to get at something I really want to look good because I don't feel that I work good if I don't look good." "I think the way I look has a lot to do with my attitude, so I get up in the morning early and I feel once I'm showered and I've got a little makeup on and I'm dressed I'm ready for the day, for whatever might come along."

Some wait to dress for the day until after they've done the housework: "I cannot clean in real clothes. I have a certain outfit I wear to clean with. But I wouldn't leave the house in." "As far as cleaning the house, it's whatever I've slept in, and then the baby goes to sleep, and then it's shower time, and get dressed time, and then we go out." Others have their appearance in mind even for the housework. "I really like to look nifty when I'm cleaning the house."

For many of these women "cosmetics" refers to makeup. Some reserve it only for when they are "going out." Others start the day with makeup and feel that the way they make up is an expression of their self-image. "I like to be up to date. . . . I wear makeup around the house. I wear the same stuff usually if I go out. My appearance is very important to me, naturally, because it's part of you." "The first thing in the morning I find that I have to go through a little routine as far as makeup is concerned . . . and I find this affects my performance."

Many of them feel their clothes are not fashionable. They may look neat and pleasant but not up to date and not even suitable for "going downtown." They would like to look "smart" and regret that they have no money for clothes now that they are not earning money. One of them, in fact, is resentful of the fact that her husband dresses fashionably but that she may not. "I have clothes from when I worked that you couldn't wear on the street today. And he doesn't understand—his clothes are all, I shouldn't say they're all new, but I mean he's always fashionable and in style, and I don't feel just because you're home—I'm not saying I should have as much as him—but you know when you go out you still like to look nice."

Their yearning to keep up with fashion seems to be a strong motivation for their desire to go to work someday. "I would get more dressed up to go to work. In fact, I was even going to wear a dress today until I put it on and it was a little short and I can't believe I ever wore my dresses that short! I would really like to get dressed up, and to wear a smart dress. I love to come into the city and see what everybody's wearing and who I think is well dressed. I like to look nice. I like to dress nicely, and I like to spend money on clothes. I always did." "With three boys and food bills and everything else, I wait for gifts from my family and very very rarely do clothes shopping and I find it very intimidating coming into the city—when you look around and see all the styles and you're still back in 1960 somewhere. . . . I would like to be more stylish and more up to date, with a lot of new things and a nice wardrobe, but it's just not going to be for a while."

Their perception of working women is that they dress fashionably, not in "a faddish manner" but "up to date." They believe working women dress better because they have more money to spend and want the sense of personal confidence that comes with the assurance that they are appropriately dressed. "Just to get you to the point where you feel confident that you are either in style or in clothes that are comfortable for you or your job or the situation you're in. And when you feel confident that you look the best you can, that you're dressed right and look appropriate, I feel you have a very good successful day—you're putting your best foot forward and you're giving it all you can." "[If I went to work], I would want to look charming. I have this thing almost fanatical about atmosphere, about the feel of things, and it's real important and I notice it when I'm around people I just get a feeling about a person . . . the way you dress and look, are you neat, or cluttered, or give the illusion of simplicity or casualness or very sophisticated."

They think of grooming as an intrinsic part of going to work. Whether or not they now use makeup regularly or keep their hair as neat or fashionable as they'd like, they all agree that the working woman must look her best, whatever her style, and must look her best all the time. And the need and the right to do this are one of the most attractive aspects of working. It is one of the things they miss. "Grooming would be very important. I might try and improve it, you know. I don't know too much about makeup, hair—I do everything myself. I never go to the beauty parlor. Right now I still feel very housewifey . . . really not up to date. I mean I'm a little behind the times, you know—I just haven't caught up with the in crowd, so to say, and I'd like to be more a part of the world than what I have been; I feel I've been hibernating." "If I went to work I would be better groomed and dressed more fashionably. I would invest in a neat but casual wardrobe, a better makeup and would make it my business to go to a beauty parlor regularly to keep my hair styled and shaped." "My clothes wouldn't have to be the best, but I would like expensive accessories—leather bags and shoes, gold earrings, et cetera." My fetish is my complexion. I would like to be able to go to a dermatologist salon every so often."

"Neat and well-groomed. . . . I would continue to wash my hair every day. . . . Smell good too." "I would buy better makeup." "My husband came back unexpectedly this morning and caught me looking like hell. If I were working I would have to get my act together sooner."

"Just a job" working women know they look better than they would if they were at home. Several contrasted the way they used to dress when they were housewives with their present standard of grooming. They frankly admitted that when they were full-time housewives they wore either jeans or "PTA uniforms." "Before I went back to work last year, I had been home for years with my children. I had jokingly said I had three PTA uniforms, outfits, or whatever you call them and that's exactly what they were all for, the little meetings or whatever you had. Everything else was the cutoffs and the jeans."

Some equate going to work with the desire to look more attractive. The job gives them the justification to spend money on clothes and cosmetics. Some seem to have chosen to work just so they could indulge in personal grooming. "That's one reason I went back to work, because my husband and myself thought that I needed a different outlook, a change of pace, because I was running around in jeans and tennis shoes and Scholl sandals and sloppy tee-shirts. I like that look sometimes, but not all the time." "I think the whole thing is that when you're working you feel like you've got to make the investment because you're going out the door everyday. When you're not working, you're on a tighter budget and you've got other things that you want to spend that money for, but if you're going out every day you know that you've got to have the pantyhose and the nail polish and the whole bit, so you spend part of your income for that." One young woman in Chicago uses her free time for a beauty ritual at Elizabeth Arden: "I need it and deserve it for myself."

They are conscious of styles and enjoy clothes. "I wear dresses to look stylish and feel good about myself." "I like removable layers." "I go to the hairdresser for a *today* look, but not overish." "I want the 'downtown' look; what the magazines stress." "I like casual mod; wish I could wear scarves like Rhoda." "I don't use less makeup now, just different kinds for a natural, casual look." "I like having a reason to look my best."

They are also conscious of dress codes and, to some extent, the image they project. But more often it is a matter of conformity: "My office is casual." "I'm the only girl in the office, I meet customers, I have to look decent." "I'm in an office; you can't wear jeans; no one tells you you can't but you just don't." "My law office has a strict dress code—to look professional; I love clothes and like a reason to look my best." "My boss wants me to conduct myself and look like a professional woman." "We're in a back room—nobody has the incentive to dress—it's sad."

These women make a clear distinction between the way they dress for work and the way they dress at home. Their home attire is the housewife's uniform—jeans. "I dress differently for work from how I dress at home—when I'm at home I'm usually scrubbing and cleaning and cooking." "I wear jeans at home. I have two pairs of jeans and I have tee-shirts or something, that's what I wear and some of the times I wear jean tops. Basically, that's a little uniform I have, and I think most young mothers wear at home." "Casual. Nobody ever says anything about how I look when I'm at home. It doesn't seem to matter to them."

However, when they go downtown to work, they are very conscious of how they look. The particular styles they choose are directly linked to the atmosphere of the places where they work and the nature of their jobs. The women who are in contact with people are concerned about how they look to others, but they don't want to look too extreme or high-style. "When I was a leasing rep for a very large company, the big thing was your looks, you know, you didn't wear hose that had runs in them and you just had to really look nice, because you were the first person the client saw when he came in and so on and so forth. So I bought an awful lot of dresses because I just feel more fashionable in dresses." "I want to look stylish but not a model, you know what I mean. I like to have a today look but not overish. I like to feel comfortable . . . in slacks, slack suits."

On the other hand, the kind of work they do may require more functional dressing. Even then, they are concerned with maintaining a standard of neatness. When their work does not bring them into contact with other people, they are more concerned with comfort than with image. "In my type of work I have to wear slacks because I'm climbing up on ladders and stuff part of the day so I have to wear slacks, but I like to see that dresses are coming back. I like to see that, but I just think neat." "I have very little contact with people, so sometimes I wear slacks to work. I find them very comfortable."

One woman in Atlanta articulated the thought that when she knows that she looks good, she feels better about herself: "I like the way this dress makes me feel. . . . I feel like I approach the day differently when I have something that feels good on me."

A few expressed yearnings for more fashion know-how. They have an image of how they'd like to look but don't know how to achieve it for themselves. They would like to know how to cope with accessories such as scarves and jewelry and how to plan their wardrobes so they can go from work to dinner. "I think they really look nice and on a lot of people they make the outfit, the scarves and the jewelry. I see a lot of people, young girls, that come in the store, and older women too, that look really good in scarves, and I wish I would look like that, but I can't." "I think there's a difference in dressing downtown than there is away from downtown. I feel that in Atlanta there definitely is and we are verging on downtown. I'd like to also have the type of look that you could go straight from work into the evening . . . if someone said, well, let's go to dinner. That is what all the magazines stress, buy this and it will carry you through any situation. Maybe I need a lesson to learn how to do this, but that's more of what I want to achieve."

A common theme running through all of the *career women's* discussion of clothes and grooming was the feeling that grooming is an expression of their perception of themselves. Many of the career women said that grooming was a reflection of their sense of their own self-worth: "It's important for myself. It's a respect and love for yourself." "I have found out a long time ago that I wear makeup and clothes to suit me, not to suit anybody else or any man that I go out with. I realize that what is important to me is the way I look to me."

Some indicated that the knowledge that they are well or appropriately groomed adds to their assurance, which, in turn, enables them to deal with the demands of their work with more confidence. "Your attitude is much more positive if you are confident in your appearance. It is the first thing that people see, and that's their impression of you. They're going to go on that no matter how hard you try. It's really important in your attitude and your performance." "I feel my appearance is important to me. This is how people are going to judge you by the way you're dressed and by the way you look. I think if you feel like you're dressed like a slob that day, you feel like one." "If I've got a good outfit on and my makeup and hair are right, I feel marvelous. I just feel marvelous and it just helps me immensely to face the day. But there are people who could care less."

They were also conscious of the fact that the image they project is an important element in the way their professional peers and associates relate to them. Many of these women seem to regard fashion and cosmetics as an important professional tool. They are aware that they have to define and create the image they wish to project. "You know, you have to make the impression. You have to play the role." "The image . . . you definitely know the image that you want them to have of you is the one you have got to create.''

There were two interesting reports from young women in these interviews. Both of these women were being pressured by their bosses to dress professionally, to assume authority, but the women were finding it difficult to take on the trappings of their positions. They did not know how to, or wish to, distinguish themselves from their still junior colleagues or, in one case, their social welfare clients. This is corroboration of the role that image plays in career achievement. In effect if they are to achieve a level of professional authority, their bosses expect them to dress the part.

The way they go about achieving the desired image varies enormously. Some put their emphasis on quality; they think of their wardrobes as investment spending. "I would rather buy a few pieces of clothes that are good, of good quality and that look very well, than to have many things that aren't all that good. I find subtlety very tasteful. It's not necessary to wear all kinds of elaborate, ornate things.'' "I'll sink a lot of money into a very few pieces if they are good, and I'm trying to buy only the things I like.''

Others admit to being bargain hunters. They want maximum value for the money they spend, so they plan ahead, shop the sales. "It took me a long time to get it down pat. Now I need a new raincoat. I wait until just before Christmas to buy a raincoat. But I will not buy a coat, any kind of coat now, because they're full price. But, if you wait until Christmas, you have to buy a season ahead almost, and that's how I do all my shopping.''

Not all achieve the results they desire, but each seems to have her own formula: "I would like to be a clothes horse and somehow look like I just came out of Bloomingdale's, but I just never could get to do it. It just seems like you walk in there and pick out something that looks just super and it just takes so much effort—either they don't have your size or you put it on and it doesn't look the way it does in the ad.''

Several of these women travel on business. They discussed the special wardrobe needs of the woman business traveler: "That's one problem I have when I travel. I wear multipurpose combination things: pants, skirts, and jackets that interchange.'' "I use things that are easy to pack and that can be used for a week, because when you pack for a week you've got to figure out how much luggage you're going to carry. After a while, you get tired of lugging a lot of things, so the less you take the better off you are.''

Looking their best also means being well-groomed—manicured,

neatly coiffed, and made up. One of the reasons some career women say they can't cope with housework during the week is that they need time to attend to their grooming. They may not even be conscious of the regularity with which they do this. One woman, recounting her activities, discovered during the interview that she had a twice-a-week hairwashing drill she hadn't even been conscious of. Some also attend beauty parlors regularly. "I like to dress well, I like to look well, and I like to have makeup on, I like to have my nails done, my hair. . . . I feel very uncomfortable if I'm not fairly neat and well dressed. I seldom let my appearance go. When I'm home I even put makeup on on Saturday and Sunday mornings, when I get up. I look pretty good on the weekends." They also feel that spending money on cosmetics is as much a necessity as buying clothes. One woman in Los Angeles said, "I got a clothes budget, and I'll spend that much on cosmetics."

While most of their emphasis was on their professional grooming needs, several indicated they like to look just as attractive at home as they do on the job. "Every morning, no matter what day it is or whether it's summer and I'm off or what, I get up, bathe, put on makeup, put on something very decent, because I'm the kind that if I have to run to the store, I don't want to change clothes. I'm not a clothes changer." "I think a woman should stay very attractive, too. After all, I mean you've got a man in the house and they like to see you look nice. They don't want you to dress up to look nice for all the guys in the office all day and then come home and look—you know—no makeup, hair down."

Unmarried career women may, in fact, spend a great deal of money on grooming and cosmetics. In addition to wanting to project an appropriate professional image, they also want to be attractive for their personal lives. "I have a very very nice wardrobe for dating. . . . I buy expensive things. Grooming is very, very important. I buy expensive cosmetics, and that's where a lot of my money goes—clothes, grooming—I need a haircut and a body wave now and that will cost quite a bit of money together, it's unbelievable, but I will spend that kind of money on myself—I need a new couch but that's gonna wait. I'll save, put it away in the budget. But I won't let my fingernails go because this is very expensive, this is like $40—$10 a week, $44 a month—and you can buy something nice for that, an appliance, but I just feel it's me, it's very important, appearance, more than anything else."

This review of the amount of money they spend for clothes and cosmetics and their motivations for doing so suggests some real untapped opportunities among career-oriented working women. In the late

1970s many marketers became aware of these opportunities. Among them, the Associated Merchandising Corporation sponsored a study of the career women market.[5] Many of its findings quantify the attitudes expressed in our own diagnostic exploration of their feelings about fashion.

Career women are clearly conscious that the way they dress is relevant to their being taking seriously as professional women. Two-thirds believe that they can be taken seriously at work without having to dress like men. On the other hand, they also make it clear that the way they dress for work is quite different from their choice of attire for their personal lives. They tend to dress to express a unique personal image rather than to project a variety of fashion looks. More than half say something like this: ''I have found that as my responsibilities increased in business, the look and quality I want have changed.''

When asked to describe the image they are trying to project in business, all agree with some version of the concept of projecting a professional image. Slightly more than half say they would like to look ''businesslike, professional, and competent.'' About one-third say they would like to be ''well dressed and in good taste.'' An equal number describe their ideal image as being ''neat, clean, well groomed.'' Almost as many talk about being ''coordinated, well put together.'' About three in ten use words like ''tailored'' and ''conservative'' to describe the image they wish to project. The image elements that matter to these women are clothes that make the woman who wears them look important or stand out and clothes that look as though they are expensive.

All of their projected images relate to some aspect of professionalism. Femininity is implicit in the concept of not having to dress like a man. But none of these women talk about wanting to look alluring or sexy in their business dress.

They emphasize the importance of investment dressing. They want clothes that are of good value and styles that will last a long time. This kind of approach to fashion requires versatile clothes that can work in many climates throughout the year and are easy to accessorize. Clearly, such clothes must be well made. They emphasized the importance of seams that don't split, buttons that will stay on, and fabrics that are not too flimsy to stand up.

The things they look for in the clothes they buy are clues to the fact that they are concerned with investment dressing and with quality. These women think it extremely important that the clothes they buy be functional, that they don't wrinkle. This, of course, is not only important in the course of a business day, where a woman wants to end up the day looking reasonably well groomed, but is essential to a travel wardrobe. Therefore, they think it is extremely important that clothes not get out of shape after a few wearings. And many appreciate the easy upkeep that comes with clothes that are machine washable.

With all this emphasis on practicality, they still want clothes that fit well and are becoming. Some talk about clothes that will hide their figure faults, others about clothes that will show their figures to good advantage. An article on top women executives in the beauty business describes their particular styles of dressing. While they are of different personalities and physical types, the importance of clothes and grooming as a professional tool runs through all of their comments. They share a sense of quality and, with only one exception, a rather understated classic approach to fashion.

Simone Hoffman, the senior vice-president of the Cosmetics Division of Charles of the Ritz, says: "I think we are talking grooming and we are talking pride and I don't think that has anything to do with trendiness. . . . I don't think anyone wants to look contrived. I know I don't want my clothes to detract from what I say. I like very simple, classic clothes. I'm not what you would call 'trendy' at all."[6]

Kitty D'Alessio, president of Chanel: "I believe in classics. I always have. And I believe in tradition but in taking it forward. And, of course, I believe in taste. Style is not only what looks good but what makes you feel good."[7]

Linda Wachner, president of Max Factor, says that good grooming is "after all, part of the winning feeling. I found that the way people feel about you at the start of a meeting is the way the meeting ends. . . . I've always dressed simply, and I've always loved Halston's clothes. It's better to have a few pieces that you love rather than a huge wardrobe." She adds, "I want to look feminine, but I don't want to look flippant."[8]

Carole Beller, president of Frances Denney: "I guess I'm a classic, nonfaddish person. That's true of my dressing, my style of makeup, my way of entertaining at home. More and more I find the kind of clothes you wear has an impact especially on men. I don't want my clothes to be overly dramatic. I want people to look at me for myself, not for what I wear. I don't think there is any excuse for a woman in business not to be looking good."[9]

Career women tend to do their clothes shopping throughout the year rather than at particular seasons. When they are shopping for clothes they are conscious of time pressures. They say it is extremely important, therefore, that the stores be open for a number of evenings a week. Most currently concentrate their shopping on Saturdays, some in the evening, and some at lunch time. About two in five would appreciate stores being open on Sunday.

There has been much discussion and speculation as to whether career women require special shops or special merchandising facilities to serve them. The AMC study explored the degree to which career women would appreciate having a special shop of their own available in a department store. Slightly less than half say they would definitely shop in such a department, and a sizable number said they would probably shop there. The principal reason for their response to the concept of a career woman department was convenience. Second to that is the fashion look that might be available in such a department and the sales help that would be there to serve their needs.

In recent years a number of specialized services have sprung up in and out of department stores. Many of these are fashion consultants or shops geared to the needs of career women. Clearly, there is no single path to the cultivation of this particular market. Nor will these women seek out one kind of shopping pattern. If the kind of classic, well-designed investment clothes defined by these women are available to them in general merchandise, they do not need to shop in a specific "career woman" department. That has too much the implication of a career uniform. The more sophisticated career women are, the less likely they are to want to dress like each other.

On the other hand, there are young women who are launching careers who feel somewhat insecure about grooming and about the images they project. For such women the availability of fashion consultants and special shops can be invaluable. And, of course, if the specialized departments help busy women to streamline their shopping chores by assembling the items she needs in the sizes and colors she requires, they perform an invaluable service for the busy woman, the gift of time.

Notes

1. Roberta Reynes, "The Beauty Business: New Freedom in Fragrances," *Marketing Communications,* February 1980, p. 19.
2. *Ibid.,* p. 20.
3. *Ibid.,* p. 20.
4. Unless otherwise specified, the qualitative and quantitative data reported

in this chapter were taken from "Understanding the New Demographics" and special JWT analyses of TGI data, respectively.

5. "A New Study of Career Women—A Leadership Market," sponsored by the Research Division of Associated Merchandising Corporation, 1978.

6. Francesco Stanfill, "Women in Cosmetics: Studies in Style," *Fashions of the Times* (*New York Times* insert), March 3, 1980.

7. *Ibid.*

8. *Ibid.*

9. *Ibid.*

Chapter 12

Women and Cars

Sometimes we can judge how far we have come by taking a look back to where we were. And nowhere is this more true than in the three product areas we examine in this and succeeding chapters.

Men have been traditionally considered the key customers for "big ticket" products and services. The traditional assumption was, of course, that women were concerned only with homemaking and the domestic arts on the one hand, and the pursuit of beauty through fashion and cosmetics on the other. But when it came to major expenditures, it was the man, usually the husband and the father of the family, who made the purchase decisions.

This is certainly true of the automotive market. The traditional point of view that pervaded this market until very recently is based on a number of assumptions about the nature of the car market. The conventional wisdom represented by these assumptions no longer operates in the board rooms of Detroit or on the floors of many car dealerships. Nonetheless, there are still many people associated with the manufacture and marketing of cars who still subscribe to the following:

Assumption #1: *The car market is a man's market.*
Assumption #2: *Men make the automotive purchase decision.*
Assumption #3: *If women do buy cars, they buy compacts.*
Assumption #4: *After all, men pay the bills.*

Let us review each of these assumptions and examine the current realities to see if these classic beliefs about the car market hold up in the 1980s.

Assumption #1: The Car Market Is a Man's Market

A review of the historical industry data suggests that women were a very small factor in the automotive market. Over the years from the early 1960s through the mid-1970s, women's participation in the car market ranged from just under 15 percent to slightly over 20 percent. Certainly, by any definition, this would make women a fairly unimportant or minor segment of the car market.

When we examine these figures more closely, however, we see that they are in part a self-fulfilling prophecy. Until very recently most of the standard industry reports on the nature of the car market attributed the cars owned or driven by married women to their husbands. This is an extension of the "head and master" concept, which still operates in some states in our country. Applying that point of view to the automotive market leads to the assumption that if there is a car in the house—regardless of who drives it, in whose name it is registered, or who paid for it—it belongs to the man who is the head of the household.

If the lady was married it was assumed that the family car belonged to her husband. It follows that the apparently low proportion of women who participated in the car market was *based on unmarried women only*. Since the ratio of married to unmarried women in our country is roughly sixty to forty, we begin to see how really understated industry perceptions of women's involvement in the automotive market have been.

In recent years we have begun to look at the realities of car customers in terms of who really drives the car. When the perspective of "principle driver" is applied to our market data, it becomes clear that women represent about half of the car market. Women's participation varies somewhat by type of car and by car make. However, in general, our data suggest that somewhere between 40 percent and 50 percent of the car owners and drivers in our country are women. And this pattern is fairly consistent across all types of cars.

Assumption #2: Men Make the Automotive Purchase Decisions

Implicit in this assumption is that no matter whether the woman actually buys the car and/or drives the car, she is not the one who makes the purchase decision. Therefore, since it is the man of the family who makes the purchase decision, it is his business that should be cultivated.

What are the facts? There are two ways to define decision-makers: those who made the decision alone, by themselves, without consulting another member of the family or a friend, and those who shared that decision. Our most recent information tells us that men are, in fact, almost twice as likely as women to make automotive purchase decisions by themselves. But one in three of the sole decision-makers are women.

On the other hand, more than half of the automotive purchase decisions that are made are shared decisions. And women are more likely than men to participate in those shared decisions. So, when we combine all decisions to buy cars, both solo and shared, we see that women account for just under half of all car purchase decisions made in the United States. Their participation in the car decision-making process has increased slightly from year to year. So even taking the conservative view that women are not fully equal to men in the extent to which they make the car purchase decision, it is clear that women do represent greater opportunities for the car marketer than Detroit used to believe. We have come a long way from the old assumption that the only role a woman played in purchasing a car was to choose the color of the upholstery.

Of course, the claim of having shared in a purchase decision is a subjective one on both sides. Amusingly, in the early 1970s when I first began studying this particular market, a far higher proportion of women than men claimed to have shared in the purchase decision. Since we can't really follow each couple into the car dealership as they make their purchase, we have to take their own testimony as to whether or not they really did share in the decision. Taking the conservative view, we could discount the higher proportion of married women who claimed to have shared in the decision, and we still see that there were many more shared decisions than industry pundits had assumed in the past.

But, certainly, there are no self-delusions in the percentage of women who report that they made the decision all by themselves. While they represent, perhaps, only about one in six of all car purchase decisions, cultivating the business of that crucial proportion of car buyers could give a car marketer a competitive edge.

Assumption #3: If Women Do Buy Cars, They Buy Only Compacts

What are the realities? It is true that women are more likely to be found buying and driving the smaller types of cars—compacts, mid-specialties, subcompacts, small specialties, and midsize. About half, or just under half, of the drivers of these types of cars are women. When it comes to the larger and luxury cars, women's presence declines somewhat, but they still represent about two out of five of all drivers for those types of cars.

Yes, it is true that women are especially responsive to compacts. But they are responsive to almost every other type of car to the same extent as men, with a slightly lower level of participation in the large and luxury car categories. The facts are that whether we look at new cars or used cars, at women who make the decisions all by themselves or who share in the purchase decisions, the spectrum of car sizes selected by women decision-makers parallels that chosen by men.

Up until now I have been generalizing about the women's market for cars. But, of course, as in any other product area, each woman buys a car to fit her own special situation. People choose cars to fit their own driving needs, their own personal motivations, and their own life styles. The way people choose and drive cars is affected by their stage in the life cycle.

If an *unmarried* female is working, she is far more likely to be in the car market. She has more money available, and she is more likely to have a car available to her. She is also far more likely to have a driver's license. When she does drive, she uses her car more, and she is more likely to come from a multicar family. The unmarried woman is most likely to be a sole decision-maker. And if she is working, she is a strong car prospect. The unmarried working woman buys both new and used cars more often than her stay-at-home counterpart. And she is more likely to be a recent car buyer. Her kind of car seems to be a two-door sedan, especially if she is working. And when she picks out her own car, she is most likely to choose the small or racey ones.

Even *with a husband around the house,* if the wife is working the family seems to be a better prospect for cars. They have more money to spend. They are slightly more likely to own *any* car. And the wife is far more likely to know how to drive. The working wife does more driving. And two-paycheck families are more likely to have two or more cars. While both working and nonworking wives are more likely to share in the decision than decide by themselves, if she is working she appears more likely to be consulted.

Working couples seem more likely to buy both new and used cars than families where the wife does not work. And two-paycheck households are more active in the car market. Childless couples in which the wife works are likely to buy two-door sedans, four-door sedans, or convertibles, while families with the nonworking wives are apt to pick the sensible four-door sedan. In families where the wife shares in the decision, both working and nonworking wives without children selected the full spectrum of car sizes.

Apparently *the presence of children* is likely to put mother in the driver's seat. The nonworking wives with children are more car-involved than any other nonworking group, but in most cases the working mothers are still better car prospects. These are the most affluent families. They are both likely to own cars, but the working wives are slightly more likely to drive. The working mom does more driving than her nonworking counterpart. While both types of families are above average in multicar ownership, that second paycheck seems to lead to that second or third car. Both working and nonworking wives and mothers are more likely to share in the purchase decision than pick a car by themselves. If she is working, she seems to be a little more likely to have a voice in that decision. Both types of families were similar in the extent to which they buy cars new and used. That second paycheck seems to suggest more activity in the car market. Although these families seem to respond to all car styles, mothers of children under eighteen are far more likely than other groups to own station wagons. This is the one area where the nonworking housewife is even a better customer than her employed neighbor.

When there is *no man around the house,* if mother goes to work, she is far more likely to be a prospect for cars. The husbandless working mother has a higher income. She is far more apt to have a car available, and even more likely to know how to drive. And if she does drive, she drives a lot. Both working and nonworking mothers without husbands use their cars a great deal. They are second only to the working single women in the number of miles they drive each year. Surprisingly, the nonworking female head of household appears to be more likely to live in a multicar household.

In fatherless households, if mother is working, she is far more likely to decide on the car purchase by herself. The working mothers without husbands were more likely to have bought both new and used cars to a greater extent than their nonworking counterparts. If mother is out working, she is more likely to be active in the car market, and particularly more apt to have bought a car in the last year. With no man around the house, if the woman goes to work, she is more likely to buy a two-door or four-door sedan, and she is above par in choosing convertibles. The affinity of station wagons and children is confirmed again. And when she selects her own car, the husbandless working mother favors compacts, intermediates, and imports. The stay-at-homes choose full-size, medium-priced cars as well.

Both life cycle and New Demographic considerations help to identify which women would be most likely to be good prospects for which kinds of cars. There is no market where it is more important to keep both New Demographics and life cycle in mind. If we are really to understand the dynamics of women's responsivesness to cars, we need to consider their employment status, their attitudes toward work, and their personal living situations.

For example, if we examine the last car purchased in a household, we see that an equal number of new cars and used cars are bought in a year. However, career women are far more likely than any other group of women to live in a household where a new car was bought. Plan-to-work housewives and "just a job" working women are somewhat more likely to live in households where the last car purchased was a used car.

If we look at the decision to buy a new car, we see that career women are the only one of the four New Demographic segments who were substantially above the norm of the total population in having made that decision on their own. On the other hand, stay-at-home housewives, as well as career women, were particularly likely to have shared in the car decision. "Just a job" working women were somewhat under the norm in having participated in a shared decision.

Stay-at-home housewives are most likely to live in households where there is only one car. The other three groups are more likely than stay-at-homes to live in two-car households, with career women being particularly visible in this category. And when it comes to the household where there are three or more cars in the garage, the two types of housewives are far below the norm, career women are above the norm, and "just a job" working women are just over the norm. So we see that the presence of a paycheck in the homes of both job and career women is translated into more cars in the household. In the case of the career women, it also means that more of those cars are bought new.

However, it is the balance of the New Demographic segmentation with a woman's position in the life cycle that really pinpoints her relative value to the car market. In general, if we define a woman prospect as someone who has participated in the purchase decision for a car, and if we consider a woman who made that decision by herself twice as valuable to the car marketer as one who shared in the decision, then we have a framework for assessing the relative value of individual women as prospects for the automotive market.

By this definition, two out of three women prospects are women who work, both job and career women. Career women are especially valuable. They represent twice their actual numbers in the population to the purchase of cars. Again, the unmarried working women, both job and career, are twice as valuable to the car market as their numbers in the population. While childless career wives are a small number of all women, they are three times as valuable to the automotive marketer as their numbers in the population.

So we see that it is not enough just to recognize that there is a woman's market, it is essential to identify which types of women are particularly valuable to which types of cars. After all, we don't sell cars to markets, we sell cars to *people,* one at a time.

A national survey of women who bought cars and registered them in their own names was released recently. This study confirms some of our other data about the women's car market. While the typical woman car buyer was thirty-six years old, they represent a large cross-section of the population, according to J.D. Power, president of the firm that conducted the survey. Mr. Power said, "Some twenty-one percent are under twenty-five years of age, and twenty-one percent are fifty-five years of age or older."[1] He points out that there are a sizable number of older women with a good deal of money. He also noted that 60 percent of the female car buyers have attended college, while only 26 percent of the total adult women in this country have gone beyond high school. More than two-thirds of women car buyers are employed full time.

The role of life cycle is very clear here. One-third of the registered women car buyers are married, while two-thirds of all women are married. The remaining two-thirds are either single or formerly married. As Mr. Power said, "There's nothing surprising about the higher than average proportion of unmarried women. These women must depend more on their own abilities to buy and finance their own means of transportation. As with many women, getting credit approved to buy a car is a problem."[2]

Half of these women made the automotive purchase decision by themselves. The other half turned to members of their families to help them: They turned to their husbands, fathers, or brothers to help in negotiating a price with the dealer.

Importantly, about half the women felt they were treated differently by the car dealer from the way that a man would be treated. They generally felt "that the auto salesman talked down to me," or "didn't take me seriously." Some said that the salesman "tried to take advantage of me." Mr. Power observed that "auto salesmen like to see a husband and wife come into a showroom, but they don't like to bother with a woman who enters alone." He says, "Salesmen are used to the traditional way of selling cars."

According to an article in September 1979 *Advertising Age,* the automotive industry has become aware of the women's market, and there are varying philosophies on how to reach these newly discovered customers. James H. Graham, marketing director of Pontiac Division, is quoted as saying, "The fastest growing segment of the driving population is female. We expect that licensed drivers will be one to one male to female by 1985. I would suspect that with the bulk of our cars, the principle driver is female since most housewives do most of the chauffeuring and so on."[3] This perspective reinforces the traditional view that it is the full-time homemaker driving the station wagon on her round of household errands who is the major female driver.

On the other hand, the article points out that auto executives do talk about the importance of the two-income family or the multiple-job household. As the author says, "These executives leave unsaid what lies behind these terms. A wife or a female roommate gets a job and buys her own car." Several of these executives predicted sales growth for particular kinds of vehicles because of the multiple car ownership in two-income households. The former director of marketing at Buick says, "Two people work, and they both need an automobile. You know we're talking about some pretty heavy incomes. They can afford to own something a step above basic transportation."[4] The marketing manager at American Motors Corporation believes that the four-wheel drive Jeep Cherokee and wagon are substitutes for the conventional family station wagon and are typical of the trend toward trucks and alternative vehicles that are sought by multiple-job households.

Most auto executives say that women seem to be looking for the same things in an automobile that men are. As the Buick spokesman said, "It's not just a pretty face to a woman. She's looking for a car that offers her a package value. She wants interior comfort, convenience, and also a car that is economical and easy to park." We seem to have come a long way from the concept that all she is worried about is the color of the upholstery.

Some luxury car marketers believe that women are a factor in that market as well. The marketing director of Cadillac says, "It used to be the wives of successful Cadillac owners. Now you're getting professional women buying Sevilles on the basis of their own achievement.

They're seeking a symbol of their own success, just as men have always done."[5]

Assumption #4: After All, Men Pay the Bills

While women may, in fact, be driving cars, and some of them may participate in the purchase decision, it is the man whose business should be cultivated, because, after all, they pay the bills.

This is a more complex and circular situation. Until very recently, most car dealers did not cultivate women's business. If a woman came into a dealership to buy her own car, she was often told to "go back and get your husband, honey, and bring him in to make the deal."

Since most cars are sold on credit, the dealers and banks tended to make it difficult for a woman to establish credit on her own. It was easier for the woman to purchase a car through her husband or through a male family member. Since the mid-1970s the Equal Credit Opportunity Act has made it illegal to refuse credit on the basis of sex. But there have been experiments conducted where a man and woman have walked into the same dealership with precisely the same set of credit references, and the man is more likely to get credit than the woman.

One of the problems in this kind of situation is that the question of whether women are reliable credit risks cannot be answered on past history. Since women didn't particularly seek credit on their own and were not given it easily, it has been difficult for them to establish themselves as reliable credit risks.

However, whatever evidence does exist suggests that women are at least as reliable as men, and possibly even more dependable as credit risks. In 1973 Barbara Schack, assistant director of the New York Civil Liberties Union, said in a hearing on discrimination against women by the banking industry, "There are no statistics or studies to support the suspicion about women's credit worthiness. As a matter of fact, there is strong evidence that women are better credit risks than men."[6]

As far back as the early 1940s David Durand said in *Risk Elements in Consumer Installment Financing* that the "classification of borrowers by sex and marital status indicates that women are better credit risks than men, and the superiority appears to be statistically significant."[7]

Another early endorsement of women as credit-worthy came from Paul F. Smith in "Measuring Risk on Installment Credit": "A 1964 study of more than 100,000 loans over a five-year period by a moderately large commercial bank showed that the bed account probability for single and married women was substantially lower than for men with the same marital status."[8]

And in 1973 Thomas A. Jones, executive director, Neighborhood Housing Services, Inc., said: "Similar results were reported by the director of an organization providing home improvement loans to elderly and low income families. Many of the loans have gone to women who are heads of households. They, as well as the other program beneficiaries, were considered high risks and were, therefore, unable to get conventional financing. The program has a delinquency rate of only four percent; there have been no foreclosures. Most significantly, of the families headed by women, the delinquency rate is estimated as two percent. The program's director believes that female heads of families 'demonstrate better fiscal responsibility than other households.'"[9]

In the early 1970s there was a groundswell of concern in both the public and private sectors about women's role in the economy. It culminated in a bill entitled the Equal Credit Opportunity Act, enacted in 1974. This bill was sponsored by Senator Brock of Tennessee, who said: "The definition of credit-worthiness for women has too often been obscured by irrelevant questions and outmoded customs and beliefs. Credit is the lifeblood of our economic system. If women are denied credit solely on the basis of their sex, they are denied full participation in the free enterprise system. I would be the first to argue that credit should only be granted to credit-worthy individuals. The bill I am proposing would not mean that women ought to be granted credit because they are women. Rather it would insure that women must not be denied credit because they are women."[10]

Actually, enlightened businessmen realize that inviting women's credit is just plain good business. A banker, Eugene H. Adams, asked a bankers' gathering: "Is it possible that outdated assumptions, if they are outdated, are blinding us to a potentially very profitable market right on our own back doorsteps?"[11]

A credit executive, Hugh M. Martin, wrote in *The Credit World:* "Perhaps, over the years, some credit executives have lost sight of the value of the female consumer and are only concerned with legalities. Perhaps some of us credit executives are not keeping up with the times, and as a result, we could lose some very profitable business. By refusing to open an account because of sex, we definitely discourage the applicant to purchase from our company. We lose her business and the company we represent is placed in a position of ridicule and adverse publicity."[12]

And the president of BankAmericard has said: "But perhaps the most important misconception is that bank cards are more readily accepted by men than by women. The facts from some rather extensive research we have done contradict this misconception. In only thirty-eight percent of the homes we interviewed who use this type of product, does the man dominate discretionary spending. In other homes, women dominate discretionary spending. Of those homes where men dominate, forty-one percent of the men had accepted the product, but fifty-two percent of the women had accepted the product. The facts we have to live with are that in all probability today use and acceptance of the product, BankAmericard, is dominated by women, and will be increasingly dominated by women. It has to become responsive, in my view, to their needs."[13]

What does all this have to do with selling cars? The assumption that "after all, men still pay the bills, don't they?" still permeates parts of the industry in marketing planning, in advertising, and at the dealer level. The opportunity is manifest for automotive marketers who don't permit past prejudices to blind them to the realities of the market place. The first auto marketer who seriously invites women's business by offering them credit based on an objective appraisal of their ability to pay without reference to sex or marital status will reap the rewards of opening new sales opportunities and capture the respect and share of mind of an increasingly important segment of the automotive market.

Notes

1. Dan Jedlicka, "Women Car Buyers Angry at Treatment," *Chicago Sun-Times,* 1977.
2. *Ibid.*
3. Julie Candler, "Women—A Part of Every Segment in the Market," *Advertising Age,* September 17, 1979.
4. *Ibid.*
5. *Ibid.*
6. Barbara Schack, statement prepared for hearings on discrimination against women by the banking industry in the extension of credit of the Assembly Standing Committee on Banks, October 11, 1973.
7. David Durand, *Risk Elements in Consumer Installment Financing* (New York: National Bureau of Economic Research, Technical Edition, 1941).

8. Paul F. Smith, "Measuring Risk on Installment Credit," *Management Science 2* (2), November 1964, pp. 327-40.

9. Thomas A. Jones, private communication, April 18, 1973.

10. Letter 40 United States Senate, May 17, 1973.

11. Eugene H. Adams, remarks before the Florida Bankers Association, June 23, 1973.

12. Hugh M. Martin, "Sex vs. Credit," *Credit World,* November 1972.

13. Dee W. Hock, Proceedings of Symposium on Women in the Economy, sponsored by *Ladies' Home Journal,* National BankAmericard, Inc., and Bank of America, September 21, 1972.

Chapter 13

Women and Travel

Travel is a unique product and therefore is uniquely linked to the social context. In some ways the special nature of the "travel product" is more visibly interconnected with the fabric of society than are more tangible products such as a tube of toothpaste, a pack of cigarettes, or a lipstick. The product that the travel marketer has to sell is an experience; you can't put it on a shelf, and it doesn't come in a box. It costs a good deal more than most things that do come in boxes or packages. And that travel experience doesn't occur in limbo. It takes place within the constraints and cross-currents of government regulations, the direction of the economy, the quality of the environment, and the availability of energy. It also occurs within the context of changing social values and changing life styles.

Over the years we have heard reports on the attitudes that predispose people to travel. These are almost a self-fulfilling prophecy. We are told that people who are not adventurous and who are home-oriented tend to seek non-travel-oriented vacations in familiar surroundings. People who are interested in experiencing new things, learning about other cultures, or exploring new horizons are responsive to travel.

We can gain another perspective on consumers' predispositions toward travel by observing the changes in their personal priorities that have occurred in the past few years. Many of the changing life styles that have occurred recently have a fairly direct relationship to the travel decision. After all, the travel marketer is competing for discretionary dollars along with the sellers of durable goods, housing, and considerations of long-range financial security and savings. Changes in social values or priorities create a climate of acceptance for travel as an option in the consideration of how those discretionary dollars are spent.

One of the changes that occurred in the late 1960s and through the 1970s is that people have become more interested in living than in acquiring, and that change in emphasis favors the travel industry. The

192

move away from a desire to own things toward a desire to experience things has had direct benefit for travel marketers.

There was a time when the American dream centered on acquisition—the house in the suburbs, the well-stocked linen closet, the silver chest, the appliances, the second or third car, clothes, jewelry. The cliché about "keeping up with the Joneses" measured achievement in terms of possessions. It was only after all of the visible trappings of success were obtained that a family might plan a once-in-a-lifetime trip. The development of mass travel has made travel more accessible, but the changes in their own priorities have made many people more receptive to travel as an option.

No social change that has occurred recently has more direct impact on the potential of the travel market than the changing role of women. In 1973 I had the privilege of addressing the Annual Conference of the Travel Research Association. The title of the paper I gave at that time was "Working Women: The Invisible Consumer Travel Market." As a matter of fact, at that time women were not only a truly invisible travel market, their potential was totally unrecognized by most travel marketers. The conventional wisdom was that men are the prime customers for travel.

Therefore, until very recently, the marketing of most travel products has been directed to men. The assumption seemed to be that the heavy business travelers are, of course, men. It was further assumed that since holiday travel represents a fairly major expenditure, men, of course, were the key decision makers for that kind of travel as well. It has taken a long time for travel marketers to recognize the potential of women as customers for travel.

This was the first public presentation of my analysis of the changing role of women and its implication for marketers. It was before the New Demographics concept had emerged, so my analysis was based on a comparison of working and nonworking women within life-cycle. I raised the question of whether working women would be more likely to be good customers for pleasure travel than women who do not work, and whether certain life style segments among working women might be better prospects for pleasure travel than others. In the course of the speech, I reviewed foreign travel, use of travelers' checks, domestic air travel, and the use of and stays in hotels and motels on domestic trips.

I first asked a question, *"Are working women better customers for pleasure travel than women who do not work?"* To answer it, I began with a review of the median household incomes of working and nonworking women within life cycle. While household income levels in

1973 are far lower than their equivalent in the 1980s, the conclusion is still relevant. At that time I said that certainly one prerequisite for pleasure travel is the presence of discretionary dollars. A comparison of the median household incomes of working and nonworking women within each life cycle segment indicated that in every case, working women simply have more money available to them than women who do not work. When life cycle, (that is the presence of a husband and/or children) is held constant, in every case working women are far more likely to participate in pleasure travel than women who do not work. Therefore, the answer to the opening question was, and still is, a clear-cut "yes!"

To answer a second question, *"Are some women more valuable than others as prospects for pleasure travel?"* I reviewed the extent to which working women in the four life cycle groups traveled overseas, used travelers' checks, took domestic air trips, or stayed in hotels and motels. It became clear that the presence of young children is a real deterrent to travel. The unattached working women with neither husbands nor children at home and the childless working wives who either have not had children or whose children have left the nest are clearly better customers for travel than working women with family responsibilities. Both the unmarried and childless married working women take more foreign trips than working mothers with and without husbands at home.

Their patterns of travel diverge in other ways. Unmarried, working women—that is single, separated, widowed, or divorced—are apt to be heavy users of travelers' checks and somewhat more likely to take domestic air trips than childless married women. And although these live-alone women do more flying around the country, they are less likely to stay at commercial lodgings.

In order to confirm that it is both the absence of young children and the presence of a paycheck that make these women particularly good prospects for travel, we compared the travel behavior of working and nonworking women within each of the childless life cycle segments. It became clear that single, widowed, and divorced women without children in their homes would not be able to travel if they didn't go to work. The fact that they do so, even though their median household incomes are lower than those of the married women, suggests that they represent a valuable market segment for the travel business.

Nonworking married women without children at home are more likely to travel than any of the other nonworking life cycle segments. Nevertheless, childless working wives are far more likely to participate in travel than their nonworking sisters. Apparently the absence of young children in the home provides the ability to get away to take a trip, but the presence of that second paycheck and the attitude that led to working in the first place triggers the travel activity.

Working mothers are apt to do less traveling than the two childless groups. However, the presence or absence of a man around the house appears to result in different kinds of travel patterns. Married working mothers are somewhat above the norm in the degree to which they travel abroad, use travelers' checks, and stay in hotel or motel accommodations. They are less likely than women in any other stage of the life cycle to take domestic air trips. On the other hand, working mothers with no husbands at home do go in for plane travel in this country. And when they travel they are somewhat more likely to stay at hotels and motels than unmarried, childless working women.

Although the presence of children seems to limit the travel activities of working mothers, the fact that they go to work seems to bring them into the travel market. When we compare the travel involvement of working mothers with that of mothers who are full-time homemakers, it becomes clear that if a mother is a working woman, she is far more likely to travel than if she is a full-time housewife.

Therefore, the answer to the question, "Are some working women more valuable than others as prospects for pleasure travel?" is an overwhelming "yes!" While all working women travel more than nonworking women in equivalent life cycles, working women with no young children at home are particularly valuable customers for travel.

There is no doubt that the travel needs and interests of unmarried women traveling alone or together are vastly different from those of the traveling married couple. The fact that both groups are free to travel, have the motivation to do so, and have the money to take them there makes them valuable prospects for the travel marketer. I speculate that the presence of children as a deterrent to travel activity is a temporary condition. Working mothers have indicated far more involvement with pleasure travel than their stay-at-home counterparts. As their children grow up and leave the nest, these women will be in a position to indulge their desire to travel without concern for the responsibilities that currently keep them close to home.

Of course, up to now we have been discussing discretionary travel, that is, vacation or holiday trips. Business travel is another prime segment of the travel market. In my 1973 discussion of the "Invisible Consumer" travel market, I said, *"The business traveler is a man—or is he?"* Of course, the business traveler is a situational traveler. His or her business trips are essential to the conduct of business. The business traveler has no say as to whether or not a particular trip is necessary. But for most major destinations, the business traveler does have a choice as to how he or she will get there: the selection of a particular airline, train, or car rental service, and of where he or she will stay on arriving at the destination.

Most analyses have shown that while the number of people traveling on business are a minority of the population, they represent an extremely heavy user group. Therefore, the travel industry has courted their business. This is reflected in a multitude of facilities and special conveniences tailored to the needs of the business traveler—special departure lounges, carry-on luggage racks, computerized car rentals, car rental credit cards, and one-phone-number hotel reservation service. All of these are designed to streamline the business travel experience.

Back in 1973 I reviewed a cross-section of travel advertising. This included advertising for airlines, car rentals, destinations, and lodgings. I said at that time, "If this advertiser reflects the viewpoint of the travel industry, it would appear that women almost never travel, and that they certainly don't travel on business. We see an endless parade of businessmen carrrying attaché cases getting on and off planes, in and out of cars and hotels, but nowhere is there any indication that a woman ever travels on business. As far as travel marketers are concerned, the woman as a business traveler is almost invisible." Yet in 1973, according to TGI, one in four business travelers was likely to be a woman. This was not the "take-me-along" wife but the traveler who was traveling "for business reasons paid for by your firm." At that time the woman business traveler patronized hotels and motels on her business trips in that same one-to-four ratio with the male business traveler, although she was somewhat more likely to stay at hotels than motels.

Women are still not equal to men in the degree to which they participate in business travel, but their presence in the business travel market has increased. Women are approximately 40 percent as likely as men to have participated in a business trip in the past year, and slightly more than half as likely to have stayed in a hotel or motel while on that business trip.

We have begun to see some recognition of women business travelers in some travel advertising. However, on an objective basis I don't believe that the presence of women business travelers in advertising is as yet proportionate with their actual presence in the market.

In 1973 I said: "Certainly there are opportunities for travel marketers to cultivate the woman business traveler and serve her special needs. It will, no doubt, be many years before women will be involved in all levels of business responsibility and, therefore, as active as men in business travel. However, the trends in women's education and their increasing commitment to professional activity suggests that the women's market for business travel is in its infancy."[1] An example of one travel marketer's cultivation of the women's business travel market is the program mounted by Western International Hotels. The objectives were "to learn more than any other hotel company about the needs and concerns of the traveling business woman so as to position Western International as the industry leader in service to women; to reinforce among employees management's commitment to service the woman guest fairly and completely; to reach the traveling woman, particularly the business woman, with the message that Western International is aware of her needs and intent on meeting them."

The hotel chain conducted a research program to identify the wants and needs of women business travelers. Regina Henry, who is currently the director of advertising and public relations for the Plaza Hotel in New York City, reported on the results: "What did women tell us? Well basically, just like men, their primary concern is for clean, comfortable guest rooms. Most of their criteria for selecting a hotel were the same as men, but women did place a higher value on such items as security, a hotel chain's reputation and downtown locations. However, these same respondents also told us they felt their needs were somewhat or very different than those of traveling men. And it was the women who traveled most who were most mindful of these differences.

"Along with practical needs, like full-length mirrors and skirt hangers, women also expressed the opinion that they were not offered the same high caliber of service by the travel industry as that offered men. Whether this was true or not in the past was something we at Western International cannot be sure. But since the majority of women did feel that way we wanted to deal with it and we wanted to reach women with the message that our hotels recognize women business travelers, want to serve them well, and based on the results of our comprehensive survey, can serve women better than any other hotels."[2]

These findings were implemented in a Woman Business Traveler Program, which dealt with tangibles, such as mirrors, electric outlets, and skirt hangers, and the more subtle and serious intangibles of staff attitude. Ms. Henry explained that "in order to stress the point that women do travel independently, I went along to our hotel cities and addressed the hotels' staffs on the increasing numbers of women travelers and told them the corporate commitment to women was one we felt would make the traveler experience better for all. Women's requests for things like full-length mirrors and even skirt hangers were not for the exclusive comfort and use of only women. Obviously, men would use a full length mirror and any guest could hang a pair of slacks from a skirt hanger.

"Today men travel with hair dryers and an expanded list of toiletries. They benefit, too, from convenient electrical outlets, vanity space and mirrors.

"I also shared with the staffs that sometimes intangible thing known as attitude. And that is women feeling they are taken for granted . . . not given the same respect as men. The film we did illustrates, I think in an only slightly exaggerated way, four situations which can be irritating to women when the personnel is not alert. The film shows a businesswoman and a businessman arriving at a hotel in an airport limo and the doorman greeting them incorrectly by assuming they are a "couple." Then the correct greeting is offered by the same doorman. We follow the woman into the hotel's front desk where a roomclerk embarrasses not only her but the gentleman checking in ahead of her. After the corrected check-in procedure there are two dining scenes—the woman dining alone and then entertaining a gentleman at dinner.

"Obviously, the message to our staff personnel is that one cannot be careless and presume or assume anything. Each guest deserves individual and courteous service. And it is up to each department head in each of our hotels to reiterate and reinforce the fact that it is the responsibility of each employee to serve well our women guests."[3]

When we apply the New Demographic perspective to the travel market, we see that it is not just life cycle or the presence of a paycheck that identifies the most promising prospects for travel.[4] In every case, with incredible consistency, career-oriented working women are by far the most valuable customers for travel. Whether we examine women who have taken a domestic trip of a hundred or more miles, women who have taken a scheduled airline trip, those who have participated in foreign travel, those who use travelers' checks, or those who have valid passports, it is career-oriented working women in each case who are most actively involved in travel activities.

In our earlier review of life cycle, we saw that women's likelihood to travel was clearly affected by whether they go to work or are full-time homemakers. Their patterns of travel behavior were also clearly affected by whether or not they were married or had children under eighteen living in their households. When we consider the New Demographic perspective, we see that the life cycle situations of the four New Demographic groups also impact on their patterns of travel behavior.

Childless career women, both married and not married, are far more likely to take domestic trips or fly scheduled airlines, to have traveled internationally, to use travelers' checks, or to have passports than any other segment of women. Working wives with children at home are more likely to travel than the husbandless working mothers. However, in every life cycle situation these career-oriented working women are far heavier travelers than their "just a job" counterparts and either housewife group.

"Just a job" working wives without children at home are more active travelers than "just a job" working wives with children under eighteen in their households. Among the unmarried "just a job" women, certainly the childless group are more likely to travel than the "just a job" working mothers without husbands at home.

The two types of housewives are far less likely to participate in travel than either of the working women segments. However, plan-to-work housewives seem to live in hope. The married plan-to-work housewives do have valid passports at the ready! And those without children at home have, in fact, traveled domestically, used airlines, gone overseas, and used travelers' checks, although not nearly to the extent that the career women have.

Club Med is a travel marketer that has responded to changing life styles. As Roz Gibbons, vice president for advertising and sales, said at a TTRA symposium: "For the 'Changing Markets' of the 1980s, I am going to speak about 'soloists' and 'paired parties' instead of 'singles' and 'couples,' adding a new dimension to the traditional demographic breakdown as we see it at Club Med. . . . In the past, 'single' had the connotation of 'swinger'. If a single was not a swinger, one assumed he preferred to be otherwise in another 'state,' ultimately married. Today, the single person remains, or becomes, single by choice—not pressured by society or parental guilt to be married or to stay married. They have chosen a 'solo' lifestyle, a lifestyle which compliments and enhances their career and personal ambitions. And because of this 'soleness,' there is a current inward drive toward 'self,' the emergence of the 'ME generation'—a rebirth of individualism, self-identity, self-awareness; and self-help programs have flourished universally. The solo person will be older as a result of the post–WW II baby boom and as a result of the increase in the divorce rate among middle-aged married;

retired, widowed people who are staying fit longer and increasing their travel will often fall into this category. They will be richer as a result of better education and training, and will have more sophisticated vacation needs as they will have traveled in the past much more extensively because of inexpensive airfares and hotel prices in the sixties and seventies.

"Taking a new look at the 'couple,' couples no longer consist of the traditional 'husband and wife' union, but rather 'paired parties' such as father and son, mother and daughter, or vice versa, two men, two women, et cetera, resulting from the increased divorce rate, the decline of the traditional marriage, and the low birth rate. They, too, will have more discretionary income for leisure activities with the predominance of the two-career people and emergence of the working woman."

Ms. Gibbons explained how the Club Med concept is tailored to fit the needs of specific life cycle groups: "We at Club Med are marketing a total leisure experience, based on this philosophy and formula, as opposed to marketing and selling a hotel room, or a specific destination. . . . The Club's philosophy: to ensure that the most precious and irreplaceable time of the year—your vacation—be the best ever, filled with happiness, joy, discovery, plus a touch of enchantment. The formula, which is a rather practical one, is to provide reasonably priced, all-inclusive packages that usually include air transportation, transfers, comfortable accommodations, three all-you-can-eat meals per day with unlimited wine at lunch and dinner, sports instruction and equipment, disco, nightly entertainment, et cetera, plus taxes. Tipping is not permitted. You know exactly what you will spend before you go. . . . Contrary to popular belief, Club Med is not a swinging singles organization, which brings me back to my opening statement that 'singles' are soloists, and couples, 'paired parties,' very apropos lifestyle segmentations for the eighties. . . . Club Med is analyzing, very closely, the product and how it can be changed to accommodate the needs of its market—primarily soloists and paired parties in the eighties. These changes are already taking place."[5]

Continuing the New Demographic perspective, no matter which facet of travel activity we examine, we see that career-oriented working women are really the core of the women's travel market. They are far more likely than the total population or than any other group of women to have used travel agents and to have stayed in motels or hotels when they've traveled. They are more likely than any other to have traveled by car, by plane, or by train. The one area of travel where "just a job" working women are more active customers than any other segment of women is in the use of bus travel.

We have talked about the value of career women to the business travel market. Career women also dominate the personal trip and vacation trip market as well. They are more likely than any other segment of women to have traveled domestically, on either a vacation or a personal trip.

As women gain in travel experience, they also gain a sense of self-confidence and assurance. They learn that they can cope on their own, and they are no longer timid about the unknowns of the travel situation: "I find that when you travel alone—the hustle and bustle of getting on a bus to get to the airport or how you're going to, you know, renting a car and studying maps on how to figure out how to get across Boston to Wellesley, you know, and things like that, when I first started doing it I was just petrified. Now, I sort of, well, when I get lost or if I can't find my way, I stop and ask directions. I don't have fears, you know, of people or situations any more. I sort of like it. I meet a lot of interesting people."

"I've had to travel on several occasions with this new job I have and I made my own reservations, rented my own car, and made my own airplane reservations. When I was single I went to Europe by myself. I went everywhere—Montreal, New York, the islands . . . Europe by tour . . . as far as traveling with business I felt completely confident in handling my own arrangements."

There are other ways in which people use their discretionary time, and this may not necessarily be linked to travel-simply a matter of the extent to which they participate in hobbies or sports or dine out.

We observe that career women are more likely than any other group of women to dine out at all and to participate in the decision to go out to dinner or to select the restaurant. "Just a job" working women are slightly above the norm in dining out; however, they do not appear to participate in the decision-making process. And both groups of housewives are far below working women in being consulted on whether to eat out and in selecting the restaurant.

There has been a move in recent years toward drinking wine as an aperitif or for the cocktail hour. We see that the support for use of wine comes predominately from career-oriented women, echoed somewhat by the plan-to-work housewife. Tina Santi, vice president, Colgate-Palmolive Company, commented on the white wine phenomenon and the fact that marketers were not perceptive enough to capitalize on this trend. "Everyone knows women no longer order their drinks with an offhanded 'I'll have the same.' Women no longer follow drinking trends; they create them. The spectacular growth of white wine as a pre-dinner drink can be attributed to women. They wanted an even lighter drink than the light drinks liquor marketers were offering. Women by the millions began asking for white wine before dinner. And in time, men by the millions were saying, 'I'll have the same.'

"Did the wine companies foster this changeover? Did they encourage it? Did any one producer step in to preempt this emerging market for itself?

"The answer is no. It was business as usual at the wineries. Producers continued to promote white wine in the traditional way: as a drink with dinner. Any sales increases from the pre-dinner market accrued by accident, not design.

"Just imagine that one producer had gone after the pre-dinner market while it was still in its formative stages. Imagine that this producer had positioned its Brand X white wine as the clear choice before dinner. At cocktail parties and in bars across the country, we would now hear requests for 'a glass of Brand X, please,' instead of just 'a glass of white wine.'"[6]

Reports in the trade press in mid-1979 reflected two wine marketers' belated recognition of the value of the women's market for wine. Christian Brothers is starting "a serious effort to reach women" because of the increased wine purchases in supermarkets. The Christian Brothers print budget will rise 10 percent next year to add women's magazines for the first time, and 30 percent of the winery's total $3,000,000-plus 1980 budget will be put into advertising aimed at women. Canandaigua's Bisceglia, a California table wine, is running a test campaign in five markets, based on findings that showed women are responsible for 70 percent of wine purchases.[7]

All women are less likely than men to drink regular beer, but there are differences. Stay-at-home housewives are least likely to be beer drinkers. Career women are somewhat closer to the norm of the total population in drinking beer.

In recent years a lower calorie form of beer called "light" beer has been introduced. The women's response to this product is really a perfect example of segmentation. Stay-at-home housewives are far below the norm in supporting this kind of product; career women are far above the norm; and plan-to-work housewives and "just a job" working women are slightly below and above the norm, respectively.

Another way people might spend their leisure time is reading. We observed in Chapter 9 that career women were the most likely to read magazines and that plan-to-work housewives were second in magazine reading. A similar pattern carries over to the reading of books. Whether we examine the purchase of paperback books or hardcover books or participation in book clubs, career women are the most active readers among the four New Demographic segments, and plan-to-work housewives are second to them. "Just a job" working women are somewhere between those two and the stay-at-homes. They do buy paperbacks to a fairly great extent, but not nearly as much as the plan-to-work housewives or career women. Stay-at-home housewives are below the norm in buying books. They and the "just a job" working women are just slightly above the norm in belonging to book clubs.

What about sports? When it comes to swimming, in either outdoor or indoor pools, the pattern is similar. Career women are the most likely to swim in either type of pool. They are echoed in this activity by plan-to-work housewives. "Just a job" working women are just a little bit above the norm, and stay-at-home housewives are far below it in swimming in either indoor or outdoor swimming pools.

When we examine other sorts of outdoor sports, such as tennis or golf, we see that career women are most likely to play tennis. They are seconded in this activity by plan-to-work housewives. "Just a job" working women go in for tennis, but not nearly to the same extent as the other two segments of women. And stay-at-home housewives are far less likely than any other group of women to be found on the tennis courts.

Golf is clearly a man's game. All segments of women are below the norm in golfing. Career women are just one percentage point above it in the extent to which they play golf. One interesting exception is the stay-at-home housewives. Although as a group they are very unlikely to be golfers, those few who do play golf are ardent golfers. They play more often than any other segment of women.

Participation in other sports, such as horseback riding and ice skating, show similar patterns. Career women and plan-to-work housewives are most likely to ride horses or go ice skating. "Just a job" working women participate in these sports to a lesser extent. Stay-at-home housewives are far below the norm in climbing up on a horse or getting out on the ice.

Career women are far more likely than any other group to get out on the ski slopes. Again, although stay-at-home housewives are less likely than any other segment of women to go in for skiing, those few stay-at-homes who do ski pursue the sport more often than the golfers in any other segment of women.

Notes

1. "Working Women: The Invisible Consumer Travel Market," speech given by Rena Bartos at The Travel Research Association Conference, August 14, 1973 (photocopied), p. 14.
2. Regina Henry, "A Case History: The Woman Business Traveller and Western International Hotels," *Research and the Changing World of Travel in the 1980s* (proceedings of the eleventh annual conference of the Travel Research Association), June 1980, p. 105.
3. *Ibid.,* p. 106.
4. Unless otherwise specified, the qualitative and quantitative data reported in this chapter were taken from "Understanding the New Demographics" and special JWT analyses of TGI data, respectively.
5. Roz Gibbons, "Singles and Couples" in *Research and the Changing World of Travel in the 1980s,* pp. 113–114.
6. Tina Santi, "Men Still Don't Know How to Sell to the New Woman," *The Forum,* January 1979, p. 19.
7. *Advertising Age,* July 9, 1979.

Chapter 14

Women and Money

It has been traditional to assume that financial matters—banking, insurance, investment—are of concern only to men. Financial institutions have therefore concentrated their marketing efforts at reaching the men whom they assumed were their potential customers. The assumed target for all of their financial products and services was the husband and father head of household. Certainly insurance salesmen concentrated on the male head of house. Bank marketers and investment specialists also targeted their efforts to men. Banks or other lending institutions issued credit to the man of the house, never to his wife.

The "masculine mystique" implied that men are experts about money and finance and investments, while the "little woman" needn't trouble her pretty head about such mysterious and esoteric matters.

However, in the 1970s there were some dramatic changes in the marketing of financial services and in the perceptions of financial marketers as to who are the potential customers for those services. The Equal Credit Opportunity Act, passed in 1974, changed the legal framework dramatically. As time passed, marketers of financial services became aware of the lucrative potential of the women's market and began to address it. The attitudes of both men and women about women's relationship to financial decisions have also begun to change.

Virginia Slims sponsored a series of studies of women's attitudes and life styles during the 1970s and into 1980. A comparison of women's involvement with financial matters in 1972 and again in 1980 gives a dramatic snapshot of what has occurred. Women became more financially active during the eight-year period between 1972 and 1980. In addition, women were increasingly likely to have their financial assets and financial records in their own names.

The 1980 special report on this project says: "Women today have a higher incidence of such things as checking accounts, mortgages, and personal loans than they did eight years ago. Moreover, having such items in one's own right rather than jointly, has risen markedly. This is particularly true of single women, divorced women and working women. But even among married women, where there are practical and sometimes even legal considerations for having 'joint tenancy,' the incidence of such financial assets and obligations in one's own right has risen."[1]

In reviewing all the areas of financial activity, the Roper–Virginia Slims report has a consistent theme. Women are more financially active than they were eight years ago. They are more likely to have their financial assets in their own names.

Clearly, both life cycle and employment are key factors in the degree to which specific women are financially active. Unmarried women are more likely than married women to have their financial assets in their own names. And women who work are more likely than women who do not work outside of the home to have their own savings and checking accounts and credit cards.

Following is an overview of the changes in women's financial activities between 1972 and 1980 as reported by the Roper–Virginia Slims poll.

"Savings and Checking

A large majority of women have money in savings (77%) and checking accounts (81%). Overall, 28% of women today have savings or checking accounts in their own name. This represents an increase over 1972 when 15% had savings accounts in their own name; 16% had checking accounts in their own name. However, among single women, 61% have checking accounts and 63% have savings accounts in their own name—up sharply from the 36% and 46% who did so eight years ago. Two out of five women who work full-time have checking accounts in their own name, while this is true of only one-third as many married women (where 'joint tenancy' often has both practical and legal advantages)—the incidence of checking accounts and savings accounts in one's own name has clearly nearly doubled among married women.

"Credit Cards

A majority of women today (64%) have credit cards; 27% have their own. Those most likely to have their own credit cards are women (42%) and women with full-time jobs (37%). Only one in five (19%) married women have credit cards in their own name.

"Loans

Nearly three in ten women (29%) have installment loans; 7% in their own name. One out of five women (20%) has a personal bank loan; one out of twenty-five in her own name. More than two out of five women (42%) have mortgage loans; one out of twenty (5%) in her own name. Among single women installment loans in one's own name has risen from 7% to 17% since 1972; personal bank loans from 6% to 9%, mortgage loans from 2% to 5%. But, it is worth noting here that a majority of women (51%) think women are descriminated against when applying for loans, mortgages and charge accounts. This figure is down, but not significantly from that of 1974 (56%).

"Common Stock

One out of every five women (21%) own some shares of common stock, 7% in their own name. Among single women, this has risen from eight percent to eleven percent in eight years."[2]

Since there is a clear suggestion that the women who work are more financially active than women who don't work, let us turn to the New Demographic perspective to see if there are any differences in the financial behavior of the two types of housewives and the two types of working women.[3]

Stay-at-home housewives are less likely to be financially active than any other segment of women. They are less likely than the population as a whole to have checking or savings accounts.

Plan-to-work housewives are more involved with financial matters than their stay-at-home neighbors. They are above the norm of the total population in having checking and savings accounts. They are more likely to say "charge it" in department stores with their department store charge cards than are either stay-at-home housewives or "just a job" working women. They are somewhat above par in having bank charge cards. In contrast, stay-at-homes and "just a job" working women are somewhat below the norm for this activity. However, plan-to-work housewives are very unlikely to use travel and entertainment credit cards, and they're slightly below the norm for the total population in being involved in investments.

An analysis of the financial behavior of *"just a job" working women* confirms the importance of the New Demographic perspective. While it is true that working women as a group are more financially active than housewives as a group, it is clear also that working women who feel their work is "just a job" are a very distinct segment. In no way does their financial behavior resemble that of their career-oriented counterparts. They are actually less active financially in a number of areas than plan-to-work housewives. They are just over the norm in having checking accounts. They are slightly above par in putting their money into savings accounts. They use their department store charge cards to about the same degree as do the stay-at-home housewives. However, they are less likely than the total population to use bank credit cards. And they are clearly inactive in the market for travel and entertainment credit cards. They are less likely than any other group of women to make investments.

Career women are in sharp contrast to their "just a job" working counterparts. Career women are the most financially active and financially sophisticated of all segments of women. They are sharply above the norm for the total population in having checking and savings accounts. They are strong supporters of all types of credit cards. They tower over other segments of women and the total population in their likelihood to use department store charge cards and bank credit cards. And they are the only group of women who are really good customers for travel and entertainment credit cards. They are also more likely than any other segment of women to be active investors.

The evidence has been that women have become more financially active during the 1970s. However, once we get behind that general trend, it becomes clear that career women were the core of the heightened financial activity among women.

What does this new information about women tell us about the customers for financial products? Well, for openers, if financial managers aren't actively cultivating the business of working women, they should be. Certainly, career-oriented working women are valuable customers by any standard. For the most part if an institution has their business today it could be because they have no attractive alternatives. It is only in the last few years that the law has forbidden sex discrimination in lending. However, old stereotypes die slowly. How many financial marketing and advertising programs invite their business? How many financial institutions instruct their retail staffs about the new realities?

Let me share two true stories. One is about a career woman—an officer in a major corporation, who applied for a travel and entertainment card about ten years ago. She received it only after the issuer checked her *husband's* credit rating.

The second took place in 1974. A career woman about to take off on an unexpected business trip to Europe decided to take her bank card as well as her travel and entertainment card with her, because the latter was somewhat limited. She and her husband had had a joint checking account with a major bank for many years. When bank credit cards were first issued, this bank sent them a couple of cards, which they never used. She noticed that although the checking account was in both names, both of the credit cards were in her husband's name. Therefore, she went into a branch of the bank and asked that a card be issued in her name. The teller answered, "Your husband will have to write a letter asking permission."

These anecdotes point up the fact that the *financial institutions involved regarded these women as nonpeople.* Their financial identities were defined in terms of their husbands' credit ratings, not their own. This is what I mean when I say financial institutions may have their business because there are no more attractive alternatives. But what will happen when some financial marketers really court these valuable customers and try to understand their needs? Since many women are new to the management of money, they are hungry for information. They don't pretend to be experts about an unfamiliar subject. On the other hand, they need to be treated with respect and without condescension. The first marketers to cultivate their business properly will reap rich rewards.

Some financial institutions have begun to recognize the potential of the women's market and have begun to cultivate it. In 1979 Interbank launched a campaign aimed at working women. In a report on that campaign in *Advertising Age* the reporter pointed out that the member banks of the Interbank consortium had not recognized the opportunities inherent in the women's market. "Over ten years ago Carte Blanche introduced the pink credit card for women. This spring Master Card is trying to sell them 'clout.' Master Card's marketing strategy is as much designed to hasten a belated recognition of women . . . by the banking industry, as it is to swell its own base card holders. Behind the gruff respect accorded women in its new ads which states forcefully, 'I'm in charge,' Master Card concedes the banks that make up its licensing consortium, Interbank, have failed to identify a potent financial market."[4]

The Interbank Senior Vice President of Marketing who launched this campaign said, "We want to stimulate banks to look at the women's market in general and not incidentally to push Master Card more aggressively."[5] The editor of the *Credit Card Marketing News-*

letter says that although banks have become more aware of the potential of segmented marketing, they still haven't recognized the value of cultivating the women's market. "When it comes to women, banks still have not come of age . . . it's a man-oriented industry. When a bank thinks of a household it still thinks of the man of the house."[6]

As women become more interested and involved in financial activities, the banking community has gone through its own evolving awareness of the value of the women's market. The 1970s saw the dawn of a new type of financial institution, the women's bank. At that time, women were being discriminated against by conventional banks and lending institutions. The women's bank evolved to give women who are credit-worthy their own channel into financial activity. At the time the first women's bank was founded there was real discrimination against women among conventional banks.

In 1977 laws against sex discrimination in banking changed the situation dramatically. In addition, women are becoming increasingly sophisticated about money matters. They want banking services without reference to the gender of the bank's management.

This change in context is paralleled by a change in emphasis by the management of the First Women's Bank. The current president, Judy E. Hendren Mello says that "a bank by any name must first of all be a bank." As reported in the *American Banker:* "Above all, Ms. Mello said, First Women's must be a professionally managed, successful bank. 'We have to be operationally perfect,' she said flatly. 'If a person is a successful professional,' she said, 'the last thing she or he wants to do is deal with a bank that is not successful.'"[7]

Madelon Talley, director of investing for New York State, is quoted as saying: "One-branch women's banks can't attract customers just because they are women. People want a bank close to them at home and in the office. You won't walk twenty blocks to cash a check just to do something for womankind."[8]

Judy Mello points out that the First Women's Bank is not competing for mass market retail services but rather for specialty services: "We encourage our clients to maintain a second account for convenience and transactional services at a big bank if that is important to them." Ms. Mello explained her approach as follows: "A Bank by any name has to be a Bank and has to be judged accordingly, which means 'bottom line'. Three objectives are required: a fair return to its investors; good service to its customers; and it has to be a credit to its community. As a women's Bank we have an additional responsibility to provide fair and non-discriminatory services to women and women's organizations in our community. The Board of Directors of the First Women's Bank not only accepted that premise but they have given me full support."[9]

"There are now eight women's banks around the country in San Francisco, Los Angeles, Denver, Richmond, Washington, Rockville, Maryland, Greenwich, Connecticut, and New York. To a woman, their profit-oriented presidents say that the idea of a bank set up primarily to serve the special needs of women had become obsolete . . . thanks to laws against sex discrimination in banking, to the major banks' discovery of the marketing among women, to the growing sophistication of women and the desire to join the mainstream. 'The concept of a women's bank was transitional,' said Eve Grover, president of The First Women's Bank of Maryland, established in 1979, in a suburb of Washington. . . . 'As women become more and more integrated into the financial community, we are all evolving into full-service community based banks. Our bank might well be the last women's bank to be formed.'

"The president of Connecticut Women's Bank echoed the thought: 'Everything I'm doing here is for growth and the botton line,' said Mabel E. Hamilton, who like Mrs. Grover, spent more than thirty years in banking. 'I don't distinguish us from any other small bank except that we take an extra personal interest in our customers.'

"Rita Hauser, partner of the law firm Stroock, Stroock, & Lavan, has said: 'When this women's bank thing started the big banks were still unresponsive to women, but they finally woke up to the fact that they have a great clientele in women.'"[10]

One major bank has begun an active program to reach that "great clientele." In 1980 Chase Manhattan, the third largest bank in the country, launched what the *New York Times* described as "an aggressive marketing program" to cultivate the women's market. According to the report, Chase has identified women, especially those in business and the professions, as a potentially lucrative segment of the banking market. The program is built around the Chase Exchange, which "was designed to serve the specific banking needs of women." But neither David Rockefeller, the chairman of the bank, nor his colleagues were very specific about how these needs differed from men's banking needs. Among the services being offered for an annual fee of $36.00 are booklets about sound financial planning, a newsletter, seminars, a referral service for financial professionals, and a "hot line" to find out about Chase services.

The concept of a banking facility designed to meet the special needs of women customers is analogous to the development of special career departments and fashion counseling services, which have grown up among fashion retailers. In both cases major marketers have become aware of the need to cultivate the women's market. Whether or not special career departments or special banking centers are the most effective way to accomplish that cultivation remains to be seen. Catherine Willis, the Chase second vice president assigned to run the Chase Exchange, says, "A separate banking facility for women was necessary because women are different from men in confidence levels and in willingness to take risks. The differences," she added, "are in degree rather than in kind."[11]

How does their position in the life cycle impact on women's financial activities? We have seen that just under three out of five of all women are married. The Virginia Slims report indicated that unmarried women are more independent in financial matters than their married sisters. To sort out the relationship of marital status and New Demographic typology, let us consider the financial behavior of married women among the four New Demographic segments.

Marriage and Money

How does marriage relate to money and what does this tell us about the changing customers for financial services? The way that a couple handles their money and their attitudes about it tell a great deal about their relationship. Pat Carbine has said that money is the ultimate intimacy. And in many ways it is. Back in the days when men were men and women knew their place, Big Daddy doled out his wife's allowance. Her only experience with money management was how to squeeze out a few pennies every week for her sugarbowl. In that kind of relationship, money is a symbol of power, and it is very clear who was in charge. As an article in *Forbes* magazine says, "The traditional women left all money decisions to husbands—but wives are now asserting their right to have a say in family financial decisions."

There is a good deal of evidence that the majority of housewives want to share in the family's financial decisions. To quote *Forbes:* "*Family Circle Magazine*—that voice of the contented homemaker—has turned up widespread evidence of wifely dissatisfaction over who controls the purse-strings. Even the most husband oriented wife is reluctant to allow him to put her on an allowance and dispose of what is

left over himself." According to the *Yankelovich Monitor,* about
three out of four women, both housewives and working women, feel
that husbands and wives should have equal responsibility "deciding
how much should be spent on major purchases and deciding on the
family financial philosophy: how much to save, how much to spend,
etc."[12]

How does this translate into the way they handle their money and
their financial activities?

• Career wives are clearly the most financially active of all segments
of married women. Interestingly, they are not seconded in their degree
of financial activities by working women who consider their work
"just a job," but rather by plan-to-work housewives. Whether we examine checking accounts, savings accounts, or investments, career
wives are substantially over the norm of the total population in their
degree of financial activity.

• Plan-to-work housewives are more likely than their stay-at-home
neighbors to have checking accounts or savings accounts.

• Although "just a job" working women are slightly above the
norm in having these kinds of bank accounts, they do not do so to the
same extent as the plan-to-work housewife.

• The one financial area in which stay-at-home housewives are
more active than their plan-to-work neighbors is in investments. Here,
"just a job" women are below the norm. However, career wives tower
over any other segment of married women in the degree to which they
participate in investing.

• A similar pattern carries over to the use of credit cards. Clearly,
the married women in all new demographic categories are the most
likely to have department store charge cards and use them. However,
career wives are far more likely than any other group to have such
charge cards, and they are followed in this by plan-to-work housewives. Stay-at-home housewives are above the norm in having such
cards but are less likely to have them than "just a job" working wives.

• When it comes to bank credit cards, the picture is somewhat different. Career wives dominate the bank credit card scene; they are
echoed in this, but at a much lower level, by the plan-to-work housewives. In turn, plan-to-work housewives are twice as likely as "just a
job" working wives to use such bank cards. And stay-at-home housewives are barely over the norm in using this kind of charge card.

• When it comes to travel and entertainment cards, however, it is
only career wives who work strongly above the norm. All other seg-

ments of married women are far below par in having access to Diners Club, American Express, or any of the other travel and entertainment charge cards.

What does this imply for financial marketing? It's become clear that not all bank consumers are alike and that the financial behavior of married couples differs with the employment of the wife as well as her attitude toward work. Among the families living in the traditional arrangement of breadwinner husband and homemaking wife, husbands are more financially active than their wives. However, the wives are financially active and may become more so.

Money arrangements are also a clue to commitment. Whether or not a joint bank account is a wise choice in terms of estate planning, it does signal mutual trust and mutual commitment. One of the characteristics in some of the new two-career marriages is the reluctance on the part of the wife to give up her newly won financial independence! So their money is handled on a "mine and yours" basis—not as "ours". The two-paycheck households are also two-bank-customer households. Someone has said that the two-income couples represent a new class of affluents with more disposable income and more financial options than almost any other group in the population. Are their financial needs being met? Are marketers still treating the husband as the only relevant financial member of the household?

This brief overview shows that there are real differences in the financial behavior among husbands and wives in each of the New Demographic segments. Husbands of housewives are more active than their wives in financial matters, while working wives as a group are more financially active than full-time housewives. Husbands of "just a job" working women are more financially active than their wives. However, career wives and their husbands are more financially active than any other segment of married couples. But this examination of their behavior does not reveal the dynamics of how these husbands and wives feel about money matters or the extent to which financial decisions are shared or still determined by the husband.

So in addition to considering their objective behavior, it is useful to understand the changing perceptions of husbands and wives in relation to financial matters.

Some couples follow the traditional pattern in which the husband handles all the financial matters and the wife is completely dependent on the money he doles out. Many of these women are totally unaware of either the realities or the mechanics of financial management. Some love the sense of dependency. One stay-at-home housewife in Chicago said: "My husband takes care of it and I am delighted. I feel he earns the money so he should see where it's all going to. I took care of it for a while and we had a royal battle once and I said, 'You take care of it!' and he's been doing it ever since then. I get my money for grocery shopping and a little bit extra and I think it works out real well. I do everything else in the house and that's his baby."

Some resent the need to ask their husbands for money. In some of these households the wife doesn't even have the structure of a definite allowance within which to manage her household budget. "I feel very dependent on him. . . . I don't even get an allowance. My father and mother used to give me at least that." "He feels that when I need something I can have the money but I feel that I should be doing my own budgeting. I don't know how to judge how much we're spending per week on groceries and so on . . . it's really difficult to judge. I don't like this method—little dribs and drabs, five dollars here and ten dollars there. I'm often left on Union Turnpike without a dime in my pocket for a meter." "He is from the old school—Italian—where he feels as long as I don't have to work, as long as I don't have money, I can't be a women's libber." "Men like that hold over you."

On the other hand, there is a real sense of partnership and sharing in many households. These wives feel a sense of pride in their confidence at managing the flow of money and gratification from having some control over it: "My husband is self-employed and I do the books for the business and the tax forms and the house bookkeeping and balance the checkbook. I love it. We'll generally have a discussion about the things we want to buy and then my husband will say, 'Well, if you like it, get it,' and that's it. It's nothing mapped out, but I know what's due on the first and the fifteenth, and so I know when we're ahead and when we're short. He gets income tax returns, but I keep the checkbook. He has kept it before, we just go back and forth, but . . . I have it now because I feel I can do a better job."

While these domestic dramas were being played out, a major change in context occurred in 1974 when an amendment to the Equal Credit Opportunity Act opened the way for any married women to establish a credit history in her own name. Although a high proportion of married women in all New Demographic segments use department store charge cards, for the most part those cards are in their husbands' names. As long as the name on the card says "Mrs. John Jones" instead of "Mary Jones," in financial terms Mrs. Jones remains a nonperson.

When the 1977 amendment to the Equal Credit Opportunity Act

was passed, the *New York Times* did an article on the new accessability of credit for women and the extent to which they were availing themselves of this new opportunity. The writer said: "In the past, even when a husband and wife jointly applied for a loan or a credit card and the woman was legally responsible for the debt, the bank or credit card company would record the account only in the name of the husband. In effect the wife did not exist. Today, all new joint loans or accounts must be recorded in both names, *but old accounts will continue the way they have been unless the wife asks that her name be used as well*" (Emphasis added).[13]

The new provisions of the act enable married women to begin to build up credit histories in their own names. The catch is that they have to be aware that they are able to do so and to understand why it is that it is important for them to establish financial identities of their own. The same October 1977 *New York Times* article reported on the change in the law but also commented on the fact that many women were not availing themselves of its benefits. The Equal Credit Opportunity Act guarantees married women not only the right to credit in their own names but also the potential for building their own credit histories on the basis of accounts previously listed in their husbands' names but which they had used as well. It appears, however, that many women are not taking advantage of those rights.

The insurance industry is also going through its own consciousness-raising experience. Traditionally, insurance was sold to the husband and father head of household in order to provide protection for his loved ones. This is confirmed by Phillip H. Dutter in his lecture on "Life Insurance Company Marketing: Time for a New Game Plan?" He says that "the main purpose and value of life insurance—the replacement needs of the breadwinner's income—provide adequate protection for his family. The traditional target for life insurance is the husband and father of the family, probably in his late twenties or early thirties during the years of family formation."[14] This definition of the target customer is a simple demographic one. However, it also suggests an attitudinal dimension: the traditional view that it is the man's responsibility to provide for the protection of his dependent wife and children.

Women distance themselves from discussing the subject of insurance, as it might imply a self-serving mercenary approach to their marriages. Therefore, in traditional households the decision on the technicalities of insurance remain part of the masculine mystique and something that the wife does not understand. "My husband is in the insurance business, so he takes care of the whole thing and it's bad because I'm completely out of it." "When the agent was mapping our insurance plan I was sitting in the background. I don't understand insurance that much—it's like when the lawyer is there to understand his language. It is very difficult, they should have a school that explains."

On the other hand, the increasing trend toward sharing and partnership in financial matters occurring in the households of many married couples across the land is also occurring in relation to insurance decisions. In 1979 *Advertising Age* reported, "Though insurance buying remains largely a male domain, women seem to be taking a bigger part than was commonly believed. A survey conducted for *Newsweek* by Scarborough Research Corporation found that two-thirds of the married women respondents claim decisions to buy life insurance are equally shared."[15]

In 1979 the Insurance Department of the State of New York issued an excellent brochure entitled *Insurance and Women*. The introduction to the brochure recognized the changing roles of men and women in relation to financial matters: "Why women need to know about insurance—insurance is a part of each of our lives . . . traditionally mortgage payments, financing an automobile, homeowners protection, and purchasing of life insurance were considered part of a husband's responsibilities. As women become increasingly involved in family affairs, and contribute to the family income, their need to know more about insurance becomes apparent." This brochure also addresses the contribution of the full-time homemaker to the family's well-being and the reasons why a nonemployed wife should be insured: "As a manager of the home you should be aware of the availability of life and health insurance so that in the event of disability or death, insurance will pay for a person to perform the household duties and responsibilities."

In detailing some of the reasons why women need insurance, one statement is addressed to working wives: "As head of a household or a contributing income producer, you must know how to protect your income for the benefit of your dependents in the event of your disability or death."

These changing perceptions about women's need for insurance began to permeate the state capitals in many parts of the country. In 1977 *Business Week* reported: "The government has opened a new front in its campaign to equalize the treatment of men and women: the 150 billion dollar insurance industry. The full range of insurance practices has come under attack—how insurers select their customers, how they set their rates and how they make up employee benefit packages for companies. Because insurance is regulated primarily by the states, the rules are being changed state by state. . . . In an attempt to achieve national standards, The National Association of Insurance Commissioners has recommended that all states adopt rules of sex bias under their existing powers to define unfair insurance practices.

"'Society is moving toward recognition of equal rights of males and females and this is part of that general movement', says Richard Hemmings of the NAIC's executive staff in Milwaukee. The NAIC model code suggests that pregnancy complications, but not pregnancy itself, be covered like other illnesses; that men and women be equally eligible for all types of insurance; and that marriage have no effect on how much insurance a woman can buy. It would allow women to list their husbands as dependents and ensure that women who work at home or for relatives be considered gainfully employed in situations where men are so considered.

A 1977 *Business Week* article states: "The need for anti-bias rules was dramatized in 1975 by the Illinois Insurance Department which sent hypothetical policy applications to hundreds of insurance companies asking if they would sell the requested disability insurance to a man and woman and at what rate. In one-third of the answers, the insurers said that they would not sell to the woman, even though all other facts about the situation were the same as for the man. Insurers willing to sell to women were quoting rates as high as double those charged men. As a result Illinois made new insurance regulations last July."[16]

Against this backdrop of change, it is not surprising that some insurance companies have begun reassessing their products and their pricing policies toward women. In September 1980 the *New York Times* reported that "one-third of all life insurance policies now being written cover women and insurance companies expect the demand to increase as more families become solely or partly dependent on the income of women and it becomes accepted that work done in the home without pay has monetary value. The new awareness of the women's market has led to new pricing policies and products aimed at women.

"Charging women less for insurance because as a group they outlive men and so are liable for more years of payments is not new. For many years insurance carriers have granted women what is known as a three-year 'setback.' A woman buying a policy at age thirty-five, say, would pay the same amount as a man aged thirty-two, but now that gap in life expectancy has broadened to eight years (77.1 years for females,

69.3 years for males), some companies are moving to equalize life insurance premiums further.

"The Sun Life Group of America became the latest to do so with the introduction of the "Her" life insurance policy, which is based on female life expectancy instead of the three-year setback formula. Those who meet health qualifications and who buy a minimum of $25,000 worth of insurance will pay premiums that Gerhardt M. Hoff, president, said represented a 25 to 40 percent reduction from previous fees.

"The Equitable Life Assurance Society of the United States started giving discounts to women in 1957 and last year began issuing a new classification of policies based on the the current mortality figures for women. The New York Life Insurance Company used a slightly different method for change. In 1978 it added discounts to the three-year setback system."[17]

And of course the change has spilled over into advertising approaches. In 1979 *Advertising Age* reported the prediction of their columnist Sid Bernstein on how advertising will change in the 1980s. Bernstein used an illustration of insurance advertising as an example of how change has impacted on advertising. "Setting the scene with U.S. census reports population shifts and the number of women now working," Mr. Bernstein illustrated how advertising depicts these shifts. "For instance, a 1970 New York life insurance printed ad featured the head of the household as a man who felt 'Ten Feet High,' as protector and provider for this family. The company's current ad featured the family's two bread-winners, the husband and the wife."[18]

Money and the Unmarried Woman

What about the other side of the life cycle spectrum, the unmarried? Two out of five American women are not married. This group includes single women who have never married, the divorced, the separated, and the widowed. Of these, 35 percent have neither husband nor child in their homes at present. Not all people without spouses are necessarily swinging singles. The unmarried cluster at both ends of the age spectrum. And, of course, the financial needs of the two age groups are very different. Let's take a look at the financial profiles of unmarried working women.

• Among unmarried women in the work force, as among their married sisters, career-oriented working women are the most financially active group. They are above the norm of the total population in having checking and savings accounts and slightly above par in investing.

• Unmarried "just a job" working women, on the other hand, are somewhat below the norm in having checking accounts. Although they are likely to have savings accounts, they do not do so nearly to the extent as their career-oriented counterparts.

• When we examine the credit card picture, it becomes clear that unmarried women who consider the work they do just a job are not a factor in the credit market at all. They are even below the norm in having department store charge cards.

• On the other hand, unmarried career women are substantially above the norm of the total population in charging at department stores, in using bank credit cards, and in using travel and entertainment credit cards.

If ever there was evidence that the New Demographic typology defines two very different segments among the working women's market, the use of credit cards is a clear discriminator.

Unmarried working women, particularly career women, represent real opportunity markets for financial marketers. Women in this segment are building toward their independence. While this might have been customary for men, this is a new dimension for women. As *Forbes* says, "As single women, they are using investments to cushion their lives now and when they retire."

The New York State booklet on insurance points out one of the main reasons why unmarried women should be knowledgeable about insurance is that they need to plan and prepare for their own future: "As an income producer, you should be concerned with adequate financial preparation for retirement. What type of insurance can help most in a basic retirement program? Do you need insurance to fund a retirement plan?"

As unmarried women gain understanding on the need to be responsible for their own financial futures their financial priorities are changing. This has made them very good prospects for investment. A 1977 *U.S. News and World Report* article states: "Just a decade or so ago, the investment office along LaSalle Street, the heart of Chicago's financial district, dealt almost exclusively with men. That is no longer the case. More women customers are showing up and the same thing holds true in financial firms in other cities. As increasing numbers of women are joining the work force, more of them are trying to build financial security through savings and investment . . . money managers know the female investor has become a steadily growing force in financial markets.

"'Just in the past five years,' said one Midwestern banker, 'we've seen a turning point in the way single women and perhaps women in general relate to financial matters.'"[19]

The article cites a few case histories of unmarried women who are taking charge of their own financial affairs.

• "Karen Munson, 32 and single, a classical music critic for a Chicago newspaper . . . jolted by the comment of a friend who told her it was time to stop assuming that a husband would support her in the future, Munson visited a stockbroker. By investing about ten percent of her income, she has kept ahead of inflation, 'Now I come home from writing about music and open up the paper to the market quotations,' Munson says. 'I think about how I can take care of myself financially—even if I'm married.'

• "Susan Darby, A Chicago stockbroker . . . finds that 'single and divorced women used to be frightened at the prospect of walking into a brokerage firm or even a savings institution. Now they come in and want to know how corporate stocks compare with municipal bonds or savings certificates.'

• "'For many single women "investment clubs" have replaced the macramé lessons they used to take to keep busy,' says Helen McLane, herself single and author of a book about such clubs. She says that there are 300 investment groups in the Chicago area, with each member chipping in ten dollars or more a month. McLane notes, 'Women enjoy the challenge of investing as much as men do.'

• "Marge Beleckis, a Chicago securities broker, has about 200 women clients. She starts them with an investment package of A-grade utility stocks that can yield 8–9%. She encourages them to re-invest dividends. 'As their assets increase,' says Beleckis, 'women more subconsciously trim living expenses to put more money into stocks. If they marry, they are likely to retain the portfolio and add to it.'"[20]

Unmarried women are also beginning to invest in real estate, both condominiums and suburban houses. Of course, the change in the credit law has made it possible for them to do so. The Equal Credit Opportunity Act has particular relevance for the formerly married women who are either divorcees or widows.

After a lifetime of nonparticipation in financial matters, a widow is suddenly in possession of the proceeds of life insurance and possibly stocks and mutual funds as well. It is not news that women have had a higher proportion of the nation's wealth in their hands. However, by and large they have been passive in its management, leaving the decisions to their husbands or his professional surrogates. We speculate that this is probably the last generation that will be quite so passive and helpless in dealing with money.

The opportunities for financial marketers are manifest. Unfortunately, the more protective the husband, and the more he has sought to shelter his wife from the crass realities of the market place, the more likely it is that she will find the transition to financial responsibility traumatic. One unexpected legacy to the wife who has lived in this traditional life style is that in financial terms she is a nonperson. The excellent booklet on women and credit prepared by Citibank instructs women on how to establish their own identities as financially responsible individuals.

Think of the recently bereaved widow, suddenly having to cope with the unfamiliar and bewildering territory of financial management. What would happen at most banks if she notified them of her change of status, whether it involved canceling her husband's credit card, changing the the name on the bank account, and so on? In view of the trend toward automation in banking, whom would she talk to and how would she be handled? This represents an opportunity for banks to establish the kind of personal banking relationships that some of their experts talk about. If not, they run the risk of leaving the widow frustrated and bewildered if she receives an impersonal bureaucratic response.

Obviously, a widow is better able to cope if she has had some prior experience in money handling. This is one strong reason why even the most traditional-minded husband should share his financial plans with his wife. This suggests a number of opportunities for bankers and for financial marketers. They should consider some humane and personalized ways of dealing with the recent widow so that her interaction with the bank will be a comfort rather than an additional trauma. Banks should think about developing some estate planning and money management courses for married couples or for married women while their husbands are still alive. These need to be positioned carefully and positively. The insurance industry knows how emotionally charged the subject of a spouse's eventual death can be. Both husband and wife are reluctant to think about it, and many wives feel that even thinking about such matters implies a cold-blooded opportunism, so they'd rather not consider the subject at all. And, of course, if a widow has lived in a traditional life style, she probably has no financial history, and therefore in the eyes of the credit bureau she may be a nonperson.

An example of this was cited by Shoshana Cardin, chairman of the Maryland Commission for Women: "A woman who had been a widow for eleven years maintains her accounts in her husband's name with a 'Mrs.' in front of it. She decided to start using her own name. But when she applied for credit, she was turned down as unqualified because of the absence of any credit history. She will now have to show that she was the Mrs. John Doe who already had this good credit history. It will be be a step-by-step process, rather than the automatic one that would have taken effect if she had been using her name all along."[21]

Any estate planning or money management courses aimed at married women must be positioned so that the most protective, traditional-minded husband would feel he was providing his wife with the ultimate protection by preparing her to deal with the eventual financial responsibilities instead of having them suddenly thrust upon her. Mrs. Cardin suggested that it is important to educate women about their credit rights and "to explain to husbands that an independent credit history is not a threat, just a form of insurance for the future and an educational process for the woman."[22]

This kind of education in money management is extremely relevant, of course, to all younger married couples who are tending toward shared financial decision-making, even though many do not feel that they have adequate financial know-how.

Notes

1. The Virginia Slims American Women's Opinion Polls, New York: The Roper Organization, 1972 and 1980.
2. *Ibid.,* pp. 96–97.
3. Based on special JWT analyses of TGI data.
4. Josh Levine, "Interbank Touts Clout for Women," *Advertising Age,* April 16, 1979.
5. *Ibid.*
6. *Ibid.*
7. Teresa Carson, "New President of 1st Women's Vows Evaluation of Each Service," *American Banker,* June 1980.
8. Ann Crittenden, "Women's Banks: An Idea Whose Allure Has Faded," *New York Times,* August 4, 1980.
9. Judy Mello, speech given at the Third National Women in Crisis Conference, June 28–July 2, 1981 (photocopied).
10. Ann Crittenden, "Women's Banks: An Idea Whose Allure Has Faded."

11. Robert A. Bennett, "With Dainty Touches, Chase Aims at Women," *New York Times,* October 24, 1980.

12. *The Yankelovich Monitor* (annual) (New York: Yankelovich, Skelly, and White), 1972–81.

13. Frances Cerra, "Educating Women about Credit Rights," *New York Times,* October 9, 1977.

14. Phillip H. Dutter, cited in Rena Bartos "The Customer for Life Insurance: A Moving Target" (speech given to the Life Insurance Advertisers Assoc., September 15, 1976) (photocopied), p. 2.

15. *Advertising Age,* June 25, 1979.

16. "Bringing Sexual Equality to Insurance," *Business Week,* May 23, 1977, p. 116.

17. Nadine Brozan, "Insurance: New Policies Toward Women," *New York Times,* September 22, 1980.

18. "Marketing Challenge of the '80s: Shift with Times," *Advertising Age,* September 3, 1979.

19. "It's Not Only Men with Extra Cash" *US News and World Report,* December 5, 1977, p. 32.

20. *Ibid.*

21. Frances Cerra, "Educating Women About Credit Rights."

22. *Ibid.*

IV

Changing Advertising

Chapter 15

How Have the Changes in Women's Lives Been Reflected in Advertising?

We have reviewed the changes in women's lives. We have explored ways to link the new realities to our marketing procedures. And we have examined how women's changing life styles impact on the way they respond to media and how they behave in the market place. How have the dramatic changes in the way that women live, in their aspirations, and in their behavior been reflected in advertising? Depending on one's perspective and experience, this question can be answered in several ways.

Certainly, in the early 1970s there was no sudden and dramatic change in the way women were portrayed in advertising. In a seminar on this eternal subject of the image of women in advertising in 1976, I summed up the situation as follows: "I think we honestly have to agree that we have been showing women in terribly limited ways. Just pretend that you are a visitor from another planet and all you know about the women of America is what you see on TV. You would see the lady alone in her kitchen, polishing her floor, getting the whitest, cleanest, brightest wash in town and dishes you can see your face in. Once in a while she ventures out of the house to get a manicure with Madge or she drops into the supermarket to catch Mr. Whipple squeezing the Charmin. On the way home she pops into Cora's shop to get a little advice on how to make better coffee. Back at home she vacuums her living room until hubby returns from the office to announce that he smells clean. After all this she goes into a little low down music and prepares for an Aviance night."[1]

A number of academic surveys of the portrayal of women in advertising confirm the fact that not much has changed. In 1975 the National Advertising Review Board Consultive Panel reviewed the available data on the subject and reported the following:

"A study reported in the Journal of Marketing Research during 1971 found that magazine advertising reflected four stereotypes: 'A woman's place is in the home'; 'Women do not make important decisions or do important things'; 'Women are dependent on men and need their protection'; 'Men regard women primarily as sex objects—they are not interested in women as people.'

"The evidence is clear that in both broadcast and print advertising, although the situation continues to change, working women are underrepresented. A study of 'The Image of Women in Network TV Commercials' was reported in the *Journal of Broadcasting* in 1972. On the basis of a content analysis of 986 prime time commercials, the authors concluded that 'women are most often seen as decorative (sex objects) or as useful (housewives and mothers), but hardly ever as professionals or working wives.' Men were twice as frequently shown in outdoor or business settings as were women. When not in the home, women were shown in a limited number of roles such as secretaries or stewardesses. Only 18 different occupations were shown for women in contrast to 43 for men. In the sample of television commercials, there were no women lawyers, doctors, business executives, scientists, engineers, athletes, professors, or judges.

"Two different studies of the content of advertisements in general mass magazines were reported in the *Journal of Marketing Research,* one in 1971 and one in 1973. In the 1971 study, only nine percent of the women in the ads were shown in working roles, as compared with 45% of the men. Women workers were underrepresented both in numbers and in the range or variety of their occupational roles. More than half of the women shown in working roles were entertainers. If entertainers of both sexes were removed from the sample, the proportion of women workers in the ads would have been only seven percent. None were professional or high-level business executives.

"The 1973 study in the *Journal of Marketing Research* revealed an improvement in the types of women's roles portrayed in magazine advertisements. The proportion of working women rose from 9% to 21%—a remarkable change in emphasis. A smaller percentage of working women in the 1973 study were entertainers or sports professionals. More women were depicted in other responsible working capacities, such as in professional, sales, middle-level business, semi-professional, and similar occupations.

"A longer time perspective is provided by a study of 'Women in Magazine Advertisements' reported in the August 1974 issue of the *Journal of Advertising Research.* Comparing ads in mass magazines from 1950 to 1971, some increase was noted in the number of women who were shown working, although at 'traditional' tasks. The other side of the coin is that there was a substantial decrease in ads portraying women as housewives or mothers. The conclusion of the author, however, was that 'the overall results would appear to corroborate feminist charges that the images of women reflected in the ads are quite narrow.'"[2]

On the other hand, in the early 1970s change did begin to creep into the way women were shown in advertising. It was not the kind of fundamental change that might have been expected if advertisers had taken the changing role of women seriously and built it into their marketing procedures. But creative people are responsive to change. Their antennae are out. They may not have any profound information base to document why they begin to see consumers differently, but their intuitive sense of changing atmospheres and changing contexts often anticipates the changed facts of the market place.

The first breakthroughs occurred in the early 1970s. Advertisments began showing women in nonstereotyped roles. We began to see female pilots, female jockeys, and female newscasters as protagonists in commercials. These types of women were not necessarily the target consumers for the advertised product, but the fact that they were used in advertising was a marvelous creative reflection of change. Casting commercials with women in these unusual occupations seemed to freshen the advertising, add interest, and keep it looking contemporary.

One example of such offbeat casting of women was in the Champion spark plug commercial, "Florida Fly In." The point of the commercial was to demonstrate the efficacy of Champion spark plugs by reporting that test pilots use them in their own planes. Creative excitement was added to this rather standard advertising format by casting the commercial with a female test pilot rather than the expected man. Obviously the creative people were not identifying women pilots as a new marketing target. Their purpose was to add freshness and interest to an otherwise expected commercial format. And it succeeded.

Another example of this kind of offbeat casting was in the use of a female jockey in a Listerine commercial, one of a series in which the protagonist was asked by an off-screen interviewer how he or she felt about the taste of Listerine. The answer invariably was: "I hate it, but I use it twice a day." The dialogue played on the contrast between the user's dislike of the taste of the product and his or her appreciation of the efficacy of its results. Viewer involvement was created by casting each commercial with an unusual or distinctive kind of character. The series included an actor being interviewed for the part of a dock worker, a school crossing guard, and the female jockey just mentioned. In no case were any of these colorful characters intended to exemplify the marketing target of the campaign. Presumably the market for female jockeys is as limited as that for female airline pilots.

Another use of offbeat or unexpected casting is to provide creative surprise. One commercial done a few years ago by my agency starts out like a conventional product commercial. It was produced for the American Gas Association, and it obviously predates the energy crunch. It shows a young couple on a patio preparing to entertain the husband's boss. The husband expresses surprise that the wife is using her gas grill because the boss is coming for dinner. The wife explains that anything she can cook on her kitchen stove can also be prepared on this wonderful gas appliance. She demonstrates the attractive menu sizzling away on the grill. The husband responds by nuzzling his wife and telling her how wonderful she is. She acts a bit embarrassed and says, "Honey, your boss is here." The snapper ending provided the element of surprise. The boss turned out to be a tall, beautifully groomed woman!

Another commercial that used this sort of surprise ending was one for Illinois Bell Telephone Company called "The History of Dialing." This traced the use of telephones since the earliest days and showed a series of rather nostalgic vignettes in which a man is trying to make a telephone call to a girl. It goes from the earliest predialing days when the man talks to the operator by saying, "Hello, central," to the earliest use of the dial. The final scene shows a contemporary looking phone with the dial contained in the body of the phone itself. This time the person doing the dialing and inviting a member of the opposite sex to dinner turns out to be a beautifully groomed woman in an office setting. She is obviously a very sophisticated career woman. The surprise is in the role reversal. The woman is inviting the man to dinner. The voice-over says: "Now, that's progress!"

Other ways in which changing attitudes toward women were reflected in advertising were in commercials featuring women in prestigious or unusual occupations. These women achievers were used to demonstrate the advertiser's awareness of the contemporary scene. These women were meant to be either an analogy for product excellence or a symbol of the advertiser's sensitivity to change. They were not the target customers for the product advertised.

One example of this approach was the commercial for Purolator called "Hospital." This one showed a female surgeon explaining why the hospital with which she was affiliated used Purolator filters. In a sense she was cast as an endorser or testimonee in this particular commercial, particularly when she was shown in her occupational role in her operating gown. Then we saw her in her normal street clothes leaving the hospital, and getting into her car. There she continued to endorse Purolator filters by explaining that she used them in her car as well and that she found them of great value. The special feature of this commercial was that it used an authoritative, professional woman as an authority figure to endorse the quality of the product.

A slightly different use of a female professional is the Busch Beer commercial, "Zoo." This one shows a female veterinarian working with animals. While she cares for them, she talks about her lifelong aspiration to become a vet and how much she enjoys pursuing this satisfying career. The commercial draws an analogy between her commitment to excellence in her profession and the Busch Beer commitment to excellence in the products they make.

Some advertisers began shattering stereotypes by developing commercials that recognized that older women are attractive or want to be attractive. This is a refreshing break with the stereotyped approach to cosmetic advertising that cast commercials with young, impossibly beautiful glamour girls. It is addressed to target customers who might be in their thirties or forties or beyond. These advertisements make the point that middle-aged women want to and can be attractive. What's more, they recognize the fact that middle-aged women are good customers for cosmetic products or products with cosmetic benefits.

One of these is an Ivory Liquid commercial called "Young Looking Hands." An attractive and vital looking forty-four-year-old mother is shown romping on the grass with her young child. She is interviewed in what purports to be a candid interview and shows the reporter how young her hands look. The point of the commercial is that she is youthful and active and uses Ivory Liquid for her dishes because it helps her hands look young at any age.

Another commercial developed by Clairol for their Loving Care product dramatizes the trend toward middle-aged women's returning to or entering the work force. This presents a motivation for the use of a cosmetic product that goes beyond women's desire to be attractive to men. It shows how grooming can reinforce a woman's sense of self-worth. The camera shows a living room. A woman's voice talks about the fact that when her children were growing up she promised herself she wouldn't cry when they left home but that, of course, she did. As the camera shows the beautifully polished floor, table, and accoutrements of a very attractive suburban living room, she says that she could have gone on polishing the floor again or waxing the furniture or even redoing the closets, but she realized that she was the one that needed redoing. So she went on a diet, lost ten pounds, and bought some new clothes. All the while the camera is showing her hands unfolding a dress from the box. We do not see the woman herself until the very end. Then she goes on to say that she realized she didn't need gray hair. We see the back of her head in the bathroom using the product while she talks about the product benefits. She goes on to say that she then looked for a job. The final scene shows the woman herself looking impossibly young for her claimed age of forty, in which she says, "I'm forty, I've got a new job, and I've only just begun." She flings a raincoat over her shoulder and walks out of the house.

I describe this commercial in such detail because it has elicited rounds of applause from audiences every time I have shown it. It really seems to have captured one of the elements of the quiet revolution. It is a marvelously empathetic presentation of a cosmetic product. It is not a put-down, and it shows that there are motivations for women to improve their looks that go beyond the old cliché of getting or keeping a man.

Two advertisers who have reflected the demographic change we refer to as the "quiet revolution" are a bank, the Cleveland Trust Company, and Nationwide Insurance. The Cleveland Trust commercial recognizes the fact that many women are reentering the work force and that many of them are seeking to complete their advanced education before they do so. The "Back to School" commercial shows an older woman mounting the steps of a college. She explains that now that her family has grown she wants to go back and complete her own education. She talks about how the Cleveland Trust Bank has helped her achieve her goal of returning to school.

The insurance commercial is particularly interesting, because traditionally insurance companies have targeted their advertising and their sales efforts toward the husband and father head-of-household. The Nationwide Insurance "Working Women" commercial recognizes the fact that there is diversity among women in the work force. It shows a montage of working wives, of young career girls just starting out, and of widows and divorcees going to work. We see them getting on buses, driving their cars, and so on. As the commercial shows the spectrum of different types of women who are in the work force the voice-over talks about why women need insurance and recognizes the fact that women are just as viable customers as men are for financial products such as insurance. This particular commercial is a real reflection of social change.

Somewhere in the middle 1970s we began to see a variety of commercials that showed working women as valid customers for advertised products. Only then did we begin to see the new kinds of targets recognized in advertising. The Nationwide Insurance commercial just described is one example of this.

Two others in more traditional female product categories are the Stayfree Maxi Pad "Busy Reporter" commercial and the Stouffer's "Career Girl" commercial. The first uses a mini-drama in a commercial format known as "slice of life." In this two young women are rushing down the steps of a building and into a car. Their conversation identifies them as reporters. The younger reporter asks the older one how she copes with the demands of her profession. The older reporter points to a package of the product, which happens to be on the car seat. She advises the younger one to try them because they are so convenient. While the slice-of-life format of this commercial is fairly traditional, the use of two working women not only as protagonists but as target consumers for the advertised product is a reflection of change.

Stouffer's "Career Girl" is a straightforward commercial in which we see a well-groomed young woman in horn-rimmed glasses at her desk preparing to leave at the end of a busy working day. She says that she worked very hard that day, but thanks to Stouffer's she won't have to cook that night, because she's using one of Stouffer's prepared products. Again, this rather overt approach underlines the need of working women for convenience foods and does identify working women as the target consumers for this particular product.

As change occurs in women's lives, it also affects the lives of the people around them. One result of the surge of working wives into the work force is the change in attitude on the part of many of their husbands. There is a move toward sharing and partnership in many of these households. We have begun to see commercials that show husbands participating in all sorts of household chores. This type of advertising would not have been dreamed of five or ten years ago.

One example is the charming Campbell's Soup "Working Wife," which uses a rather catchy song and shows a young husband in an attractive kitchen preparing dinner. As he goes about his chores of opening a can of soup, cutting up some salad, and setting the table, he sings a song in which he says that he has a working wife and that one thing he doesn't need at the end of the day is a heavy meal. And one thing she doesn't need at the end of the day is to have to cook. So, he is helping with dinner. The wife appears in the final scene, having returned from work. The husband points out that he is using Campbell's tomato soup and says, "After all, red is her color." The young wife is wearing a red dress. The husband lights candles, and they settle down in front of the fireplace for a cozy domestic evening.

Another example of husbands' participation is the commercial done for Scott Baby Fresh Wipes. We see a young father diapering a baby. He is an attractive, credible looking young man in horn-rimmed glasses with his sleeves rolled up. He obviously enjoys caring for his child. He sings a rather engaging song to the tune of "Baby Face" in which he extols the virtues of the product. The baby's happy gurgling confirms that the baby is enjoying the procedure. The one unusual thing about this commercial is, of course, that the father, rather than the mother, is diapering the baby. This happens to be one of the commercials that was tested in the project discussed in Chapter 17. It happened to be the most appealing commercial of all those we tested. Somehow, there is universal appeal for women today in seeing a young father happily caring for his baby.

As the decade progressed, we began to see a few commercials that shattered still another stereotype: the notion that the car market is a man's market and that women's only role in purchasing a car is to pick the color of the upholstery. While this new perception certainly did not dominate car advertising, there were a few examples that showed women as credible consumers for cars or car-related products. A charming commercial done by B. F. Goodrich for its tires was called "Moosie and Cathy." In this commercial Cathy, an attractive young woman, is shown changing the tires on her car, and Moosie, a football player in uniform, is trying to get her to agree to go to the prom with him. In the course of his courtship, Moosie tries to persuade her to go to the football game with him, promising as an inducement to get her a ride on the Goodrich blimp. She obviously knows that Goodrich doesn't have a blimp, and she straightens him out on the subject. This lighthearted commercial makes the point that Cathy is even more knowledgable about tires and cars then her football-playing boyfriend.

Another commercial that makes the point that women are credible consumers for cars is a Honda commercial called "Why Women Buy Cars." In this one a young woman walks up to the camera and says she has been asked to explain why she bought her Honda. She says that's ridiculous, because women buy cars for pretty much the same reasons as men. She then proceeds to get into her car and go through a series of driving situations that are all slightly humorous. For example, she is at a stop light when a middle-aged man in the next car tries to flirt with her, and she talks about the quick acceleration of a Honda. She talks about the economy of the car as she stops off to buy some flowers. The final scene shows her arriving in front of an imposing mansion, honking the horn, and having her boyfriend come out and get into the car. She gives him the flowers. They both laugh. As they drive off, he says, "I still have to be home by ten." Although this commercial has a great deal of charm and humor in the way it is executed, nonetheless the underlying message is that the woman car owner is competent and knowledgeable about cars. This, I think, is real news in advertising land.

Another way advertisers began to reflect change was to recognize that many young women today aspire to build careers that will go beyond the traditional limited kinds of jobs available in the female ghetto. One example is a U.S. Marine Corps "Career Corps" commercial which shows a young woman getting dressed. As she dresses she talks about her ambitions. She says that she was in the typing pool for many years and then decided that she wanted something better out of life. As she puts on her makeup and buttons her blouse and so on, she explains that now she has the kind of job where she is learning about computers and can really use her mind. She has a real career in the Marines. She calls the Marine Corps the "career corps."

Another commercial that celebrates the achievements of a young woman at the beginning of her career as a professional is the Inglenook "Father and Doctor Daughter," one of a series that tells about the use of Inglenook wine at special occasions. In this case the daughter has just become an M.D., and her father is celebrating the occasion. In the course of the dialogue she reminds her father how he always encouraged her to achieve and to reach for the highest goal. This is a particularly effective presentation of the aspirations of many young women today.

But, of course, women's potential can be realized only if girls growing up understand that there is no societal limit to their aspirations. Many social critics tell us that stereotyping starts in the cradle. Little girls are encouraged to play with dolls, while little boys are encouraged to play more challenging games. Some commercials have shown the positive contribution that advertising can make to society, and they have been sponsored by major corporations. One done by General Motors called "Doll House" uses the actress Anne Jackson to articulate the message. She is shown sitting among girls' toys—doll houses, dolls,—as she explains that while these domestic concerns are wonderful and part of life, little girls need not be limited to only playing at being a mommy or a housewife. She talks about the fact that there are no limits to girls' aspirations today and encourages them to train for any kind of career they wish. She then goes on to explain that at General Motors women are people, too, and that they hire women at all levels.

Eaton Corporation's commercial "Kerry Security" is another example of stereotype-breaking. It is one of a series using the analogy of a child's imagination with the research-and-development kind of creativity that this corporation encourages. In this case the protagonist is a little girl. In this charming commercial Kerry explains that she is tired of having to clean up her own room because it is her sister who always messes it up. She shows an imaginary invention, a special kind of doorknob that locks when her sister tries to open the door. The voice-over says "patent not pending" and goes on to foretell a bright future for people like Kerry, who will be one of the inventors of tomorrow. The point of this commercial is that a little girl can do more than just play with dolls, that she has the kind of creative imagination traditionally ascribed to men.

The advertising that reflects the changing role of women, covered in this brief review, was not the dominant form of advertising in the 1970s. The commercials I have described tended to be the exception rather than the rule. As advertisers recognize the new realities, that recognition could be a springboard to a really new creative breakthrough.

The 1950s was the era of the "Unique Selling Proposition." The 1960s was the era of Doyle Dane's self-deprecation, Mary Wells's recital of life's little indignities, and the creative explosion. In the early 1970s we discovered credibility. An endless string of stand-up announcers and noncelebrity consumer endorsements flowed across the screen (and are still flowing).

The commercials that I have described are refreshing simply because they were the first to recognize change. The problem is that a year or two from now we shall be inundated with a host of imitations. We'll see an endless series of husbands of working wives demonstrating their shinier floors, whiter wash, and convenience dinners. Where do we go from here?

Of course, the safe way would be to turn our backs on consumer imagery and concentrate on the product. A lot of people are doing exactly that right now, but this could lead to another spate of look-alike, not very exciting advertising. Sometimes it's hard to realize that those stubborn consumers just aren't as fascinated by the magic ingredient in our brand of widgets as we are. This approach could be a cop-out. There's got to be a better way!

We may well ask ourselves whether recognizing the diversity in women's lives may lead to an endless series of fractionated segments. Do we really want to develop separate strategies for each type of working woman? For each type of housewife, and so on? Not necessarily.

One of the most brilliant advertising people I know has said that this fresh way of looking at consumers means we break the jigsaw puzzle apart and then put it back together again in a new way. As we put it together, we may find new dimensions that are far more compelling than the clichés of the past. That is where the real breakthroughs will occur. This is where we go beyond the facts of the market place to the art of communication. We have to go beyond the excitement of having discovered new kinds of consumers. We have to experiment and innovate to develop new ways of talking to these new kinds of consumers.

We cannot just put our marketing plans and research to music. We need to find the common threads that run through these consumers' lives and develop advertising that reaches them in their terms, not in ours. And if we do, there is no way that we can be guilty of perpetuating outworn stereotypes of women in our advertising or run the danger of creating new ones.

Of course, the practical realists among us may say that even though we deplore the stereotypes in our ads, they must be working or people wouldn't be buying the products, right? Well, let's remember that currently people don't have any choice. We don't know what will happen when a really innovative marketer studies social change and develops the kind of breakthrough advertising that will work better because it will reach people where they are today.

When that happens, we will have launched that new creative era.

Notes

1. Rena Bartos, "The Opportunities and How to Capitalize on Them," speech given to Advertising Women of New York, February 5, 1976 (photocopied), p. 1.
2. *Advertising and Women: A Report on Advertising Portraying or Directed to Women,* prepared by a Consultive Panel of The National Advertising Review Board, March 1975, p. 7-10.

Chapter 16

Stereotypes, Assumptions, and Advertising Imagery

One of the concomitants of the changing role of women has been a growing consciousness of and concern about the images of women in advertising. Many social commentators believe that the way women are shown in advertising perpetuates outmoded stereotypes and myths. They say that these stereotypes, in turn, reinforce outdated attitudes toward women among both sexes, and particularly among the young.

In the early 1970s the Commission on the Status of Women at the United Nations conducted a study on this issue in twenty-eight countries. They examined the way that women are shown in the media and in advertising. Their conclusions were discouraging: "Women are shown primarily as housewives in commercials, although they comprise from 35 to 55 percent of the labour force of the different countries in the world . . . women are offered, basically, two roles: that of the beautiful, but passive glamour girl, and that of the housewife caring for the home and children. Both are shown as dependent on men and receiving their social identity not in themselves but through men. . . .

"Advertising is the most insidious form of mass media in its portrayal of wives and mothers . . . women seem to be obsessed with cleanliness, placing above-normal emphasis on whiteness, brightness and expressing a gamut of emotions at smelling the kitchen floor or the family wash. Housework is rarely viewed for what it is: a necessary task that is performed in order to make the family comfortable."[1]

A few years later the National Advertising Review Board appointed a consultive panel representing diverse points of view to examine the situation and come up with a point of view for the industry. To a great extent the NARB conclusions parallel those of the United Nations. They too found that women for the most part were shown as either housewives or glamour girls: "One of the most frequently voiced complaints about advertising is that it portrays women too often just as housewives and mothers—shoppers, cleaners, and family cooks—minimizing their roles in the business and professional world and in community affairs. . . .

"The evidence is clear that in both broadcast and print advertising, although the situation continues to change, working women are underrepresented. . . .

"In the advertising of household products, women too often are portrayed as stupid—too dumb to cope with familiar everyday chores, unless instructed by children, or by a man, or assisted by a supernatural male symbol. Even off-camera voice-over announcements are made by predominantly male voices. In many of the commercials the implication is clear that, if carefully told what to do, a woman can use the product. Apparently, however, it takes a man to manufacture the product or to understand its virtues well enough to explain it.

"The advertising of household products often involves psychologically unflattering portrayals of women. In some instances, they are depicted as being obsessed with cleanliness, as being embarrassed or feeling inadequate or guilty because of various forms of household dirt. Other advertisements show women being mean or catty to each other, or being envious or boastful about cooking or cleaning accomplishments in the home.

"The image of the housewife in advertising appears frequently to be not only a circumscribed one, but also that of a person with a warped sense of values.

"Advertisements often feature women's sexuality to the neglect of their individuality. The charge is that advertising portrays women as 'sex objects.'

"The Panel believes there is an important difference between portraying a woman as sexy or as having sex appeal, and portraying her as a sex object. Compared to a vibrant living person with a variety of interests, talents, and normal human characteristics, the woman portrayed as a sex object is like a mannikin, with only the outer shell of a body, however beautiful. . . .

"Some women feel that such single-dimensional portrayals of women as sex objects hamper the development of friendships or love between men and women. Also, they deplore the effect on children's values. Many men share these reactions. . . .

"Even though mores are changing, nudity and suggestiveness are resented by many women. They are considered especially cheapening when the product is totally unrelated to the female body."[2]

The panel offered its conclusions in the form of guidelines for the industry. The guidelines took the form of a checklist of questions[3] for advertisers and agencies to consider as they develop their advertising executions:

"Checklist: Destructive Portrayals

Am I implying in my promotional campaign that creative, athletic, and mind-enriching toys and games are not for girls as much as for boys? Does my ad, for example, imply that dolls are for girls and chemistry sets are for boys, and that neither could ever become interested in the other category?

Are sexual stereotypes perpetuated in my ad? That is, does it portray women as weak, silly, and over-emotional? Or does it picture both sexes as intelligent, physically able, and attractive?

Are the women portrayed in my ad stupid? For example, am I reinforcing the 'dumb blonde' cliché? Does my ad portray women who are unable to balance their checkbooks? Women who are unable to manage a household without the help of outside experts, particularly male ones?

Does my ad use belittling language? For example, 'gal Friday' or 'lady professor?' Or 'her kitchen' but 'his car'? Or 'women's chatter' but 'men's discussions'?

Does my ad make use of contemptuous phrases? Such as 'the weaker sex,' 'the little woman,' 'the ball and chain,' or 'the war department.'

Do my ads consistently show women waiting on men? Even in occupational situations, for example, are women nurses or secretaries serving coffee, etc., to male bosses or colleagues? And never vice versa?

Is there a gratuitous message in my ads that a woman's most important role in life is a supportive one, to cater to and coddle men and children? Is it a 'big deal' when the reverse is shown, that is, very unusual and special—something for which the woman must show gratitude?

Do my ads portray women as more neurotic than men? For example, as ecstatically happy over household cleanliness or deeply depressed because of their failure to achieve near perfection in household tasks?

(A note is needed here, perhaps. It is not the panel's intention to suggest that women never be portrayed in the traditional role of homemaker and mother. We suggest instead that the role of homemaker be depicted not in a grotesque or stereotyped manner, but be treated with the same degree of respect accorded to other important occupations.)

Do my ads feature women who appear to be basically unpleasant? For example, women nagging their husbands or children? Women being condescending to other women? Women being envious or arousing envy? Women playing the 'one-upmanship' game (with a sly wink at the camera)?

Do my ads portray women in situations that tend to confirm the view that women are the property of men or are less important than men?

Is there double entendre in my ads? Particularly about sex or women's bodies?

Checklist: Negative Appeals

Do my ads try to arouse or play upon stereotyped insecurities? Are women shown as fearful of not being attractive to men or to other women, fearful of not being able to keep their husbands or lovers, fearful of an in-law's disapproval, or, for example, of not being able to cope with a husband's boss coming for dinner?

Does my copy promise unrealistic psychological rewards for using the product? For example, that a perfume can lead to instant romance.

Does my ad blatantly or subtly suggest that the product possesses supernatural powers? If believed literally, is the advertiser unfairly taking advantage of ignorance? Even if understood as hyperbole, does it insult the intelligence of women?

Checklist: Constructive Portrayals

Are the attitudes and behavior of the women in my ads suitable models for my own daughter to copy? Will I be happy if my own female children grow up to act and react the way the women in my ads act and react?

Do my ads reflect the fact that girls may aspire to careers in business and the professions? Do they show, for example, female doctors and female executives? Some women with both male and female assistants?

Do my ads portray women and men (and children) sharing in the chores of family living? For example, grocery shopping, doing laundry, cooking (not just outdoor barbecueing), washing dishes, cleaning house, taking care of children, mowing the lawn, and other house and yard work?

Do the women in my ads make decisions (or help make them) about the purchase of high-priced items and major family investments? Do they take an informed interest, for example, in insurance and financial matters?

Do my ads portray women actually driving cars and showing an intelligent interest in mechanical features, not just in the color and upholstery?

Are two-income families portrayed in my ads? For example, husband and wife leaving home or returning from work together?

Are the women in my ads doing creative or exciting things? Older women, too? In social and occupational environments? For example, making a speech, in a laboratory, or approving an ad?

Checklist: Positive Appeals

Is the product presented as a means for a woman to enhance her own self-esteem, to be a beautiful human being, to realize her full potential?

Does my advertisement promise women realistic rewards for using the product? Does it assume intelligence on the part of women?''

In a special note on humor the report pointed out that ''it is healthy for people to laugh at themselves, but usually this is a luxury only the secure can afford. Effective humor often has a cutting edge, and it requires extraordinary care to insure that the cut is not made at the expense of women's self-esteem.

''In the present context, for example, the Panel suggests extreme caution in making fun of efforts to improve the status of women and the opportunities available to them.''[4]

The NARB Panel called the problem of stereotypes ''an inherent part of our changing social fabric. It is real and will not go away by itself.''[5] The report concluded that changing the stereotypes of women in advertising would accomplish two important goals: It would result in a greater measure of fair treatment for women and would be an intelligent marketing decision. I agree with both of these. But I suggest that they be reversed. It's just plain bad business and bad marketing to insult your customers. And it's plain good business and good marketing to keep in touch with what your customers want and need, and how your product fits into their lives.

One of the things that worries me in this kind of discussion is that when people begin talking about fairness and social issues, they put on their good citizenship, social responsibility haloes. And when they return to the office or to the the client's office, where the real decisions are made, they get back to the practicalities of real-world marketing. Unless we recognize that these goals are two sides of the same coin, we will never solve the problem. The only real way to achieve "a greater measure of fair treatment for women" in advertising is to understand that abolishing stereotypes really *is* "an intelligent marketing decision."

If we are really pragmatic about the facts of the market place, there is no way we can write ads that show women as competitive housewives working to have the whitest wash or the shiniest floor on the block, or as simple-minded slobs, or as simpering idiots. The practical reality is that "Annie doesn't live here any more," and what's more, she probably never did.

A few years ago I was reviewing the way women are portrayed in ads for some of the top management people in my own shop. After screening ads in general, a committee of creative people who happened to be female reviewed a cross-section of commercials produced for every client of the J. Walter Thompson Company. We were happy to find that our company wasn't guilty of any of those put-downs. But at that time, in the early 1970s, all of the ads that included women showed them in strictly traditional roles. After looking at the reel, one of the management men said: "Well, many of those commercials were written by women." I answered that they weren't writing as women, they were writing as professionals. And they were working within a given strategy.

If we are going to close the reality gap between the way we show women in ads and the way they really are, we have to return to those basic strategies.

The Assumptions Behind the Way
We Define the Women's Market[6]

The assumptions about women reflected in most of the advertising we see divide women into the two categories identified by the U.N. study and the NARB: housewife and sex object.

• If the lady is married, she is that mythical heroine of many marketing plans, "any housewife, eighteen to forty-nine." Her greatest joy in life is getting the whitest wash, the cleanest dishes, the shiniest kitchen floor on the block. Her greatest hope is to make a cup of coffee that her husband will find acceptable.

• Or if she is not married, the assumption is that her single goal in life is to change that condition as quickly as possible. So we sell her cosmetics, fragrances, and sexy-looking clothes to help her snag a husband, move into that little white house in the suburbs, and start the cycle all over again.

This view of women defines them in terms of the traditional feminine mystique. The unspoken assumption behind this kind of marketing approach is that women's primary role in life is to care for the emotional and physical needs of their husbands and families. Therefore, their greatest gratifications in life come from their husbands' appreciation or approval.

It's true that many marketers have recognized the fact that women have entered the work force. However, they assume that the working woman has simply taken on a second job and that underneath she still wants to please her husband, nurture her family, and make the best cup of coffee on the block.

The people who make the marketing decisions that result in the advertising we see on the screen have a lot of dollars riding on their judgments. They are very pragmatic and bottom-line–oriented in their approach to marketing and advertising. They invest in careful research and market study before they invest those dollars. We might well ask, if they invest in all this fact-gathering, why the images on the screen are so out of step with reality. Is it because our procedures and marketing tools are out of date? I don't think so. But remember, we are all creatures of our own culture. It is almost impossible for us to have perspective on change while it is happening, because we are all part of the situation.

I have never personally observed anyone in the advertising business consciously deciding to insult, demean, or condescend to women as they go about the business of planning and creating advertising campaigns. People on Madison Avenue (or Lexington Avenue or Michigan Boulevard) simply do not sit around and plot how they can find new ways to put women down in their ads.

When you are swimming, you can't tell whether the water you are in is a pond or a lake. You get that perspective only when you are standing on the shore. We need to build changes in society into our marketing procedures if we are ever really to get those stereotypes out of our ads.

What we need to do is raise the consciousness of everyone concerned in the marketing process about what is happening in people's lives today. We don't need to invent new marketing tools, but we need to challenge the assumptions we make when we apply those tools. (This isn't women's lib, it's marketing lib.) The problem is one not of procedure but of perspective. The potential contribution of those sophisticated marketing tools may be limited by the social perspective of the marketing specialists who use them. The challenge to marketers is to subject their own personal assumptions about society to the kind of objective appraisal they are trained to do so well.

In so doing they may well close the reality gap so deplored by the social critics. In fact, they may discover that they are communicating more effectively with the changing and increasingly sophisticated contemporary consumers. As the NARB points out, "fairness to women" in advertising may turn out to be the most "intelligent marketing decision" that marketers can make today.

Lets Not Create New Stereotypes

And, if we really want to keep stereotypes out of our advertising, let's not invent new ones. As we recognize the importance of working women as a market or as we identify the outward-bound housewife who says she "plans to work," let's not create new, contemporary stereotypes to replace the traditional ones. While we are at it, let's get rid of all those ads that cast the man of the family as old dum-dum who can't do anything right.

If we want to find out how to communicate with our targets, both the old and the new, we need to know how our product or service fits into the context of their lives. And that leads me to a marvelous quotation I'd like to share with you. I saw this in the *New York Times* a few years ago. The column was about women's issues, not about marketing. But I think these words are one clue on how to avoid stereotypes in advertising:

"We are human beings, not a poll. One thing they could do is just listen to what the needs are and then they could accept that those needs are valid. *They can't just assume they know what women want*" (emphasis added).

Let's not "assume we know what women want." "*Just listen to what the needs are.*" Hasn't that always been the essence of good marketing and great advertising?

Stereotyping, of course, is not limited to the advertising industry. We all have our assumptions, our beliefs, our stereotypes about various groups in our population. For example, many social critics have their own stereotypes about Madison Avenue and advertising. They think we are hidden persuaders and manipulators. They believe we can change people's minds, influence them to buy products and even choose a president by pushing a button or sprinkling a little snake oil around.

Of course, advertisers have *their* stereotypes about social critics. Many members of the advertising community dismiss social critics by saying "they are not the mainstream," or "they're a bunch of far-out crazies," or "well, after all, they're not my customers."

Advertisers have equally strong assumptions about the nature of advertising. They insist that "advertising is a mirror of society." They say, "After all, we tested it and it works." "The consumers loved it." "It seems consumers always say, 'It insults my intelligence.' But they're buying the product, aren't they?" These advertisers seem to think that this is the final, irrefutable proof that our critics are wrong.

Where does the truth lie? Critics have their stereotypes about advertising. Advertisers have their own assumptions about women and what they really want. Actually, no one has asked the women themselves how they feel about the images of women in the advertising they see.

So we thought we would ask them. My company conducted a study to learn how a cross-section of women felt about the imagery of women as portrayed in a spectrum of advertising executions. Their responses are reported in the following chapter. Chapter 18 will discuss the issues that underlie those responses.

Notes

1. United Nations Economic and Social Council, Commission on the Status of Women, *Influence of Mass Communication Media on the Formation of a New Attitude Towards the Role of Women in Present-Day Society,* January 1974, p. 15.

2. *Advertising and Women: A Report on Advertising Portraying or Directed to Women,* prepared by a Consultive Panel of the National Advertising Review Board, March 1975, pp. 6–7, 9, 11–12.

3. *Ibid.,* pp. 15–19.

4. *Ibid.,* p. 20.

5. *Ibid.,* p. 6.

6. Parts of this chapter are taken from a proprietary report of a study conducted at J. Walter Thompson by Rena Bartos in 1979 on the imagery of women in advertising.

Chapter 17

How Women Respond to the Imagery of Women in Advertising[1]

The Recurring Questions

As I have discussed the changing role of women on a number of professional platforms in the past few years, certain questions have been asked over and over again. As advertisers and other marketing professionals hear and accept the fact that there have been important changes in women's lives, they ask:

- Does this mean they require separate strategies?
- How should we advertise to the new/working/career woman?
- Do we need to show her in her occupational role to reach her?
- How do housewives feel about seeing "new" women in advertising?
- Are housewives turned off by seeing working women in ads?

How We Answered Them

The answers to these constantly recurring questions lie in the concept of stimulus/response. The stimulus we used was a reel of twelve commercials that ran the gamut of imagery of women and creative approaches addressed to them. It cut across many product fields.

Responses to this stimulus were obtained from a cross-section of women representing the New Demographics groups in equal numbers in the course of a two-phase research program.

The exploratory phase was used to narrow down the number of commercials to be used for ultimate testing and to define the attitudinal issues to be quantified.

• The way we did this was to conduct group interviews in New York, Chicago, and Toronto. We conducted group interviews with each of the four New Demographics segments in each market.

• We showed a reel of twenty-five commercials and obtained the women's emotional responses to the commercials they saw based on a "like/dislike" scale ranging from "liked very much" to "disliked very much."

• As they discussed each commercial they were able to tell us what there was about it that they liked or disliked. These spontaneous responses gave us the basis for the attitudinal statements to be quantified in the next stage of the research.

We were able to identify the twelve commercials out of the twenty-five that elicited the sharpest range of response and seemed to be most discriminating. These were retained for final testing.

The quantified phase employed individual interviews.

• Respondents were shown the twelve commercials one at a time and given a self-administered form on which they rated them on a "like/dislike" scale.

• They then indicated the extent to which they agreed or disagreed with the range of attitudinal statements about the commercial that had been elicited in the spontaneous discussion stage.

We selected the like/dislike measure to answer the recurring questions because it was most appropriate to the purposes of our study of women and advertising. Since we wanted to learn how consumers feel about the images of women in advertising, we needed a measure that would focus on their emotional and attitudinal responses to the commercials they saw.

This study did not deal with the product message or the attention values of the commercials we studied, nor did we include the kind of "persuasion measures" that are customarily employed in conventional copy research. An equal number of New Demographic women were interviewed in eight cities coast to coast. In each of the four regions of the country we conducted interviews in a large city and a small city in order to obtain responses from women in metropolitan areas as well as smaller towns.

What We Learned

It should be noted that the women were not 100 percent positive or 100 percent negative about anything. Even the best-liked commercial was "disliked very much" by 1 percent of the women who saw it and moderately disliked by 3 percent. Conversely, the most-disliked commercial had its fans. It was "liked very much" by 4 percent of the respondents and "liked" by 13 percent.

It is clear that in all cases there is a spectrum of response, rather than a single monolithic reaction from all women. In spite of this range of response some clear patterns emerged:

- Four of the commercials elicited predominantly favorable responses from the women who saw them.
- Four had mixed reactions: they were controversial or bland.
- Four received predominantly unfavorable responses.

Overall, Women Responded Most Favorably to Contemporary Commercials

All four New Demographic groups reacted more positively to commercials with contemporary treatments and imagery than they did to any other approaches. Nevertheless, there were some differences.

Stay-at-home housewives were most responsive to commercials that showed the changing roles of women and changing life styles, which are not, in fact, reflected in their own lives. Their favorite commercial was one that showed a young father diapering a baby. They were almost equally enthusiastic about one showing a middle-aged woman getting ready to go back to work.

The career women had fairly strong responses to the advertising. They were equal to stay-at-home housewives in their enthusiasm for the young father commercial. They were more responsive than the other groups to a car commercial that showed a woman making her own consumer choices. They were also more responsive than the others to a headache remedy advertisement that showed women in a variety of contemporary roles.

One might generalize that stay-at-home housewives were most responsive to the emotional symbols of change, while career women were somewhat more responsive to cooler approaches—those that employed a light, humorous, almost ironic touch.

Plan-to-work housewives were generally less enthusiastic than the stay-at-home housewives about most of the advertising, with the exception of the car commerial, to which they were slightly more responsive. The working women who say their work is "just a job" were less responsive than the career women to all of these commercials, and only in the case of the headache remedy commercial were they more enthusiastic than the plan-to-work housewives.

Responses to the Male/Female Relationship Were Mixed

Two fragrance commercials that dealt with the man/woman relationship elicited mixed reactions. One showed a housewife at the end of a busy day preparing for the evening by taking a bath and using a fragrance product. The treatment was a tongue-in-cheek spoof on a burlesque striptease. The point of view was the housewife's own perspective as she finished her workaday chores and got ready for a romantic evening with her husband.

This approach was particularly appreciated by the "just a job" working women. Plan-to-work housewives are at home during the day performing those kitchen chores. They might be considered the target for this campaign. Ironically, they were less enthusiastic about it than any of the other segments of women.

The other fragrance commercial that drew rather mixed responses used a contemporary theme. It talked about and depicted the three roles a working woman plays in today's society, that of breadwinner, housewife, and wife. It was executed with a very traditional, sexy, flaunting kind of music and dance treatment.

One might assume that this commercial was aimed at the working women segment of the market. Interestingly, the "just a job" working women, who represent the greatest number of working women in our society, were more negative toward this approach than any of the other segments. It was best liked by the stay-at-home housewives, who might not be perceived as the target for this campaign. Those women were far more tolerant of the sexy approach than the working women to whom it was addressed. This is one case where the concept of the advertising and the way it was executed took two very different directions. This commercial gave out mixed signals.

Some Responses Were Bland

The two other commercials in this "mid" group did not elicit very strong reactions, positive or negative. One was a vitamin commercial that showed a number of vignettes of different aspects of women's lives. Women were shown participating in activities ranging from the tennis court to the dance floor. Stay-at-home housewives expressed more enthusiasm for this execution than did the other three segments of women.

The other commercial that had a bland response was an older tire commercial, which showed a woman in a frightening driving situation. This ad made the point that when a woman is driving alone the use of the advertised tire brand would be a safety precaution. Again, this was most positively received by the stay-at-home housewives. It had very little intense response either for or against from the plan-to-work housewives.

Although the two working women groups didn't have very strong reactions to this execution, they tended to dislike it more than did the housewives. This is ironic in view of the fact that if any women are potential customers for tires it is working women, both job and career.

All Groups of Women Responded Most Negatively to Traditional Approaches

The four commericals that triggered the most intense dislike used traditional imagery. Two of them were the traditional housewife type of advertising that our critics so deplore. Apparently, a cross-section of women in this country deplore them as well. Plan-to-work housewives and career women were particularly negative toward the two traditional household commercials.

The other two were disliked for different reasons. One of them was a bra commercial that used an overt sex-object treatment. This one was heartily disliked by all groups but was particularly criticized by plan-to-work housewives. Although also critical of this approach, stay-at-home housewives were somewhat more tolerant of it than their plan-to-work neighbors.

The most disliked of the twelve commercials tested was one that used contemporary imagery of the two young working women. This commercial was disliked not because of its imagery but because of the nature of the product it advertised: a sanitary protection product. Negative responses to this commercial were clearly related to the appropriateness of advertising this kind of product on TV. It might be noted that career women were slightly less critical than the other three groups.

When we average the responses of the four segments of women to all twelve commercials, each segment of women had slightly different patterns of reaction to the advertising they saw.

- Stay-at-home housewives were more approving of the commercials overall than were any other segment of women.
- Plan-to-work housewives, on the other hand, were most critical of the test commercials.
- "Just a job" working women were less involved with the advertising than any of the other segments.
- Career women had strong reactions, both positive and negative. On balance, they were second only to the stay-at-home housewives in their approval of the test commercials.

Note

1. The data presented in this chapter are based on a proprietary study done by Rena Bartos at J. Walter Thompson in 1979 on the imagery of women in advertising.

Chapter 18

The Underlying Issues[1]

Through analysis of their responses to all of these commercials, we identified a number of issues that underlie responses of women to the imagery of women in advertising. Women's responses to these issues were more intense than their responses to the commercials. The issues clustered around four basic themes:

Contemporary Issues

Issues of Sexuality

Traditional Issues

Sensitive Issues

Emotional involvement/identification with contemporary roles.

The women responded most positively to executional elements that elicited emotional involvement and identification with the contemporary roles of women. This cut across all of the New Demographic groups. Whether or not women live in the new life styles, they respond to the imagery of new life styles in advertising. They do not resent seeing cooperative husbands or achieving women on the screen, even though their own households do not fit these patterns.

Their emotional responses to these symbols of change are reflected in such comments as: "In other commercials someone is always getting put down. In this one, it was positive, loving, happy." "I was glad for her that she was able to get herself where she wanted to be."

Father participation in care of children.

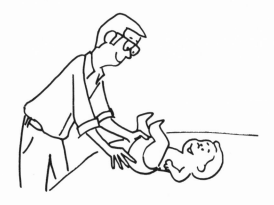

The commercial that some women described as "positive, loving, happy" showed a young father diapering a baby and, obviously, enjoying it. Even though many of these women reported that their husbands had not helped with such chores, they responded with empathy to this example of sharing: "It's nice to see a father changing the baby and enjoying it." "I had a good feeling about it because it showed that the father shared the responsibility for care of the child, not just playing with it."

Only a minority felt that the reality that mothers are more likely than fathers to care for children should be reflected in the commercial execution. They were more likely to agree with the statement: "The men I know do help take care of babies—and they enjoy it."

The multiple roles of today's women.

All of the New Demographic segments identified with the notion that each individual woman plays many roles in the course of the day: "It's believable that a woman can cook and clean and still be sexy for her man at night." "I like seeing advertisers acknowledge the many roles women fulfill."

Contemporary Imagery of women.

All New Demographic groups responded positively to contemporary imagery of women. They liked commercials that showed many kinds of women playing many different roles in our society. They responded positively to women in work situations and in achievement situations. This was true of all groups. They were aware that women are not all cut out of the same mold. They appreciated executions reflecting that diversity. They endorsed diversity of age: "It's nice to recognize that older women are still concerned with their appearance." "It showed a nice cross-section of women—young, middle-aged, holding all kinds of jobs."

They were also appreciative of advertising that reflected a diversity of life styles and motivations: "It's good that the woman wasn't only a sex symbol. She was there. She was doing her job." "It was a nice portrayal of the idea that women can be everything they want to be." "Today you're liable to pull up to a garage and a women will change the tire for you."

Respect for women's intelligence/ consumer judgement.

The approaches that implied respect for women's intelligence and judgment as consumers were well received. The fact that a woman can choose and pay for her own car and make an intelligent purchase decision was appreciated by all groups, particularly by the career women. This notion received somewhat less endorsement from the plan-to-work housewives, who perhaps have not had an opportunity as yet to exercise those kinds of consumer judgments: "It's nice to see car dealers selling women on how the car performs and not just on the looks of the car."

These women appreciated any execution that treated women with respect, whether or not they were shown in their roles as consumers: "I liked that it showed that a housewife can be an intelligent individual."

Girl gets boy-girl takes initiative in romance.

A vignette at the end of a car commercial showed a young woman car owner who called for her boyfriend in her car. She gave him some flowers as they drove off for their evening outing. The boy's voice was heard in the final scene saying, "Well, I still have to be home by ten." This obvious spoof on the male/female role was found amusing and appreciated by all four New Demographic groups. This was somewhat surprising. One might have anticipated that traditional-minded stay-at-home housewives would disapprove of this kind of role reversal: "Today the girls do call boys and give them gifts. It's how they act now." "The role change—the girl giving a boy flowers—was interesting and amusing."

Appreciate cute, sexy, teasing mood vs. sexy treatment too suggestive.

Any commercials with an overt sexy treatment, even those that were somewhat tongue-in-cheek, elicited controversy. Women seemed to be somewhat hung up over what is cute and sexy and what is too suggestive. It's hard to believe that the women who made the following remarks were watching the same advertisement: "It's more teasing than sexy and I find that appealing." "The strip act is suggestive and I find that commercial offensive."

This kind of ambivalence cuts across all groups. The most negative responses came from the stay-at-home housewives, and the most tolerance of sexy treatments came from the career women. However, the differences between them were only minor nuances.

Sexy treatment personally embarrassing; TV a public medium

Stronger differences among the four New Demographic groups were elicited by the potential embarrassment of sexy treatments. These women say that, after all, TV is a public medium. They watch TV in their living rooms with their husbands, families, and visitors, and to a certain extent they find that sexy treatments are really personally embarrassing: "It would be embarrassing if you had a young boy watching it with you." "Women parading around in their bras is the wrong thing for young children to be watching." "If I watched this cute 'stripping act' with my kids, I would feel uncomfortable."

Stay-at-home housewives were most likely to find sexy treatments embarrassing. Career women were least likely to be embarrassed.

Portrayal of women as sex objects.

More intense negative responses were elicited by advertising that showed women as sex objects. These women perceived an execution in sex object terms when it showed not just the sensuality or sexiness of the woman herself but implied that she was preening herself in order to get a man. The "just a job" working women were particularly negative here. The others were almost as negative as they were positive: "The woman was shown too much as a sex symbol." "It seemed more like a sexist striptease than an ad for working women." She's just being a stupid sex symbol, and I feel that it puts women down."

Portrayal of women as sex objects degrading to women.

   The one treatment that took the sex object approach to its ultimate implication was most strongly rejected by all four groups. This execution showed a man reacting overtly to the attractions of a fashion model who was wearing the advertised bra. The strong negative response to this issue far outweighed any strong positive reaction it received. These women feel that the portrayal of women as sex objects is indeed degrading to women: "The man seemed to be looking over these women as if they were meat in a butcher shop." "It's degrading to women. He sits there and the women get paraded out." "My first impression was of this very wealthy guy going to a high class whorehouse, with $500 in his pocket for the right woman."

Woman can't cope/make purchase decision without a man.

One of the traditional assumptions about women is that they can't cope or make a purchase decision without a man. This, of course, is implicit in all the traditional attitudes of the helpless little woman turning to the man for decisions: "I wouldn't buy a car without taking a man with me."

Another aspect of dependency is the assumption that women are concentrated on the reward of their husband's attention as their key motivation in life: "This woman seemed to live only for a [fragrance] night with her man, and that's not good."

Personal insult/family laundry/ housework woman's responsibility/ criticism is personal affront.

The implication that family laundry or housework is women's responsibility leads many women to feel that any criticism about the quality of that laundry or housework is a personal affront: "Somebody saying that is like attacking you personally. That you're not doing a good enough job."

This is a popular theme in much traditional advertising. Many of the advertisers who insist it is effective say that the consumers like it. Apparently these advertisers did not ask those consumers how they really feel about this type of advertising.

Put-down/condescension to women
as incompetent, childish, or dim-witted.

A logical extension of the assumption that all household chores are a woman's responsibility is a put-down or condescension if her performance of those chores is less then perfect: "I feel that it's not always the woman's fault. A man might do his own wash." "I find it very offensive that she feels guilty that he's embarrassed."

Any execution that treats both men and women as incompetent, childish, or dim-witted was also taken rather unkindly by all four groups: "It makes women seem incompetent. Even if they couldn't change the tire themselves, they could use other means to remain safe and deal with the problem."

Poor taste to advertise personal products on TV.

The notion of advertising personal products on TV is a particularly sensitive one to many women. These women feel that TV is a public medium, and they resent a private, personal product being shown on the screen. This concern over privacy was particularly important to stay-at-home housewives: "I really and truly resent anything that is private like that being advertised on TV."

Another aspect of this resentment over invasion of privacy is the sense that advertisers focus on the intimate aspects of women's lives but not those of men. This kind of criticism was expressed most intensely by both segments of working women. Career women were more vehement than any other group in expressing this point of view: "If they can advertise sanitary napkins for women, why not condoms for men?"

Advertising exploits women's issues by token recognition of changed roles.

The fact that advertising exploits women's issues by token recognition of changed roles was not particularly salient to most of these women. Responses to this issue were less intense than to other issues. However, on balance, feelings about the subject were more negative than positive. Both stay-at-home housewives and career women were somewhat negative toward this notion, so it does hit home: "Everybody is using the working women thing to sell their product these days. I think it's taking advantage of the situation."

Sexist tonality.

The most negative issue of all, and one with which all four groups concurred, was sexist tonality. Some advertising was perceived as sexist because of semantics. Other commercials were considered sexist because of the attitude toward women implied in the strategy.

The unfortunate use of the word "girl" instead of "woman" triggered this kind of reaction: "I don't like being called a girl. I'm frankly proud of being a woman."

A ten-year-old tire commercial had been included in the study because it epitomized a certain kind of protective approach toward women. However, a majority of the women participating in this study felt that the problem presented in this ad applied to both sexes. This point of view was held by women in all of the New Demographic segments: "I wouldn't want my husband or son stranded with a flat tire either. It's not just women." "Instead of saying, 'no man around,' I'd sooner have it say when there is 'no help around.' Some men couldn't help even if they were there."

Note

1. The attitudes described in this chapter are from a proprietary study conducted at J. Walter Thompson by Rena Bartos in 1979 on the imagery of women in advertising.

Chapter 19

The Challenge to Management

Of course, the bottom-line question is, How can we use what we have learned about women to make more effective advertising? The first challenge is to answer the recurring questions.

"Does This Mean They Require Separate Strategies?"

The answer to this question is "probably not." However, this question must be answered on two levels. It has marketing as well as creative implications.

The fundamental answer, of course, is a marketing one, because the basic strategy on which advertising is built is a marketing decision. Therefore, in order to learn if there are differences in the product needs, product use, and product benefit priorities of the four New Demographic groups, we need to build the New Demographic framework into the marketing process.

If the marketing analysis shows that one strategic position for the product is relevant to all four groups, the answer is simple. If, on the other hand, it shows that they do have differing kinds of priorities in relation to the product, then their needs and responses can be factored into the strategy definition in proportion with their relative value to the brand.

Once that marketing strategy has been set, the question is, How should they be addressed in the advertising itself? Is there one creative approach that will be relevant to all four groups? The chances are that a single creative strategy will work if it is built on positive, contemporary imagery and avoids put-down clichés.

Depending on the relative value of each New Demographic segment to the market for the product to be advertised, the creative approach can be fine-tuned to gain maximum responses from the key targets.

"How Should We Advertise to the New/Working/Career Woman?"

This question can be answered quite simply. Advertise to her with relevance, with respect, with recognition of the changing roles and changing attitudes of all women. Above all, communicate to her with warmth, with charm, and with a light touch.

Note that career women are particularly responsive to contemporary imagery. Advertisers should be warned that career women are particularly turned off by sexist tonality. Those practitioners who have dismissed criticism of stereotypes in advertising with the assumption that the social critics "are not my customers" should take heed.

In many product fields career woman are, in fact, the most valuable customers of all, and their business is well worth cultivating. If they are as sharply critical of sexist tonality as their responses in this study indicated, the prudent advertiser would be well advised to proceed with caution.

"Do We Need to Show Her in Her Occupational Role to Reach Her?"

The answer to this question is "not necessarily." It is clear that women react to the attitudes symbolized by the imagery of the advertisement they see, not to the literal playback of situations or occupational roles.

"How Do Housewives Feel About Seeing 'New' Women in Advertising?"

They are surprisingly responsive. Even though stay-at-home housewives don't live in new-values life styles, they respond with empathy to symbols of change.

"Are Housewives Turned Off by Seeing Working Women in Ads?"

Not at all. If the attitude projected by the ad is one they can relate to, it doesn't matter if the women are working or not.

What Have We Learned About Women and Advertising?

The most striking result of this study was that all segments of women have much more in common than we might have assumed.

The *surprise,* which was a true surprise, was that all groups—housewives as well as working women—responded most positively to contemporary commercials and contemporary imagery and most negatively to traditional ones.

The news is that women in traditional life styles really endorse the new values. Whether or not women are living in "new values" life styles, they respond very positively to symbols of change.

Apparently the quiet revolution is a fact of life. While we have perceived "the quiet revolution" as the demographic fact of women flooding into the work force, it appears to reflect profound attitudinal changes as well. Changes in women's lives have permeated the hearts and minds of all women, whether or not they themselves have gone to work and whether or not they themselves live in traditional life styles.

On the other hand, endorsement of the changing roles of women does not appear to carry over to their sexual roles. There are real ambivalence and controversy in relation to women's sexuality. The notion of portraying women as sex objects is particularly abhorrent to women. While they do not reject sensuality per se, there is a very fine line that needs to be drawn between showing that women want to be attractive to the men in their lives and the inference of sex object exploitation.

Some of the broader implications of this study challenge many assumptions about women implicit in the way some advertisers still perceive the women's market.

Some advertisers seem to feel that working women and housewives are sisters under the skin, and therefore the traditional approaches will appeal to both groups. They should take note that while working women and housewives showed surprising agreement in the way they responded to advertising, the directions of that response was light years beyond the traditional assumptions about women and how they feel about themselves. Even the most traditional-minded housewife resents condescension and put-down.

The Growing Skepticism of Our Best Customers

This study also suggests that social critics who accuse advertisers of stereotyping women are not just a lot of far-out crazies. Career women who are extremely valuable customers for many products and services are acutely sensitive to sexist tonality. The National Advertising Review Board (NARB) report pointed out that "the more vocal critics of advertising as 'sexist' are younger, better educated, more articulate women who often are opinion leaders. On the average, they have more discretionary income. As their numbers increase (with increasing educational and job opportunities), their challenge to advertising will probably become greater, unless constructive action is taken."[1]

It is conventional wisdom that consumers love to complain that advertising insults their intelligence, but still go out and buy the products. Well, for one thing, they have no choice. They may be buying the products in spite of the advertising.

Recently the National Advertising Review Board appointed another consultive panel to study consumer complaints about advertising. Most of the complaints centered on issues relating to taste. The report said: ". . . we believe that people buy products *despite* being offended by their advertising *not because* it offends them.[2] And some of them get angry enough so that they may not do even that. Like the character in the film *Network,* some are "mad as hell and aren't going to take it any more."

Following are a few excerpts from a letter I received recently from a career woman in Phoenix, Arizona. It was a totally unsolicited letter. She wrote in response to a newspaper article that quoted me on the subject of stereotyping.

> I am a career woman, and I can assure you that if a TV or radio commercial depicts women as being insipid, mechanically or intellectually inferior, I will *never* buy that product. . . .
>
> Commercial advertisers have verbally abused, humiliated, and demeaned women into using their products, but the fact is that most women feel that these commercials are silly, therefore, the company, advertiser, and product is not attractive to them.

Many marketers spend a great deal of time and money devising ways to cultivate the business of these desirable customers. And those companies that are increasingly concerned with building positive corporate reputations and with advocacy advertising are particularly sensitive to the good opinion of the better-educated and more affluent segments of the public. Aside from being good customers for the products and services marketed by those companies, they are also most likely to be present or potential investors. In addition, they are most likely to be opinion leaders and politically active. If they are irritated and alienated by advertising, they are likely to be receptive to demands for regulation.

A consultive panel appointed by the NARB in 1980 sought to determine how well advertising's self-regulation process is working. It commissioned an objective national survey conducted by the Gallup Organization to learn the nature and scope of consumer complaints about advertising.

Half of the respondents told Gallup there had been at least one time in the past year when they wanted to complain about advertising. Only 8 percent of the population (or 16 percent of complainers) actually took the trouble to register a complaint. The study found that most of the unvoiced complaints were in the area of taste. The taste complaints found advertising either "insulting to my intelligence," "in poor taste," "offensive," "distasteful," or "too overtly sexual." Other complaints focused on the intrusiveness of TV advertising. Respondents said that commercials are "too long," "too loud," and "repeated too often."

According to the panel, objective tests have demonstrated that TV advertising is not actually louder than programs. Therefore, it is possible that perceptions of intrusiveness are another facet of consumer irritation or dislike of executional elements. As the report says: "If a viewer *does not like* a particular commercial, he may hear it as too loud or too repetitious."

The panel acknowledged the importance of public perception of good taste as a major element in the reputations of their brands: "Advertisers know that their advertising is often the most visible part of their corporate structure and they know that they will be judged for its honesty, accuracy, and good taste often as critically as they are judged by the quality of their products."

The Gallup Report pointed out that the "incidence of wanting to complain is greatest among those in the upper socio-economic groups." The more affluent, better-educated consumers, who are the best prospects for many advertised products, are the very segments who are most displeased by advertising. This finding is consistent with all other studies done on public attitudes toward advertising.

To date the industry's self-regulatory procedure has dealt with honesty and truthfulness in advertising, not with matters of taste. As the report points out, taste is very subjective. However, it goes on to say: "The Panel believes that a serious effort must be made to identify things done by advertising people which significantly displease substantial numbers of the public since it is this audience on whose response the entire advertising industry ultimately endures or perishes." And, of course, the "things done by advertisers that displease large numbers of people" lead back to consumers' emotional responses to advertising that they find "insulting to my intelligence," in poor taste, or offensive. And that has direct relevance to the way advertising is tested and the decision criteria employed as to which advertising is run and which is rejected. The research design employed for our study of how women respond to the image of women in advertising suggests ways to overcome these issues of taste and consumer alienation.

It so happens that we used a "like/dislike" scale because it fitted the purposes of our particular project. We did not intend to do a methodological study of the measure. We experimented with its use in order to screen some twenty-five commercials down to a manageable number for testing. We wanted to base that selection on consumers' responses rather than our own judgment.

We found that respondents could relate to a self-administered five-point like/dislike scale very easily. It turned out to be a very discriminating way to sort out the commercials that would be most appropriate for our study. It also turned out to be an excellent vehicle for evoking underlying feelings about executional elements that explain why consumers like or dislike a commercial.

The like/dislike scale worked so well in the qualitative stage that we continued it in the quantified phase of the research. The attitudes reflected in the spontaneous discussion were translated into a series of closed-end attitudinal statements. We found that a like/dislike scale is easy to administer, it is something that consumers can relate to, it discriminates, and it is a nonbiasing way to elicit underlying emotional and attitudinal responses. The dimension of "like and dislike" is not usually measured in conventional copy tests. As a matter of fact, it is conventional wisdom that a certain amount of irritation is necessary for advertising to be effective. Many practitioners believe that if consumers like the advertising they see it may be too soft to break through the competitive clutter. Therefore, since they either consider "liking" as irrelevant to effectiveness or believe that a certain amount of "dislike" is a necessary ingredient to achieving effectiveness, they either don't measure it at all or ignore it if it surfaces in their findings.

Many of us have tended to dismiss consumer criticism of advertising as "consumer expertise" or "consumer noise." We have not taken it seriously. We should take these responses very seriously indeed. There is clear documentation that dislike of advertisements correlates with negative attitudes toward our industry overall. To date, no one has examined the effect of this kind of consumer dislike on the credibility of individual company images and brand names. Nevertheless, the inferential evidence is so strong that it would be prudent to heed these warning signals. *Until the hypothesis that advertising which consumers say "insults my intelligence" is proved to have no deleterious effect on brand image and credibility, we should proceed with caution.*

The Relation of "Dislike" to the Erosion of Credibility[3]

For a number of years now every public opinion survey has documented increasing consumer skepticism about advertising and business. There is a groundswell of industry concern over consumer distrust of advertising and the slippage in credibility.

There is no direct proof of a link between the dimension of "dislike" and the erosion of brand credibility. However, there is an increasing body of inferential evidence that links consumers' dislike of advertising to their distrust of advertisers. The recent American Association of Advertising Agencies study, *Advertising and Consumers: New Perspectives,* provides some indirect evidence about the potential impact of dislike on the credibility of a company or brand.[4]

In the mid-1960s the AAAA conducted a study of what consumers thought of advertising. The results of that benchmark project were published in *Advertising in America: The Consumer View,* co-authored by the late Raymond Bauer and Stephen Greyser of Harvard. In the 1970s the AAAA Board of Directors felt it was necessary to update that basic study. Each of these surveys was based on projectable samples of approximately 1,800 consumers representing all persons in the United States eighteen years old and over, drawn by a national probability sampling technique.

The 1976 study identified a number of specific issues that had surfaced during the years since the first survey. These were expressed in more than forty attitudinal statements. The results were subjected to rigorous factor analysis in order to determine to what extent these attitudes clustered into specific issues and to what extent the issues related to positive or negative opinion of the advertising industry.

The factor analysis enabled us to identify eight issues, which represent the principal ways in which consumers look at advertising. These issues vary in salience and intensity. Several of them generate a good deal of comment and conversation but don't contribute much to people's basic opinions for or against the advertising industry as an institution. We identified three issues as crucial to people's opinions of advertising. *Two of these three key issues relate to like and dislike.* They are "credibility" and "entertainment value."

In the AAAA study we observed a decline in the number of people who agreed with positive statements about advertising and an increase in the number who feel that advertising often "persuades people to buy things they should not buy" and that most advertising "insults the intelligence of the American consumer."

When viewed in the context of other institutions in American life, the credibility of advertising was higher than that of labor unions, big business, and the Federal government. Nonetheless, the most intense spontaneous criticism of advertising dealt with credibility. The issue of credibility is potentially negative. To the extent that consumers are skeptical about what we say and show in our advertising, they are apt to be negative toward the industry overall.

What does this have to do with like and dislike? Following are the attitudinal statements that were among the top loading components of this factor:

- "Most advertising insults the intelligence of the average consumer."
- "Most advertising is boring."
- "Most advertising is in poor taste."
- "The way an average family is shown in commercials is not true to life."

When we were designing that study, our committee developed a set of statements relating to the aesthetics of advertising. These were carefully balanced to include an equal number of positive and negative statements. We had assumed that these would cluster together in a single factor, which would reflect the continuum of positive/negative attitudes toward aesthetics. Much to our surprise, the negative statements were linked statistically with other attitudes of skepticism and distrust. We concluded that when consumers say that advertising "insults my intelligence," or that it is "boring" or "in poor taste," they are not merely making an aesthetic judgment. These criticisms of advertising appear to be manifestations of an underlying disbelief of the advertising itself.

The interviewing for the AAAA study was conducted in the fall of 1974. Fortunately, William D. Wells, director of research at Needham, Harper, & Steers, trended some of these questions from 1975 through 1980. The AAAA analysis demonstrated that the consumer perception that "most advertising insults my intelligence" correlates with lack of credibility. Regrettably, that perception has increased in the years since the AAAA study was completed.

Advertising Insults My Intelligence

			(% Agree)			
	1975	*1976*	*1977*	*1978*	*1979*	*1980*
Males	61	62	61	64	66	66
Females	60	62	61	61	69	67

SOURCE: William D. Wells, Needham, Harper, & Steers Advertising, Inc.

The Relation of "Liking" to Positive Brand Imagery

A fascinating result of the AAAA study was that *liking* of advertising *is relevant to good opinion of our industry*. In our quest for measuring effectiveness, we have tended to dismiss any consumer pleasure in or enjoyment of advertising as irrelevant. As has been pointed out, some practitioners say that if consumers like an ad it is probably too soft to be truly effective. Yet the AAAA study established a clear correlation between liking of advertising and positive opinion of the advertising business. When consumers say an ad or commercial is "funny or clever," "artistic," or "enjoyable," they have more positive opinions of the advertising industry. As yet, no one has made a direct connection between this new insight that enjoyment of advertising improves opinions of the industry overall and its potential for protecting or improving individual brand or company images.

However, the inferential evidence is so strong that I believe "liking" can be the secret weapon in the battle to build the kind of brand personalities that will inspire trust instead of distrust. An interesting footnote on this subject comes from Great Britain. The trends there have run counter to those in the United States, according to a series of studies conducted by the Advertising Association of Great Britain. The low point in British opinion of advertising came in 1966, when only 23 percent of the British public admitted to liking TV advertising, while 32 percent said they disliked TV advertising. These attitudes were reversed during the 1970s.

The most recent report, issued in September 1980, tells us that 50 percent of the people in the United Kingdom like advertising on TV, while only 15 percent say they dislike it!

Like/Dislike of TV Advertising over Time

	SEPTEMBER 1961 %	AUGUST 1966 %	APRIL 1972 %	MARCH 1976 %	SEPTEMBER 1980 %
Like	35	23	43	48	50
Dislike	29	32	24	16	15

SOURCE: Advertising Association of Great Britian.

A synthesis of opinion among practitioners in the United Kingdom attributes this improvement to a number of factors: Television is no longer an unknown quantity, and therefore people are not afraid of its power to persuade or manipulate, and a more informed public can appreciate the basic economic function of advertising and has become knowledgeable about advertising executions. These practitioners believe there is a clear relationship between enjoyment of advertising and approval of the industry. "People are willing to acknowledge that they quite like advertising: its wit, its subtlety, its cleverness, its use of celebrities. Certainly over the decade there has been conscious attempt on the part of agencies to make advertising that entertains, so that in that respect, our product is more popular and has helped the climate of public opinion."[5]

Ironically, during the same period when confidence in brands and the credibility of advertising have eroded in the United States, our cousins across the Atlantic have recaptured public approval of advertising through the simple strategy of creating advertising that consumers really enjoy.

The Schizophrenia of the American Corporation—

There is a curious schizophrenia in the way many American corporations function today. On the one hand, corporate managements, their chief executive officers, and their consumer affairs officers spend a great deal of time, thought, and money on maintaining credible postures for their companies. On the other hand, marketing departments and their associated research and advertising specialists pursue the chimera of advertising "effectiveness" with enthusiastic zeal.

Top managements are sensitive to the quality of their companies' reputations. They are aware that the implicit threat of advertising regulation can be countered only by voluntary, constructive self-regulation. They are aware of the growing sophistication and skepticism of the best-educated and most affluent segments of our society, who represent valuable customers for their products. According to the NARB, "advertisers know that their advertising is often the most visible part of their corporate structure . . . and they will be judged for its honesty, accuracy, and good taste often as critically as they are judged by the quality of their products."[6] And yet we hear the growing groundswell of criticism of and alienation from much current advertising.

Neither corporate managements nor their marketing experts appear to recognize the linkage between the day-to-day business of marketing and its potential impact on the quality and credibility of their companies' reputations. The right hand of corporate management may not only be organizationally separate from the left hand of the marketing function, but the two may actually be working at cross purposes. In their zealous pursuit of "effectiveness," marketing departments may be exacerbating some of the very problems their top managements are attempting to solve.

It is understandable that corporate managements would not concern themselves with the details of copy testing methodology. The way advertising research is conducted is a minor and technical aspect of the total marketing process and one that they leave to their marketing specialists. *Yet it is possible that the unmeasured aspects of communication are undermining the efforts of top managements to enhance the credibility of their companies' reputations.* It is also possible that institutionalized advertising research procedures are compounding the problem.

Marketing specialists devise decision-making procedures and "go/no go" systems of advertising research evaluation in order to maximize the "effectiveness" of the advertising campaigns they run.

In fact, there is no agreement in the professional community as to how to measure effectiveness. The controversy over whether recall or a shift in purchase intention or communication of copy points or some combination of the above is the optimum way to evaluate advertising has been raging for at least a generation. Apparently, none of the antagonists in this debate consider the possibility that advertising may have effects other than those usually measured by copy testing. There seems to be an unspoken assumption that "if we don't measure it, it doesn't exist."

The underlying assumption behind what they do measure is that somehow indicators of attention or purchase intention are manifestations of sales effectiveness. Questions of taste and emotional response are not considered. And some industry leaders question whether these currently accepted criteria really measure advertising effectiveness at all.

—and How to Cure It

Since the problem appears to stem from a narrow definition of advertising "effectiveness" and from institutionalized testing systems built on that definition, a conservative solution would be to expand our decision criteria to include the currently unmeasured dimensions of like and dislike. In March 1980 I made a speech to the Annual Conference of the Advertising Research Foundation entitled "Do We Have to Make Them Mad to Sell Them?" In it I urged members of the industry to add a like/dislike measure to their ongoing copy testing methods.

Evidence of the relationship of like and dislike to imagery and credibility has appeared only in global studies of opinions of the advertising industry overall. The only way we can find out how like and dislike relate to the positive or negative images of individual brands or companies and to their credibility is through adding a like/dislike measure or some related questions to ongoing copy tests and by studying the results over time.

At the very least we shall be able to learn what kinds of executional details evoke positive and negative response. Over time we can also learn whether, in fact, we do "have to make them mad to sell them." We should be able to develop advertising that meets current criteria of message registration, "persuasion," and/or attention and that at the same time does enhance the quality of the brand image and does not undermine its credibility.

The most difficult barrier to implementing this simple solution will be habit. Once marketing specialists agree to try this expanded definition of effectiveness, I am sure they will experiment with some of the possible measures of affect. There are many in the literature. Some agencies have used some version of emotional response as standard criteria in their copy testing procedures for years. Interestingly, none of these agencies has been associated with the kind of advertising that has elicited the most anguished cries of resentment from consumers.

The only way we can test the hypothesis that like and dislike have an impact on brand imagery and brand credibility is to check it out. If we focus on these previously unmeasured aspects of communication, we should be able to learn how these dimensions relate to the criteria currently employed to evaluate advertising. Many practitioners insist that we have no way of knowing how or whether like and dislike relate to sales effectiveness. I agree. But, I think it behooves us all to find out before the situation deteriorates further. And, of course, this kind of consumer feedback is the best insurance of all against the perpetuation of alienating stereotypes of women in advertising.

Actually, we may be rescued by the explosion of change in media technology. Even if individual advertisers do not respond to the groundswell of consumer alienation and irritation with advertising, the sheer force of history may cause them to try to woo their customers rather than bludgeon them into buying the products. As the media context changes, the dimension of liking could be a crucial criterion of advertising effectiveness. A happy by-product of the change could be greater consonance between a corporation's goals and purposes and public perceptions of its advertised brands. When positive emotional response becomes an essential sales tool, top managements may find that they are not only selling their products, they are improving the images of their brands and enhancing the credibility of their companies' reputations.

Notes

1. *Advertising and Women: A Report on Advertising Portraying or Directed to Women,* prepared by a Consultive Panel of The National Advertising Review Board, March 1975, p. 6.
2. *Advertising Self-Regulation and Its Interaction with Consumers,* prepared by a Consultive Panel of the National Advertising Review Board, 1980, p. 16.

3. Rena Bartos "Ads That Irritate May Erode Trust in Advertised Brands," *Harvard Business Review,* July–August 1981.

4. Rena Bartos and Theodore F. Dunn, *Advertising and Consumers: New Perspective* (New York: American Association of Advertising Agencies, 1976).

5. Private communication from Judie Lannon, Vice President and Director of Research, J. Walter Thompson, London Office, September 1980.

6. *Advertising Self Regulation,* p. 6.

Afterword

There can be no such thing as the final word on a subject as dynamic and constantly evolving as women. Even before this book goes to press, the realities of the women's market will have changed.

Part I reports data about women through the year 1980. I suggest that anyone continuing to track those trends obtain the January issue of the *Employment and Earnings Report,* published monthly by the Bureau of Labor Statistics. It is this report that is the source of the occupational profile presented in Chapter 1 and the data on the ratio of working women to housewives in our population. I hope interested readers will update these data and continue to track these trends.

I am very conscious of the many aspects of the subject that have not been included in this book. Originally I had hoped to do a final section on women and society that would trace the ripple effects of the quiet revolution that go beyond its implications for marketing, media, and advertising. However, time and space precluded such an ambitious conclusion. Readers who are concerned about the social implications of the quiet revolution can join me in tracking change every time they read their newspapers and magazines or watch television. Change is all around us. The documentation of that change is accessible to all of us.

One of the obvious implications of the quiet revolution is the changing role of the family. I have touched on this in a somewhat limited way in relation to women's changing aspirations and how this might impact on their continuing presence in the work force. However, the constantly evolving redefinition of the family concerns all of us in ways that are far more fundamental than the narrower question of whether or not women go to work.

All of the evidence I have seen says that the family will be alive and well through the rest of the twentieth century and on into the twenty-first. However, it may never return to the traditional model of breadwinner husband and homemaker wife. That kind of patriarchal pattern also implies a power relationship between the sexes. Most of the data I have seen suggest that this perception of family relationships is on its way out.

This does not mean that there will not be dependent women and authoritarian men in our society. Of course that pattern will no doubt continue. However, it also becomes clear that more and more younger people are undertaking family life in partnership terms rather than in terms of the dependency/power relationship that so marked the nineteenth-century view of marriage.

Certainly children will continue to be born. However, the indications are that families will be somewhat smaller, that educated, career-oriented women may delay raising their families until their careers are launched, and that these mothers will, for the most part, return to professional life. This raises problems not just for the family but for society as a whole. Who will care for these children? How will they be acculturated? How will the family unit adjust to this major change?

This is an issue of special relevance to corporations and to personnel specialists who are concerned with reconciling the career ambitions of men and women with their family responsibilities. It may be one of the major issues of the 1980s. It will be interesting to look back at this particular question from the vantage point of the next decade to see how people did, in fact, cope with this new kind of problem.

The quiet revolution has tremendous implications for our educational system. Society's goals are transmitted to the young through education. The way that male and female roles are presented in the schools will have direct impact on whether young girls and women growing up will be able to realize their full potential.

Many industry leaders who honestly want to accommodate women's accelerating desire to participate in the mainstream of corporate life report that the young girls who have been steered away from achievement in the hard sciences and mathematics because of stereotypical thinking in the schools and among guidance counselors limit their potential achievement throughout the rest of their lives.

Therefore, one of the ripple effects of the quiet revolution will be the ways in which gender is destereotyped in our educational system and the ways in which guidance counselors are sensitized to encouraging talent to find its own level regardless of the sex of the young person involved.

The quiet revolution has many implications for corporations and their managements. As women move up the career ladder, more and more of them will be working alongside men as professional colleagues. Managers can no longer assume that receptionists or secretaries are the only women in business. If they are conditioned to thinking of women solely in personal terms—as wives, daughters, or a cute bit of fluff to flirt with—they may find it traumatic to deal with them on a peer basis.

However, as young managers move up, these kinds of adjustments will be less and less painful, and less and less necessary. Many of the younger men exemplify social change in their own personal lives. Many participate in a two-paycheck marriage or may have delayed marriage in favor of a less formal living arrangement. In either case they are comfortable with and accustomed to women as partners and as roommates. They don't see women as a separate race. Then, too, managements will necessarily begin to see a changing mix in their employee population and will necessarily need to adjust their personnel policies and their attitudes toward their employees to the new realities.

As women do move up into positions of responsibility and authority, they will surface not just as colleagues within a corporation but as representatives of client organizations or as business colleagues representing the myriad of services and companies with which a corporation does business. In either case they will be in a peer or sometimes in a power relationship to the corporate man who deals with them. The latter will necessarily learn to relate to women clients and women business colleagues in their professional roles and not merely as members of the opposite sex.

It is inevitable as women achieve more in corporate professional life that they will begin to appear on boards of directors with increasing frequency. They will begin to have a voice in how corporations are managed. Boards of directors will be less and less an "old boys' club" and more and more a collegial group of diverse individuals joined together for a common purpose. Learning and adjustment will be necessary on all sides.

As women achieve more in their professional lives, they are more and more likely to have money available to them for investing. Corporations will number more women among their stockholders. While it is true that historically women have controlled a good portion of the wealth in our country, it is usually because they inherited that wealth from their husbands. Although the assets were in their names, for the most part they deferred to their husbands' surrogates, the lawyers, accountants, and investment advisers, who counseled on how those assets were to be managed.

With the increasing sense of self that accompanies women's ascendancy into levels of management and responsibility, the new breed of women investors will police their own investments and appraise the performance of the corporations whose stock they hold. As women have begun to take charge of their own lives in the work place, they have also begun to want to control their money. They have begun to learn how to deal with money matters. Although there is still a certain amount of math anxiety among women, this is rapidly being overcome, particularly among the younger women.

Another way that the changing role of women could impact on corporate life is the clear finding that with increasing sophistication, career-oriented women also become very critical as consumers. They are particularly sensitive to issues of social responsibility and, as noted in Part IV, are very concerned about stereotyping in advertising and about sexist tonality.

Women's changing self-perceptions are reflected in how they relate to authority figures. Women traditionally deferred to their doctors as supremely knowledgeable beings whose word could not be challenged. Now women are beginning to challenge the pronouncements of their doctors and medical experts. They want to know *why* a particular course of treatment is recommended. They seek second opinions. They read about medical subjects and realize that professionals with whom they deal are extremely knowledgeable but not necessarily infallible.

Although women have had the vote for more than fifty years, they are just beginning to realize the potential of their political clout. In recent years women have become more politically active. They are running for office. They are making their voices heard in the legislatures across the land. They are still a tiny minority of all elected officials, but it is something of a revolution that currently the mayors of at least two major cities in the United States are women, Diane Feinstein of San Francisco and Jane Byrne of Chicago. As we go to press, a third major city has elected a woman mayor by a strong majority of nearly 63 percent of the vote. It boggles the mind to think of a macho city like Houston electing a woman as mayor. In commenting on the election of Kathryn Whitmire, the *New York Times* (November 22, 1981) said: "In politics, 'What do women want?' is becoming less and less a cheap joke and more and more a serious question. Vote seekers can't afford to call a female opponent 'that little lady,' as did Mrs. Whitmire's rival. As candidates—and as voters—women have turned into a potent political force."

Groups such as the Women's Political Caucus and the Women's

Campaign Fund have sprung up to raise funds for women candidates of both parties and to develop a bipartisian consensus among women in office on issues of common interest to all women.

As this book goes to press the ERA has not, as yet, been ratified. We shall know the results shortly after publication day. My judgment is that if the Equal Rights Amendment is not actually ratified by June 1982, there is an inexorable move toward equality that sooner or later will be expressed in the Constitution. All of the poll data show that a majority of both men and women believe that women should be equal citizens under the law. While the quiet revolution I have described in this book is not a political movement, it is clear that women are moving toward full partnership in all aspects of our society. Therefore, it is inevitable that this will find its expression in the political and legislative arenas as well.

Finally, one of the fascinating manifestations of the changing role of women has been the growth of an entire new industry, which I call the "woman industry." In the last ten years all sorts of specialists on women have appeared on the scene. Several magazines published today would not have been developed if it had not been for the changes in women's lives. *Ms.* magazine was the first voice for change among women. However, think of *Working Woman, Savvy, Working Mother,* and *Self.* The very concepts behind these magazines are a direct response to the dramatic changes that have occurred in the past decade.

The traditional women's magazines have also responded strongly to the changing context of women's lives. If one reviews the table of contents of traditional women's magazines, the high-fashion publications as well as the general home-oriented magazines, almost every article deals with some aspect of women's adjustment to changing roles and the changing context of their lives.

Just recently I noted that *Newsweek,* one of the major dual audience news publications, publishes a special edition that goes only to its women readers. Apparently there is a feeling that the professional executive and forward-thinking women who read their publication constitute a sufficiently important market for them to create a special edition of the magazine of interest to advertisers who want to reach this particular segment.

As this goes to press, New York City is about to celebrate its Third Annual Women in Business Week. An entire week of events, seminars, and activities is scheduled.

Accompanying these more obvious examples of change are all of the organizations that have sprung up to express women's interests or to cultivate them as a market. There are personnel experts and "headhunters" who specialize in placing executive women. There are career counselors who assist women in developing the game plans for career development and help them track their way through the corporate jungle. There are any number of seminars, training programs, and special courses aimed at assisting women in learning more about finance, helping reentry women to hone their skills in order to establish a foothold in the job market, or helping entry-level or middle-level working women to develop their careers.

Any number of "how to" books have been written on the subject. There are speakers, lecturers, seminars, and programs, all stemming from the simple demographic fact identified by Professor Ginzberg as being the single outstanding phenomenon of the twentieth century. Many of these programs and activities are extremely productive. Frankly, some of them strike me as somewhat exploitative. However, the very fact that a number of sharp promoters have joined the pack is evidence that the changing role of women is really a basic change in our society. These entrepreneurs apparently sense that this is where the mainstream of women's lives is headed. Such people don't cling to unprofitable or lost causes. Ironically, the very presence of these opportunists is evidence of the inevitability of the quiet revolution.

In the past few days I have had several conversations on the subject that is the core of this book, the changing role of women and its implications now and in the future. The first occurred at an industry luncheon. One of my tablemates asked what I did at J. Walter Thompson. I mentioned that among other things I track the changing role of women. He assured me that "the women's movement has peaked" and predicted that women would be returning to the kitchen in droves. I asked what evidence he had for this. He said he felt these things run in cycles and, just as the women's movement "died out" after women got the vote, the presence of women in the work force and in the professions in recent years was a temporary trend and would be reversed.

I cited some of the evidence covered in this book, including the changing attitudes of all women, both those who work and those who don't, and the role that education plays in women's presence in the work force. But he was not convinced. Finally, I said, "Why don't we meet here ten years from today and let's find out what really happened!"

That evening I had dinner with a two-career couple. The husband is an eminent psychiatrist on the staff of a major teaching hospital. The wife has gone through all stages of the life cycle. She had been a fashion designer, then stayed home to raise four children, the youngest of whom is about to enter college. During the years that her children were growing up, she juggled a freelance career as an interior decorator with being a mother, wife, and hostess. As the prospect of an empty nest loomed in the last year or so, she has evolved a second and very successful career in retailing. I told them about my luncheon conversation with the man who predicted women's return to domesticity. The doctor said that that man could not be more wrong. He pointed out that more than half of the residents in training in his hospital are now women and that about two out of five students enrolled in medical school are also female. He felt that women would play an increasingly powerful role in all phases of life, and that there is no turning back.

The next day I had a fascinating luncheon meeting with the president and top management of a major corporation. The purpose of this lunch was to discuss changing consumers and the implications of social change for the various enterprises with which this company is concerned. I found it particularly reassuring to hear at first hand that the decision makers of a major corporation are really aware of social change and are building their perceptions of that change into their business planning. It reminded me of a phrase suggested by one of my colleagues when we first evolved the Moving Target as the title for our study of the changing women's market. He said, "The duck hunters tell us that the way to hit a target is to aim at where it's going to be, not at where it's been." As I thought about my luncheon conversation of the previous day, it was clear to me that this corporation, at least, is aiming its strategic planning at where those moving targets are going to be. They do not believe that the trend is going to reverse itself and they are making bottom line decisions based on that judgment.

The final conversation occurred a few hours later. An editor of one of the major women's magazines interviewed me for an article she was doing on what's ahead for women. I reviewed the familiar ground covered in this book and reported the three conversations I have just described. I tried to explain to her that the quiet revolution is not just a matter of demographic change but that it represents a profound emotional and attitudinal change that will not be reversed.

I explained the notion that women have moved from defining themselves in terms of derived status, that is, as someone's wife, someone's daughter, or someone's mother, and that they are moving toward wanting a sense of personal identity beyond those private domestic roles. As we discussed this I remembered a phrase from one of Gretchen Cryer's songs that seems to express it as well as anything I have heard:

> Twice I was a mother,
> Once I was a wife,
> Tore off all the labels,
> Now all that's left is life.*

And, I think, perhaps that is as good a way as any to close this never ending saga of the Moving Target.

---

*From *Changing,* lyrics by Gretchen Cryer, music by Nancy Ford. Copyright 1973 by Multimood Music, Inc., and Marylebone Music, Inc. Used by permission.

Index

Index

A

Achievement, 32–33
Adams, Eugene H., 189
Advancement, 48
Advertising, 65, 66, 227–283
  assumptions behind definitions of
    women in, 243–245
  car, 187, 234–235, 258
  changing attitudes toward women in,
    229–233
  credibility issue, 276–278, 279, 281
  criticism of, 273–276
  household products, 238, 239, 243,
    265
  husband's participation in home-
    making and child care and,
    233–234, 255
  insurance, 219, 232–233
  research, 280–281
  responses of women to imagery in,
    247–269
  sexist, 228, 239, 243, 260–263, 269,
    273
  stereotypes of women in, 227–228,
    235–236, 238–242, 245–246, 273
  travel, 69, 196
  wine, 202
  see also Media behavior
Advertising Age, 209, 217, 219
Advertising in America: The Consumer
    View (Bauer and Greyser), 276
Advertising Association of Great
    Britain, 279
Advertising and Consumers: New Per-
    spectives (AAAA), 276
Affirmative action, 41
Age, 70, 85, 87, 90, 93, 108–109

American Association of Advertising
    Agencies, 276–278
American Banker, 210
American Women Today and Tomor-
    row (Bryant), 37, 39
Associated Merchandising Corporation,
    176, 178
Attitudes and self-perceptions of
    women, 3–4, 28–29, 111–112,
    116–128
  of career-oriented working women,
    125–128
  of "just a job" working women,
    123–125
  of plan-to-work housewives, 120–123
  of stay-at-home housewives, 118–120
Authority figures, relationships with,
    287
Automobiles, *see* Car ownership
Axiom Market Research Bureau, 105n

B

Baby boom generation, 9, 34, 40
Baca, Randy, 31
Backlash, male, 34, 41–42
Ball, George, 59, 60
BankAmericard, 190
Bauer, Raymond, 276
Beaumont, Dina, 54
Beleckis, Marge, 221
Beller, Carole, 177
Bergman, Barbara, 54
Bernstein, Sid, 219
Blue-collar jobs, 45, 49, 50
Boards of directors, 286
Books, 203